Data Mining with Confidence™

2nd Edition

Clay Helberg for SPSS Inc.

For more information about SPSS® software products, please visit our Web site at *http://www.spss.com* or contact

SPSS Inc.
233 South Wacker Drive, 11th Floor
Chicago, IL 60606-6307
Tel: (312) 651-3000
Fax: (312) 651-3668

1 2 3 4 5 6 7 8 9 0   06 05 04 03 02

ISBN 1-56827-287-1

Preface

The world of data mining has changed significantly since the first edition of this book was published. In particular, there are a lot more people doing it. (Chances are good that your competitors are doing it.) Tools for data mining have matured, and some consolidation in the data mining software market has occurred. Database vendors now routinely include low-level data mining support in their database engines. *Business intelligence* and *customer relationship management* (CRM) have become the management phrases of the day. Data mining has established itself as a commonplace tool for business process improvement.

The second edition has been revised in a number of ways. First, we have replaced the original "Five A's" approach to data mining with the Cross-Industry Standard Process for Data Mining (CRISP-DM™) methodology. This methodology was developed by a consortium of companies that were pioneers in data mining even before it became a buzzword. It lays out a detailed and complete strategy for data mining, from elaborating the business problem to monitoring the effectiveness of the solution. It is a general model and can be applied to any data mining project, regardless of size or problem domain.

Second, we've included new data mining examples, representing three common applications of data mining: public sector fraud detection, retail CRM, and Web mining. This broader set of examples provides a good illustration of the power of data mining to solve diverse problems and makes it easier to find examples that are meaningful to you and your individual situation. These three examples run throughout the book, with other smaller examples occasionally used to illustrate specific points.

Finally, in constructing the examples, we have used the newer and more powerful generation of data mining tools available today. Data mining tools continue to grow in power and ease of use. Today's tools are better at handling large data, provide better and more polished graphs and output, and provide improved embedding capabilities for deployment of data mining results.

The book retains its two-part format. The first part, chapters 1–8, covers the CRISP-DM approach to data mining. The second part, chapters 9–13, provides an overview of data mining methods and techniques. The software appendix, glossary, and bibliography have been expanded and updated.

As with the first edition, this book is not a comprehensive data mining handbook. It is meant to introduce the important concepts of data mining. To really dig into the details, you will want to seek out the relevant additional resources listed in the chapters and in the bibliography. In particular, the modeling methods used in data mining can be complex and subtle, and a thorough understanding of them will go a long way toward avoiding difficulties in your data mining endeavors.

Acknowledgments

I wish to thank many helpful people at SPSS Inc. for their support and assistance throughout the writing of this book. Special thanks to Bob Gruen for unfailing support and encouragement (and the occasional nudge when my priorities threatened to stray); to Chantal Foster, Peter Caron, Dave Watkins, and John Held for insightful comments and reviews that significantly improved the structure and content of the book; to the SPSS editorial and production staff for taking my raw copy and refining it to a polished product of which any author would be proud; and to all the others who make SPSS a wonderful and stimulating place to work. Additional thanks go to Ronny Kohavi at Blue Martini Software for making the Web data from Gazelle.com (used for the KDD-Cup 2000 competition) available for general use. Finally, heartfelt thanks go to my wife and daughter for their infinite patience during long days and nights of writing and data analysis.

Clay Helberg
April, 2002

Contacting SPSS

If you would like to be on our mailing list, contact one of our offices, listed on page v, or visit our Web site at *http://www.spss.com.*

SPSS Inc.
Chicago, Illinois, U.S.A.
Tel: 1.312.651.3000
or 1.800.543.2185
www.spss.com/corpinfo
Customer Service:
1.800.521.1337
Sales:
1.800.543.2185
sales@spss.com
Training:
1.800.543.6607
Technical Support:
1.312.651.3410
support@spss.com

SPSS Federal Systems
Tel: 1.703.740.2400
or 1.800.860.5762
www.spss.com

SPSS Argentina srl
Tel: +5411.4814.5030
www.spss.com

SPSS Asia Pacific Pte. Ltd.
Tel: +65.245.9110
www.spss.com

SPSS Australasia Pty. Ltd.
Tel: +61.2.9954.5660
www.spss.com

SPSS Belgium
Tel: +32.163.170.70
www.spss.com

SPSS Benelux BV
Tel: +31.183.651777
www.spss.com

SPSS Brasil Ltda
Tel: +55.11.5505.3644
www.spss.com

SPSS Czech Republic
Tel: +420.2.24813839
www.spss.cz

SPSS Denmark
Tel: +45.45.46.02.00
www.spss.com

SPSS East Africa
Tel: +254 2 577 262
spss.com

SPSS Finland Oy
Tel: +358.9.4355.920
www.spss.com

SPSS France SARL
Tel: +01.55.35.27.00
www.spss.com

SPSS Germany
Tel: +49.89.4890740
www.spss.com

SPSS BI Greece
Tel: +30.1.6971950
www.spss.com

SPSS Iberica
Tel: +34.902.123.606
SPSS.com

SPSS Hong Kong Ltd.
Tel: +852.2.811.9662
www.spss.com

SPSS Ireland
Tel: +353.1.415.0234
www.spss.com

SPSS BI Israel
Tel: +972.3.6166616
www.spss.com

SPSS Italia srl
Tel: +800.437300
www.spss.it

SPSS Japan Inc.
Tel: +81.3.5466.5511
www.spss.co.jp

SPSS Korea DataSolution Co.
Tel: +82.2.563.0014
www.spss.co.kr

SPSS Latin America
Tel: +1.312.651.3539
www.spss.com

SPSS Malaysia Sdn Bhd
Tel: +603.6203.2300
www.spss.com

SPSS Miami
Tel: 1.305.627.5700
SPSS.com

SPSS Mexico SA de CV
Tel: +52.5.682.87.68
www.spss.com

SPSS Norway AS
Tel: +47.22.99.25.50
www.spss.com

SPSS Polska
Tel: +48.12.6369680
www.spss.pl

SPSS Russia
Tel: +7.095.125.0069
www.spss.com

SPSS San Bruno
Tel: 1.650.794.2692
www.spss.com

SPSS Schweiz AG
Tel: +41.1.266.90.30
www.spss.com

SPSS BI (Singapore) Pte. Ltd.
Tel: +65.346.2061
www.spss.com

SPSS South Africa
Tel: +27.21.7120929
www.spss.com

SPSS South Asia
Tel: +91.80.2088069
www.spss.com

SPSS Sweden AB
Tel: +46.8.506.105.50
www.spss.com

SPSS Taiwan Corp.
Taipei, Republic of China
Tel: +886.2.25771100
www.sinter.com.tw/spss/main

SPSS (Thailand) Co., Ltd.
Tel: +66.2.260.7070
www.spss.com

SPSS UK Ltd.
Tel: +44.1483.719200
www.spss.com

Contents

1 Overview of Data Mining 1

What Is Data Mining? 1
Data Mining and Statistics. 3
Data Mining Hype. 4
History of Data Mining. 4
Uses of Data Mining 6
Who Uses Data Mining?. 8
Understanding Data 10
Characteristics of Data. 10
Organization of Data 11
Shape of Data 13
About This Book 15

2 Overview of the Data Mining Process 17

General Process Model 18
Examples 20
Example 1: Customer Relationship Management. 20
Example 2: Public Sector Fraud Detection. 20
Example 3: Web Log Analysis 20

3 Business Understanding 21

Determining Business Objectives 21
Background 22
Business Objectives 23
Business Success Criteria. 23
Assessing the Situation 24
Inventory of Resources 24
Requirements, Assumptions, and Constraints 25
Risks and Contingencies. 26
Terminology 27
Costs and Benefits 28
Determining Data Mining Goals 29
Data Mining Goals 29
Data Mining Success Criteria. 29
Producing a Project Plan 30
Project Plan 30
Initial Assessment of Tools and Techniques 31
Summary 32

4 Data Understanding 33

Collecting Initial Data 33
Describing the Data 34
Exploring the Data 36
Verifying Data Quality 39
Summary 41

5 Data Preparation 43

Selecting Data 43
Selecting Rows. 44
Sampling 45
Selecting Columns. 48
Fine-Tuning Data Selection Criteria 49
Cleaning Data 49
Missing Data 50
Data Errors 51
Coding Inconsistencies 52
Bad or Missing Metadata. 53
Constructing Data 53
Derived Attributes 54
Generated Records 56
Integrating Data 57
Formatting Data 58
The Data Set. 58
Summary 59

6 Modeling 61

Selecting a Modeling Technique 61
Modeling Assumptions 63
Generating a Test Design 64
Measuring "Goodness" of a Model 64
Defining Test Data 66
Building the Models. 67
Parameter Settings 68
Models 69
Model Descriptions 70

Assessing the Models 70
Model Assessment 70
Revised Parameter Settings 73
Summary 75

7 *Evaluation* 77

Evaluating Model Results 77
Reviewing the Data Mining Process 80
Determining Next Steps 81
Summary 82

8 *Deployment* 83

Planning the Deployment 83
Planning Monitoring and Maintenance 85
Producing the Final Report 87
Reviewing the Project 90
Summary 91

9 *Methods* 93

10 *Online Analytical Processing (OLAP)* 95

What to Include in the Table 97
Counts and Percentages 97
Sums and Averages 98
Measures of Variability 100
Getting the Most from OLAP 101
Summary 103

11 Exploratory Graphics 105

Types of Charts . . . 105
Bar Charts . . . 105
Distribution Charts . . . 107
Pareto Charts . . . 108
Histograms . . . 109
Line Charts . . . 111
Pie Charts . . . 112
Web Graphs . . . 114
Point Charts . . . 115
Chart Enhancements . . . 120
Selecting the Right Chart . . . 122
Match the Chart to the Data . . . 122
Show the Relationship of Interest . . . 123
Maximize the Information in Your Chart . . . 123
Summary . . . 124

12 Models for Identifying Groups 125

Segmentation Methods . . . 126
Discriminant Analysis . . . 127
Logistic Regression . . . 130
Tree-Based Methods . . . 132
Neural Networks for Segmentation . . . 134
Association Rules . . . 136
Clustering Methods . . . 138
Hierarchical Clustering . . . 139
K-Means Clustering . . . 143
Neural Networks for Clustering . . . 145
Further Reading . . . 147

13 Models for Numeric Outcomes 149

Forecasting Methods 149
ARIMA Models 150
Correlation-Based Models 153
Regression Models 156
Linear Regression Models 157
Cox Regression Models 160
Stepwise Regression Methods 162
Neural Networks for Prediction 163
Summary 165
Further Reading 165

Appendices

A A Brief Review of Statistical Reasoning 167

What Is Statistical Reasoning? 167
Fundamentals of Statistical Reasoning 167
Sampling 167
Variation 168
Probability 169
Modes of Statistical Reasoning 169
Statistical Testing 169
Modeling 174
Combining Statistical Testing with Model Building 177
Some Pitfalls of Statistical Reasoning 178
Statistics and Data Mining 181

B Guide to SPSS Products Used in Data Mining 183

Clementine/Clementine Server 183
SPSS/SPSS Server 184
Options for SPSS 184
SmartViewer 185
SmartViewer Web Server 185
AnswerTree/AnswerTree Server 186
Neural Connection 186
DecisionTime/WhatIf? 186
LexiQuest Mine 187

Glossary 189

Bibliography 203

References Cited in Text 203
Books on Data Mining 203
Books on OLAP 204
Books on Data Visualization 204
Books on Statistical Modeling 205
Books on Neural Networks 205
Resources on the World Wide Web 206

Index 207

Chapter 1

Overview of Data Mining

> Knowledge is power.
>
> —Francis Bacon

What Is Data Mining?

Data mining is a diverse process involving ideas from business, marketing, and public administration, database management, statistics, and computer science. Because of this diversity, there are many different ways to define and think about data mining. The following are examples of published definitions of data mining:

> Data Mining—(1) The process of utilizing the results of data exploration to adjust or enhance business strategies. It builds on the patterns, trends, and exceptions found through data exploration to support the business. It is also known as data harvesting. (2) A technique using software tools geared for the user who typically does not know exactly what he's searching for, but is looking for particular patterns or trends. Data mining is the process of sifting through large amounts of data to produce data content relationships. This is also known as data surfing.
>
> —Applied Technologies Group (1997), p. 15

> Data Mining, as we use the term, is the exploration and analysis, by automatic or semiautomatic means, of large quantities of data in order to discover meaningful patterns and rules.
>
> —Berry and Linoff (1997), p. 5

> Data Mining [is] the process of efficient discovery of non-obvious valuable information from a large collection of data.
>
> —Berson and Smith (1997), p. 565

> Using advanced techniques in mathematics and artificial intelligence, data mining uncovers complex patterns or models in data. Those models are then used to help solve business problems that come up in direct marketing, credit-risk evaluation, fraud detection and other areas.
>
> —Wilson (1997), p. 74

> Data mining uses sophisticated statistical analysis and modeling techniques to uncover patterns and relationships hidden in organizational databases—patterns that ordinary methods might miss.
>
> —Two Crows Corporation (1998), p. 1

> Data mining is the process of discovering meaningful new correlations, patterns and trends by sifting through large amounts of data stored in repositories, using pattern recognition technologies as well as statistical and mathematical techniques.
>
> —Erick Brethnoux, Gartner Group

The common thread in all of these definitions is *finding useful relationships in large data sets*. As we use the term, **data mining** refers to a process, a strategic approach to deriving valuable information and insight from available data. (The process itself will be described in detail in subsequent chapters.) Several of these definitions also mention that the information discovered should be non-obvious and that hidden relationships should be revealed. Hence, one of the strengths of data mining, as opposed to more traditional database or statistical methods, is that you don't necessarily need to know exactly what you're looking for when you start.

The term *data mining* is sometimes applied to a set of *techniques* used in the data mining process. We will try to avoid this usage, however, because data analysis techniques are only a part of the process we are presenting. They are an important part, to be sure, but they are not the only part. Our discussion of techniques will generally be in the context of solving business or organizational problems.

Data Mining and Statistics

Statistical methods form the core of many data analysis techniques used in data mining. Statisticians have been in the business of extracting information from data for a long time, and they have developed a lot of powerful methods and techniques. These techniques are the key to discovering subtle but interesting patterns in your data. Data miners routinely rely on statistical and machine-learning methods to extract information from data. Of course, as you will see in the next chapter, building data mining models is only one part of the data mining process.

The collaboration between statistics and data mining has not always been so congenial. Originally, most statistical techniques were designed for the purpose of *confirming theories*, mainly in the context of scientific research. Those techniques were not well suited to exploratory data analysis or data mining. To use such methods for exploring data, without proper precautions, can lead to serious problems. Because of this, data mining has historically had a negative connotation for some in the statistics community (see Selvin and Stuart, 1966).

However, more recently, as the value of data mining has become more and more apparent, statistical methods have been developed and adapted for the specific purpose of exploring data and generating new hypotheses. Many prominent statisticians now proudly claim the title of "Data Miner." In addition, recently popularized methods for *validation* allow data analysts to apply powerful traditional methods in exploring data but to protect themselves from the errors that plagued earlier attempts at exploratory data analysis.

This combination of statistical methods and validation techniques helps you to get the most out of your data and forms the basis of data analysis in the data mining process.

Data Mining Hype

Pick up any computer-industry or business magazine and you will probably find at least one article on data mining. Some reports in the media give the impression that data mining is a magic wand, giving instant solutions to business problems. Unfortunately, this is not a very realistic view. Successful data mining requires hard work and, more importantly, careful thought and planning.

Another important point to remember is that data mining should not be viewed as an end in itself. Data mining is not a solution to anything; rather, it is a *process* you can use to find solutions to substantive organizational problems.

History of Data Mining

Data mining has only recently emerged as a recognized field; however, many of the techniques that it uses have been around for decades. It wasn't until the necessary computer and statistical technology had evolved that data mining took its rightful place in business intelligence.

The foundation of data mining is, of course, data. In the 1940s and 1950s, businesses, universities, and government agencies began to use digital computers. Still, at this early stage, many organizations were skeptical about the impact that computers would have on their day-to-day operations.

In the 1960s, database technology was developed that allowed data to be stored and accessed systematically and efficiently. Organizations began to understand the advantages of being able to store information about customers (or constituents) and transactions. Unfortunately, early methods for extracting and reporting information from these databases were primitive and difficult to use, usually requiring extensive programming to generate even simple reports. This meant that end users—the decision makers—had to rely on canned reports for the information they needed. Customized reporting simply wasn't feasible. Additionally, the computers of the day were expensive and slow, which meant that only queries of the highest priority were executed.

The 1970s brought further advances in computers and database systems. Networking technology allowed computers at remote sites, such as retail outlets, to send data back to the home office for processing. Companies began accumulating large databases, and the demand for efficient and easy access to the data grew. In the 1980s, **online transaction processing (OLTP)** systems, which allowed transactions to be encoded and captured without human intervention, led to a huge new source of data.

Further advancements in computer technology provided the means to store this new abundance of data.

The introduction of the PC in the 1980s revolutionized the way people thought about computers. The computer, previously a monstrosity requiring its own room and a specialized staff, was transformed into an everyday business tool that any employee could operate and benefit from. Spreadsheet software for microcomputers gave many business people their first exposure to data analysis, and they discovered the power of data to aid decision making.

Meanwhile, during the 1970s and 1980s, scientists in universities were engaged in statistical and artificial intelligence (AI) research. In statistics, researchers were developing techniques for automatic relationship detection, model validation, and data visualization. In AI, researchers were beginning to explore the possibilities of neural networks, rule-induction systems, and genetic algorithms.

In the early 1990s, these technologies matured. Large databases became accessible to end users with PCs via local area networks (LANs) and client/server technology. User-friendly statistical and database software made it possible for end users to perform their own analyses and generate their own reports. Software packages began to incorporate the developments of the last two decades from AI and statistics. A new way of reporting and examining data, known as **online analytical processing (OLAP)**, was a significant advancement for the business world. OLAP provided techniques for setting up different *views* of the data and, thus, the means to go beyond the arduous programming of customized reports by an individual. The interactivity and speed of OLAP allowed business users more freedom to look at their data in fresh, novel ways and to discover new patterns. With more powerful technologies available, businesses began to organize special data storage systems for the purpose of providing company-wide access to usefully structured data. These new data stores, known as **data warehouses**, provide the raw materials for large-scale data mining.

Additionally, the 1990s have seen the resurgence of the service paradigm in business and government. Many companies now realize that they can profit from improved customer loyalty by adding service value to their products. It has become clear that the best way to accomplish this is to get to know the customers so that you can give them what they want (and avoid wasting resources trying to give them something they *don't* want). For all but the smallest companies, this means collecting data and searching it for patterns. For government agencies, learning about constituents provides a way to streamline processes, eliminate waste, and generally improve the efficiency of operations.

Finally, the growth of the Internet has spurred a new computer revolution, where computers are no longer considered as standalone machines but rather as nodes in a world-wide network of information resources. Businesses are using the Internet to get information to, and more importantly *from*, their customers. They are using intranets (small, private mini-Internets within an organization) to disseminate mission-critical information to their employees, making their jobs easier and maximizing the value of information in the enterprise. Government agencies are also making the most of the Internet, encouraging learning and participation among their constituents and collecting and disseminating information in the public interest.

In the early to mid-1990s, researchers began putting all of the pieces together. Since then, the value of data mining has become apparent to computer scientists, statisticians, and business people alike. We now see regular conferences on data mining or "knowledge discovery" (as it is commonly known in the AI field). Technical journals dedicated to the topic have appeared, as have numerous books, papers, and theses. Software developers now offer integrated data mining suites that offer a wide range of techniques, ease of use, and convenient integration with existing data infrastructure. Data mining has emerged from the lab and found its place in the real world.

Uses of Data Mining

Data mining can be applied to a whole range of substantive problems. Basically, any problem that can be solved using new information is a candidate for data mining. Of course, your success with data mining will depend on the relevance of the available data to the problem that you are trying to solve. However, assuming that you have pertinent data, you should be able to extract useful information by mining the data.

You can use data mining to solve problems through the *discovery* of new patterns and *confirmation* of suspected relationships.

Discovery. The primary use of data mining is to find something new in the data—to discover a new piece of information that no one knew previously. This is sometimes referred to as the "bottom-up" or "data-driven" approach because you start with the data and then build theories based on discovered patterns. This approach tends to rely more on methods derived from computer science research, such as neural networks and tree-based methods, as well as visualization techniques.

Confirmation. This approach starts with an idea about a possible relationship (a **hypothesis**) and seeks to verify or refute the hypothesis based on the data. This application is strongly related to traditional statistical approaches, with their emphasis on *hypothesis testing* and *model building*. This is sometimes referred to as "top-down" or "theory-driven" data analysis because you start with a hypothesis and then check the data to determine whether it is consistent with the hypothesis.

These two approaches are complementary and are often applied iteratively in an alternating sequence. You use discovery methods to detect new patterns or relationships, and then you use confirmation methods to make sure that the new patterns represent reliable information that you can act upon. As you build your knowledge base by adding new information, new questions arise, and these new questions lead to new avenues of exploration and discovery.

The following are examples of situations in which data mining was used successfully:

- Mellon Bank needed a way to identify prospects with high profit potential so that they could be targeted for credit card offers. Data mining allowed the bank analysts to identify such customers and to enjoy significant savings in their marketing campaigns.
- Proctor & Gamble spends enormous amounts of money on clinical trials for new drugs and wanted to leverage that to get more return on investment (ROI). The company now uses data mining to gain additional insights into the strengths of and problems with new drugs based on the clinical trial data collected.
- NationsBank needed a way to quickly and accurately rate new loan applications. Data mining gave the bank the techniques necessary to improve the loan approval process and increase profits while reducing risk.
- Bell Atlantic wanted to develop methods for detecting fraudulent phone activity, especially within the wireless market. The company now uses data mining for increased ability to detect fraudulent phone activity early and to minimize the losses that result from such activity.
- The Louisiana Commission on Law Enforcement wanted to examine the effect of policy changes on law enforcement and crime. The commission turned to data mining to track the results of policy changes and to get ideas for increasing the effectiveness of law enforcement efforts.

Who Uses Data Mining?

> Do not worry about your difficulties in mathematics. I can assure you mine are still greater.
>
> —Albert Einstein

Historically, the kind of analysis being done now with data mining—when it was possible at all—was performed by highly trained specialists. If your company was large enough, you had a dedicated group of statisticians and database programmers who responded to requests for data analysis from throughout the company. If your company was small, you probably had to hire high-priced consultants to do this kind of analysis, or you simply had to do without it.

To use data effectively depends on two things—knowledge of the substantive problem and the ability to apply data analysis techniques. The drawback with the old system was that these two things were seldom found in the same place. The product managers knew what their goals were but didn't have the analytical skills to do the analysis. The data processing group had the ability to do the analysis but didn't really understand the business problem. So the two groups had to work together to solve the problem. If communication between the groups was good, they found a solution. However, in many cases, poor communication and logistical problems resulted in wasted time and effort or opportunities missed because of long turnaround times.

With the advent of computer technologies such as PCs, LANs, client/server data warehouses, intranets, and user-friendly data analysis software, data can be accessible to almost everyone in an organization. From the CEO down to assistant sales clerks, employees have opportunities every day to use information to improve the work they do. Those involved in day-to-day processes are the ones who understand the organizational problems. Making the data accessible and putting capable, easy-to-use data analysis software in their hands gives them the ability to extract information they can use. It eliminates the need for you to explain the problem to a statistical specialist, plead your case for programming or computer resources, or pore over canned reports, hoping to piece together the information you need. Now you can go to the data warehouse (or data mart), get the relevant data, and find your own answers, often in a fraction of the time that the old system would have taken.

Of course, this does require some data analysis expertise on your part, and the amount you have will determine how far you can go on your own before calling in an expert. Most organizations have four types of data miners:

- **Information consumers.** These are people who monitor day-to-day or month-to-month activity by examining summary reports. Such users can benefit from basic multidimensional OLAP reporting and visualization methods. These interactive methods can help them find the information they need more quickly and reliably than they could by scanning pages of prepackaged output. It also gives them the ability to look for something new without extensive reprogramming of the report generator.
- **Knowledge workers.** These people are more accustomed to working with the data—rearranging it, looking at it in different ways, and trying various approaches to understanding it. They generally have the skills necessary to apply multidimensional OLAP reporting, visualization, and simple analytical techniques to data. Good data analysis software provides methods for looking at the data in ways that are difficult or impossible with standard spreadsheet software.
- **Model builders.** These people usually have formal training in statistics or data analysis. They are familiar with the advantages and drawbacks of various data analysis approaches. They are proficient with data analysis software and have the expertise to generate complex models from the data. They use sophisticated mathematical techniques such as regression, classification trees, and neural networks, as well as the basic tabulation and visualization methods.
- **Application developers.** These are the people who make it easier for everyone else to do what they need to do. They know the analysis process inside and out and are generally responsible for creating prepackaged reports and analyses. As software evolves to become more and more powerful and flexible, developers can add value by customizing analytical software to meet the needs of users. They can automate large portions of the data mining process so that end users can focus on the substantive business problem.

There will always be situations in which users need to consult with model builders or application developers on difficult problems. In fact, even model builders and application developers sometimes need to consult with other experts when a problem gets too large or complex. However, many important everyday questions can be answered quickly and effectively by OLAP reports and visualization methods that can be used by almost anyone. In later chapters, we will cover these methods, from basic to advanced.

Understanding Data

One of the fundamentals of data mining is understanding the basics of data. At its most basic level, data are abstract representations of some part of reality. Data provide a way to take the complexity of your business environment and abstract, encapsulate, and store it. Each value indicates something about the real world—some aspect of one of your customers, a detail about a phone call carried by your telecommunications system, information about a taxpayer's itemized deductions, and so forth.

You can think of the data as providing a snapshot (or a movie) of your business environment. Data mining is akin to examining that snapshot with a combination of high-tech methods and a trained eye to find the important patterns. Without the picture, there's nothing to examine; likewise, without data, there's nothing to mine, and any conjecture about exploitable relationships reduces to guesswork.[1]

Characteristics of Data

Just as a snapshot has characteristics such as the field of view, sharpness, and so on, data sets have characteristics that describe them. These characteristics of the data define the questions that can be successfully addressed using that data.

The first characteristic is the **sampling scheme**. This refers to the method of selecting the data to include in the data set and the data to exclude. You rarely have *all* of the data that could possibly exist. It may be that only events that occur after a certain point in time appear in the data set, or it may be that events of a certain type are excluded. It is important to know what the limits of the data are and how those limits might affect your efforts at data mining. A tragic example of neglecting to consider the limits of the data was the Challenger space shuttle disaster. In the days before the mission, engineers examined test data to predict the performance of the rubber O-rings as a function of temperature at launch time. Unfortunately, their models were based only on cases where the O-rings actually failed. Had the model been based on all of the data, including cases where the O-rings did *not* fail, the model would have successfully predicted the outcome of the fateful launch, and the mission could have been postponed until conditions were warmer.[2]

1. Even in cases where you have ideas about relationships based on personal experience or other nondata sources, it is important to confirm those ideas with data. Testing your theories against a data set gives you the confidence to act authoritatively if your suspicions are confirmed and protects you from potential strategic mistakes if they are not.

This does not mean that all sampling is bad. Quite the opposite is true, in fact. In most situations, your data warehouse will contain far more data than you need to answer your questions. In cases like this, basing your data mining efforts on a properly selected subsample of your data warehouse can dramatically reduce the time required (and costs incurred) in data mining without significantly reducing the accuracy of your results. In this way, sampling allows you to increase your return on investment for data mining.

Another important characteristic of data is accuracy. **Accuracy** refers to how well the values in your data set match the attributes that they represent. For example, if you are measuring call duration but are rounding these values to the next minute, you are losing some information because of the rounding. On the other hand, if you measure call duration in minutes and seconds, your values will be more accurate. In general, the more accurate your measurements are, the better your data represent the real world. Knowing where your data are more or less accurate is necessary in interpreting your data mining results.

A third important characteristic is the quality of the data. **Data quality** refers to aspects such as completeness of the data, consistency of measurements, and so on. Unfortunately, because of constraints on resources, real-world data sets are rarely perfect in these respects. Too many missing values, inconsistencies in the way things were measured (for example, rephrasing questions on a questionnaire half way through a survey), data entry errors, and other such problems can make data mining very difficult. Knowing the ways in which your data quality is good or bad can be crucial to formulating correct interpretations of data mining results.

Organization of Data

Data can be organized in many different ways. The organization of the data should reflect the task at hand. There are some general concepts that apply to most data structures, however. You start by assuming that there are items you want to talk about. These items might be transactions, customers, phone calls, survey respondents, inventory units, etc. Each of these items has qualities that have been recorded. For a transaction, these qualities might consist of date and time, customer ID, sale amount, product purchased, and so on. A collection of information about items and associated qualities is usually arranged in a grid, where rows represent items and columns represent qualities.

2. For more information on the reanalysis of space shuttle O-ring data, see Dalal et al. (1989) and Tappin (1994).

Because data mining has such diverse roots, you will discover that different people use different terminology to talk about the same thing. The concepts described in the previous paragraph are referred to by various names, which are summarized in Table 1-1. In this book, for simplicity we use the database terminology, although we use the alternatives if the situation warrants.

Table 1-1
Data terminology used by groups involved with data mining

Group	Term for items	Term for qualities	Term for data grids
Database managers	Records, rows	Fields, columns	Tables
Statisticians	Cases, observations	Variables	Data sets
Artificial intelligence researchers	Cases, examples	Features, attributes	Data sets

For storing and accessing large amounts of data, the organization of choice is the relational database. A **relational database** consists of tables (data grids), each of which summarizes the details of a particular aspect of the overall business process. For example, in a transaction database, there might be one table for orders, another table for customers, and another for products. These tables are usually linked together using **key fields**. In our example, the orders table might contain a field for customer ID, which can be linked to the appropriate record in the customers table. In that way, information on a particular customer needs to be stored only once, in the customers table, rather than being stored as redundant data with each order in the orders table. Because this data structure is, in a certain sense, the simplest (it eliminates redundancy in the data), data formatted this way are called **normalized** data. A hypothetical normalized database is shown in Figure 1-1.

Figure 1-1
Relational database with three linked tables

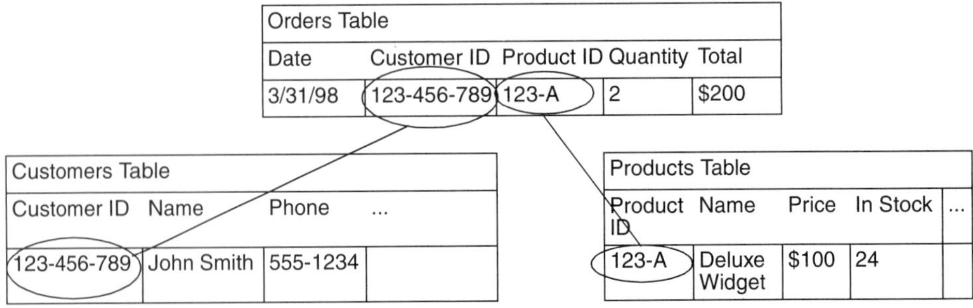

While normalization is efficient for storing large amounts of data, it makes data mining more difficult because data mining techniques are designed to operate on simple data sets where there is only one table, with one row for each record and one column for each field. Such data are called **denormalized** data because they usually contain some redundancy. The denormalized data from the previous example are shown in Figure 1-2. Notice that the product name and price appear twice in this data set—once for each row—whereas they appear only once in the normalized data set.

Figure 1-2
Denormalized data set with redundant product information

Orders Table (denormalized)									
Date	Customer ID	Customer Name	Phone	Product ID	Product Name	Price	Quantity	Total	...
3/31/98	123-456-789	John Smith	555-1234	123-A	Deluxe Widget	$100	2	$200	
4/1/98	456-789-123	Jane Johnson	555-4321	123-A	Deluxe Widget	$100	1	$100	
...									

Shape of Data

One of the most important aspects of data is that they almost always contain **variability**; in other words, not all of the records have the same value for a particular field. This variability in data is what gives them meaning. The pattern of different values for a given variable (field) defines the **shape** of the variable. (In statistics, this is called the **distribution** of the variable.) The shape of a variable can be examined using a plot called a **histogram**, which shows the different possible values and how frequently each occurs, as shown in Figure 1-3.

Figure 1-3
Histogram of hypothetical salary variable

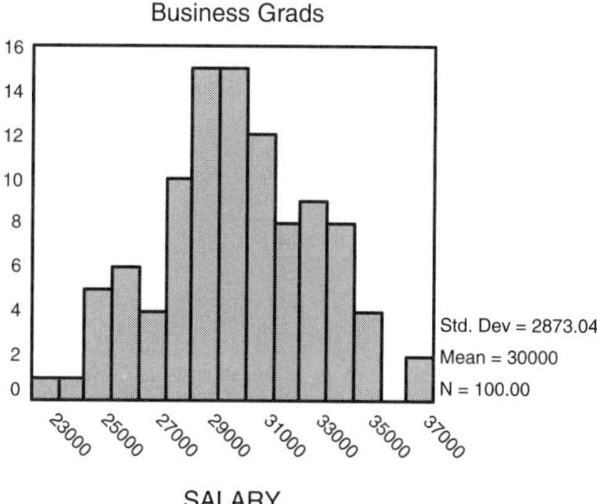

One of the biggest mistakes data analysts make is restricting themselves to looking at averages (also known as **means**). Averages are, of course, valuable for looking at your data, as far as they go. But averages are not enough—you can't get the full value from your data if you look only at averages. For example, consider the plots shown in Figure 1-4. These represent the shape of a hypothetical salary variable for three different employment groups. They all have an average salary of $30,000, but they obviously have very different shapes. The first group, business graduates, has the sort of distribution you might expect, with a hump in the middle and values getting rarer as they get further from the mean. The second group, master's level statisticians, has a very different shape with two humps, indicating that there may actually be two subgroups hidden in this group (perhaps those working in lower-paid academic jobs versus those in higher-paid industry jobs). The third group, university teaching assistants, all have the same value, their salaries being determined by the university.

Figure 1-4
Histograms illustrating different shapes of data

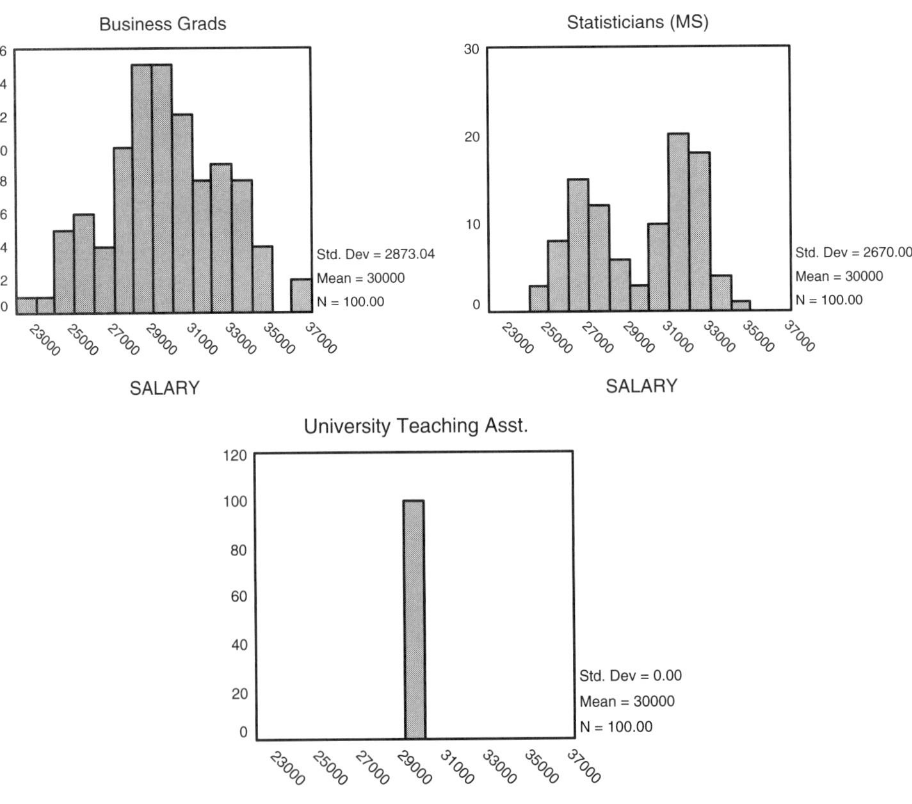

You would not want to conclude that these three groups are the same, despite their identical average values. Examining the variability within each group is the key to seeing the differences. This concept applies to all of data mining—identifying, explaining, and exploiting the variability is the source of value in your data.

About This Book

This book provides a thorough overview of how data mining is used to increase value in the context of business. Whenever possible, realistic examples are used to clarify points and to show how concepts are applied.

However, this book should not be considered a comprehensive data mining handbook. While the information presented here may be enough to get you started, data mining is a broad and complex field, and if you plan to become a regular data miner, you will want to consult the works listed in the bibliography to increase your knowledge of the topic. This will help you to get the most from your data mining efforts and to be more confident about your results.

Chapter

2

Overview of the Data Mining Process

As with all things, data mining is much more effective if you do it in a planned, systematic way. For all the hype you may have seen about data mining as "automatic data analysis," you will still need to take an active role in managing the data mining process. Even with today's cutting edge data mining tools, the majority of the work in data mining requires the careful eye of a knowledgeable business analyst to keep the process on track. This includes making decisions such as:

- What substantive problem you want to solve
- What data sources you have available and what parts of the data are relevant to the current problem
- What kind of preprocessing and cleaning you should do before mining the data
- What data mining technique(s) to use
- Evaluating the results of the data mining analysis
- Deciding how to get the most out of the information gained from data mining

The typical data mining process can become complicated very quickly. There's a lot to keep track of—complex business problems, multiple data sources, varying data quality across data sources, an array of data mining techniques to choose from, different ways of measuring data mining success, and so on.

To help you stay on track, it helps to have an explicitly defined process model for data mining. The process model guides you through the critical issues outlined above and makes sure that the important points are addressed. It serves as a data mining road map so that you won't lose your way as you dig into the complexities of your data.

The data mining process model we'll use in this book is based on the Cross-Industry Standard Process for Data Mining (CRISP-DM), a very general model developed by a consortium of organizations that saw the need for a standardized approach to data mining. This process model can be applied to a wide variety of industries and organizational problems. The remainder of this chapter will give an overview of the general CRISP-DM process model. In the chapters that follow, we'll describe in more detail the various phases of the data mining process and give examples from a set of typical data mining problems.

General Process Model

The general CRISP-DM process model includes six phases that address the main issues in data mining and fit together in a cyclical process, as shown in Figure 2-1.

Figure 2-1
The CRISP-DM process model

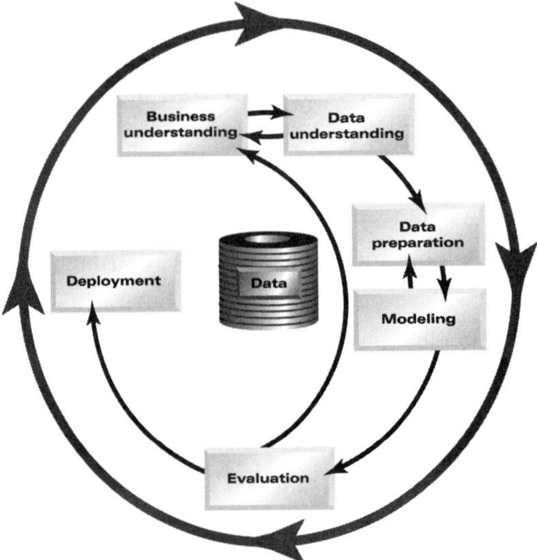

These six phases cover the full data mining process, including how to incorporate data mining into your larger business practices:

- **Business understanding.** This is perhaps the most important phase of data mining. Business understanding includes determining business objectives, assessing the situation, determining data mining goals, and producing a project plan.
- **Data understanding.** Data are the "raw materials" of data mining. This phase addresses the need to understand what your data resources are and the characteristics of those resources. It includes collecting initial data, describing data, exploring data, and verifying data quality.

- **Data preparation.** After cataloging your data resources, you will need get them ready for mining. Tasks include selecting, cleaning, constructing, integrating, and formatting data.
- **Modeling.** This is the "meat" of data mining, where sophisticated analysis methods are used to extract information from the data. This phase involves selecting modeling techniques, generating test designs, and building and assessing models.
- **Evaluation.** Once you have your models in hand, you are ready to evaluate how the data mining results can help you achieve your business objectives. Elements of this phase include evaluating results, reviewing the data mining process, and determining the next steps.
- **Deployment.** Now that you've invested all of this effort, it's time for the payback. This phase focuses on integrating your new knowledge into your everyday business processes to solve your original business problem. It includes plan deployment, monitoring and maintenance, producing a final report, and reviewing the project.

There are some key points illustrated in Figure 2-1. First, you can see that while there is a general tendency for the process to flow through the steps in the order outlined above, there are also a number of places where the phases influence each other in a nonlinear way. For example, data preparation often precedes modeling. However, decisions made and information gathered during the modeling phase can often cause you to rethink parts of the data preparation phase, which can then lead to new modeling issues, and so on. The two phases feed back on each other until both phases have been resolved adequately. Similarly, the evaluation phase can sometimes lead you to reevaluate your original business understanding, and you may decide you've been trying to answer the wrong question. At this point, you can revise your business understanding and proceed through the rest of the process again with a better target in mind.

Another key point is embodied by the outer cyclical arrow surrounding the process. Data mining is an **iterative** process. You will rarely, if ever, simply plan a data mining project, execute it, and then pack up your data and go home. Using data mining to address your customers' demands is an ongoing endeavor. The knowledge gained from one cycle of data mining will almost invariably lead to new questions, new issues, and new opportunities to identify and meet your organization's goals. Those new questions, issues, and opportunities can usually be addressed by mining your data once again. This iterative process of mining and identifying new opportunities should become part of the way you think about your enterprise and a cornerstone of your overall operational strategy.

Examples

In the remainder of this book, we will illustrate concepts by showing how they might apply to specific data mining projects. Most of the examples will be taken from one of the following scenarios.

Example 1: Customer Relationship Management

The first example scenario is a retail company selling consumer electronics. The company wants to use its data on customers, products, and transactions to find ways to improve customer satisfaction and decrease costs. The data for this example are fictitious.

Example 2: Public Sector Fraud Detection

The second example scenario is a government agency charged with administering assistance grants to farmers in need. The agency is primarily interested in reducing fraud in grant applications. The data for this example are fictitious.

Example 3: Web Log Analysis

The third example scenario is a company specializing in e-commerce, which wants to find ways to maximize the return from their online business-to-consumer (B2C) operations. They plan to do this by mining their Web logs along with other data, such as customer registration data and purchased demographics. The data for this example are actual clickstream and demographic data from a now defunct e-commerce company called Gazelle.com that specialized in selling legwear (socks, pantyhose, etc.). These data were used in the KDD-Cup 2000 data mining competition and are made available through the kindness of Blue Martini Software. (Customer identification information has been removed from the data.) For more information, see the KDD-Cup 2000 organizers' report (Kohavi et al., 2000), or visit the Web site at *http://www.ecn.purdue.edu/kddcup.* Note that the data mining process illustrated here with these data is not meant to represent analysis that was actually performed by Gazelle.com analysts or their associates; it merely represents a possible approach to mining data of this kind.

Chapter

3

Business Understanding

If you don't know where you're going, you'll probably end up somewhere else.

—Laurence Peter

Having a clear vision of what you want to accomplish is the cornerstone of successful data mining. Unfortunately, there is a common misconception of data mining as a black box into which you drop data and then "something interesting" magically appears. Successful data mining, however, rests on two principles: a solid foundation of business knowledge and a focused attack on a specific problem.

The CRISP-DM process model includes a series of tasks that help you develop the business understanding necessary to make your data mining efforts pay off. These tasks are:

- Determining business objectives
- Assessing the situation
- Determining data mining goals
- Producing a project plan

Completing these tasks enables you to understand where you want to go, where you are right now, and how the business problem translates into a data mining problem, and it also gives you a concrete plan to get the job done.

Determining Business Objectives

The first task is to develop a thorough understanding, from a *business* perspective, of what you want to accomplish. Keep in mind that successful data mining is driven primarily by business rather than by data or technology. Often, you will have many competing objectives and constraints that must be properly balanced. If you try to take on the whole world at once, you are likely to fail. On the other hand, if you plan carefully and focus on a specific, achievable, measurable goal, you will be well on your way to success.

Background

The first step is to understand the background of the problem. By *background*, we mean the details of the organization's business situation at the start of the project. This information helps refine the business goal and identify resources that can be used to reach that goal.

Example: **CRM.** The company is a consumer electronics retailer and would like to improve relationships with customers. Improving relationships with customers is a very broad goal, one that is achieved in manageable steps. There are three possibilities for improving the value of your customer relationships: decrease the cost of initiating the relationship, increase the amount and/or quality of business with the customer, or increase the length of the relationship. For now, the company will focus on the second possibility.

Increasing the amount and quality of business with customers is still too general, so the company needs to narrow the goal further. Cross-selling presents an important way to increase the amount of business with a customer. When done properly, cross-selling benefits both customers and the company. Customers have more of their needs met in one place, and the company sees increased revenue generated through additional sales. So, for this example, the company will consider how to use cross-selling to increase business volume with existing customers. ■■■

Example: **Web mining.** The company runs an e-commerce Web site selling legwear (socks, nylons, etc.). The company would like to make the site friendlier and easier to use so that visitors enjoy their experience more and are more likely to become repeat customers. ■■■

Example: **Fraud detection.** The agency is concerned about identifying potentially fraudulent grant applications and would like to find a way to use available information (from the application itself and other sources) to select suspicious applications for further investigation. ■■■

Business Objectives

Business objectives are detailed descriptions of what you want to accomplish using data mining. This always includes a primary objective and often includes secondary objectives as well. *Be specific* in defining business objectives. You must pin down precisely what you want to see happen in your business. The path to defining business objectives includes describing the problem to be solved, specifying all business questions, detailing any related business requirements, and outlining the expected benefits from data mining.

Example: **CRM.** The electronics retailer wants to use cross-selling to increase customer value and loyalty. This needs to be narrowed further to derive a useful business objective. The company starts by focusing on a new product line and would like to launch a marketing campaign to let customers know about the new offerings. However, the company has a limited budget, so the campaign will focus on the customers who are most likely to respond. Therefore, the business objective will be to identify the customers who are most likely to respond to the marketing campaign. ■■■

Example: **Web mining.** The objective is to be able to identify factors that increase the probability of a surfer leaving the site. There could be any number of factors involved here, including pages that take too long to load, problems finding the product of choice, requiring too many clicks to get to the desired page, or other unknown factors. ■■■

Business Success Criteria

This piece of the puzzle focuses on how you will measure the results of your efforts and what kind of performance will be regarded as successful. Again, each criterion should be defined from the business perspective, for example—"increase sales of new credit card accounts by X%" rather than "build a neural network with X% accuracy."

Each stated business goal should have at least one criterion, and each criterion should correspond to one of the original business goals. If you specify a success criterion that doesn't directly correspond to one of the stated business goals, you may need to reconsider whether the criterion is relevant for this data mining project. If you find that you do consider the criterion in question to be a good measure of success, you may need to redefine the business goals to better match your definition of success.

The success criteria can range from the very concrete, such as "sales will be $X for the next quarter," to the subjective, such as "we will understand why our customers are buying from our competitors." The more objective the criteria are, the easier it will be to assess your results later. However, subjective criteria can also be used to evaluate data mining results as long as you identify exactly who will make the final judgment about the criteria at this early stage of the process.

Example: **CRM.** The aim is to entice existing customers to make purchases from the company's new product line. Since this is the first foray into e-CRM/data mining, the company will start with a small project and will consider the project a success if the profit increase due to data mining is larger than the cost of the mining. That would constitute a positive return on investment for this project, and it would also demonstrate the value of data mining, providing a good justification for broadening the scope of its data mining efforts. ■■■

Example: **Fraud detection.** The success criterion here is less distinct, because the agency doesn't have historical data on fraudulent claims. The agency won't be able to make purely predictive models in this situation but can create models that highlight anomalous grant applications. That should allow the agency to focus its investigative resources on the cases most likely to reveal irregularities. ■■■

Assessing the Situation

Now that you know where you want to end up, it's time to take stock of where you are now in order to chart a course that will get you to your destination. This includes identifying available resources, constraints, assumptions, and other factors that will determine how to proceed. This information will help you formulate a realistic and achievable plan applying data mining.

Inventory of Resources

You need to know what resources you will have at your disposal during the data mining process, including the following:

- **Personnel.** Business and data experts, technical support staff, and data mining personnel.
- **Data.** Fixed extracts and/or live access to data warehouses, data marts, or operational databases.

- **Computing resources.** Hardware for performing data analysis and related activities.
- **Software.** Programs for accessing, cleaning, and analyzing data, and applications for reporting and deploying the results.

The availability of these resources will affect important aspects of your project, such as the scope and time line. Having a clear picture of what you will have at your disposal will allow you to plan accordingly and increase your odds of success.

Example: **Web mining.** For personnel, the company has a business analyst with substantial retail experience (50% time), a database analyst (50% time), and a data mining consulting firm (2 analysts, 100% time). For data, the company has a data warehouse of information derived from Web logs, registration information for many customers, and order (purchase) information. The company also has some purchased demographics that have been merged with the operational data. For computing resources, the data warehouse resides on a multiprocessor UNIX system. The company also has a dedicated, high-speed, Windows XP workstation that can be completely devoted to the data mining project. The data mining consultants will also provide some hardware support for their activities. For software, in addition to the RDBMS used to host the data, the company will use the Clementine data mining workbench from SPSS Inc. A copy of SPSS Base software is available for certain tasks that are more easily done there than in Clementine. ■■■

Requirements, Assumptions, and Constraints

In addition to understanding your data mining assets (resources), you need to understand the liabilities associated with the data mining project. These are factors that can potentially affect the schedule for the project and the quality of results, and these factors can also have security and legal ramifications.

In any large project like data mining, you will have to base your planning on certain assumptions. They may concern the data or other resources for the project, or they may concern the business model underlying the entire project. Data assumptions are relatively simple to test during the data mining process, but business assumptions can be more complicated to understand and assess. Some business assumptions may prove to be untestable, but they can still have an impact on the results of the project. Explicitly outlining these assumptions will help you to understand some of the key determinants of success for the project and will also help you to avoid potential pitfalls.

In planning the project, take the different constraints into account. Constraints come in various forms: limitations on available resources, legal and ethical restrictions, and conflicting business requirements. (An example of the latter might be "take every opportunity to expose potential customers to our products," and "don't drive customers away with overbearing marketing tactics.")

Example: **CRM.** The fundamental requirement is that the company must identify a target group of customers who will be likely to respond to a new product promotion.

Assumptions include the following: it is possible to find a model that will generate accurate (enough) predictions from the available data; the company will be able to devise a marketing strategy that can effectively take advantage of the knowledge gained through data mining; and economic conditions in the near future will be similar to the recent past, so that the model, which is based on past data, will still make sense in the deployment time frame.

The company's main constraints are a three-month implementation time frame that coincides with the launch of the new product line and, of course, resource limitations. ■■■

Risks and Contingencies

In any project, there are risks. There is the potential for events beyond your control to disrupt the process. Those events can have a huge impact on the schedule of your project and the quality of the results. However, forewarned is forearmed; by taking the time to list the relevant risks and outlining contingencies to handle them, you can avert disaster. Obviously, not all adverse events can be predicted, and some risks may not allow an adequate contingency plan. But if you can cover the majority of potential problems, you will minimize the likelihood of an unexpected setback.

In a data mining project of any size, risk comes in many forms:

- **Business risks**, such as changes in your market or in the general business climate.
- **Organizational risks**, such as staff turnover or political shifts.
- **Financial risks**, such as diversion or loss of resources in mid-project.
- **Technical risks**, such as equipment breakdowns or incompatibility between computing platforms or software packages.
- **Data risks**, such as poor data quality or access problems.

Each type of risk presents unique challenges. For each risk, consider the conditions under which the project would be compromised. As much as possible, be sure to have a contingency plan to cover each risk. In some cases, one contingency plan may suffice to cover several risks.

Example: Web mining. With control over most aspects of the project, the company can do a lot to minimize risks. Data is backed up both on- and off-site, and the company has service contracts on computer equipment to have it repaired or replaced within 24 hours. The company can't control the business environment, but evaluating various economic indicators has revealed that any major change that would invalidate the project is unlikely to happen in the relevant time frame. The time frame is short enough that organizational risks should be small. One possible wild card is the data mining consultants. If the consultants turn out to be unable to complete the task, the company will need to find someone else to do the technical work. This would create a setback to the schedule, but the company has made arrangements with the consulting agency to get a replacement up to speed quickly, if necessary. Since the company is running the data warehouse internally, it has a pretty good sense of what it contains and the condition of the data. The analysts know that the data are not perfect, but they are confident that overall the data are in decent shape. In addition, they have the source data from operational system archives. If they find severe problems in the warehouse, they can probably reconstruct the data to fix those problems, though this would clearly involve a significant cost in terms of delays and increased resource requirements. ■■■

Terminology

Every field has its own terminology or jargon. When team members from different backgrounds try to discuss a project using these specialized vocabularies, it can lead to a virtual Tower of Babel.

To help your data mining project flow as smoothly as possible, it's important to outline the terminology that will be used throughout the project. Particularly important is an understanding of how the terminology for describing the business problem and the terminology for specifying the data mining procedure mesh together. At this point, you should outline the relevant terminology from both perspectives and make sure that everyone on the team understands the meaning of each term. It is worth putting these definitions in writing, as well. A formal glossary gives team members a reference to guide them through ambiguities that may arise during the course of the project.

Compiling such a glossary may seem like a luxury that can be skipped in the name of expediency, but it is a wise investment. If you don't give this matter the attention it deserves, your project will very likely suffer from confusion and wasted effort later.

Example: **Web mining.** During various planning meetings, a designated party keeps a list of jargon and buzzwords. Part of the meeting follow-up is to agree on definitions for any ambiguous items. The designated party makes this continuously updated glossary available to everyone on the project via a central document on the company intranet. ■■■

Costs and Benefits

As with any other investment, the key to understanding its place in your business plan is a detailed cost-benefit analysis. To make your data mining project pay off, you need to understand what the project will cost and what you stand to gain by implementing it.

When estimating costs, remember to factor in items such as developing the solution and ongoing maintenance for any implemented solution. When estimating benefits, remember to include less tangible benefits such as increased customer satisfaction or improved relations with the community.

Example: **CRM.** For this marketing campaign, the cost per contact is estimated to be about $0.30 per person, plus fixed costs of about $5,000 for copy writing, design, mail handling, etc. The average profit per purchase in the new product line is expected to be about $20. The cost of the data mining project is estimated at $15,000. So, to justify the effort, the company needs to attract about 500 more buyers than it would have without data mining, given the same number of mailers sent out. ■■■

Example: **Fraud detection.** The costs involved here will be more modest, because the data sets involved are simpler and smaller than those used in the other examples. In addition, only in-house data analysis expertise will be used—no high-priced consultants. The fixed costs will be approximately $5,000–$7,000 for the data mining project. In this case, there is an additional cost of investigation for each claim identified as potentially fraudulent. However, the grants awarded by the agency generally range between $10,000 and $300,000 with some as large as $600,000. Thus, if a single fraudulent claim can be identified and rejected as a result of data mining, the effort will be worthwhile. ■■■

Determining Data Mining Goals

Now that you have developed a thorough understanding of the business problem to be solved and the general business context, the next step is to identify how data mining will help you solve that problem. Specifically, you need to identify what information you will need to obtain by mining your data. That information is your data mining goal. Here, you are mapping your business goal to a data mining goal. By achieving the data mining goal, you produce the key element for achieving your business goal.

Data Mining Goals

A data mining goal describes the requirements for solving your business problem in technical terms rather than business terms. This brings the problem to a concrete level, a level that brings to bear the powerful tools of data mining.

Example: **CRM.** The data mining goal is to build a model that predicts the purchase of a new product in response to a marketing campaign based on available customer data. The model has to be accurate enough to save time and effort by allowing the company to target the promotion to the right customers. It must also be general enough to apply to current and future customer profiles for a reasonable time window, in this case at least six months (the time for the data mining project plus three months of actual use to realize the return). ■■■

Example: **Web mining.** The data mining goal here is to produce a model (or models) that allow the analysts to identify factors related to Web site visitors leaving the site. These factors should give them insight into how to improve the site so that visitors stay longer and become customers. ■■■

Data Mining Success Criteria

When you define business objectives, you also define success criteria as a way to test how well those objectives are met. You must follow a similar pattern with data mining goals. Once you've specified the goals, you need to determine how you will assess your data mining results. In the case of data mining goals, the success criteria should be specified in technical terms, such as a certain degree of predictive accuracy.

Once again, your job will be easier if you stipulate objective criteria for judging your success. However, you can also accommodate more subjective success criteria if you specify up front who will be responsible for making the judgment and the characteristics that will be used to formulate that judgment.

Finally, in evaluating your data mining success, remember to include deployment issues. A great data mining model is not much use if there's no practical way to apply the model to your daily business routine. You don't get any return on your investment until you capitalize on that new knowledge.

Example: **CRM.** The success criteria correspond to the data mining goals outlined above. To ensure that its model is general, the company will build the model on one set of customer data and test it on a different set of known data. This will test how well the model will perform on new data. In order to have adequate predictions, the accuracy of the model must be good enough to let the company increase the response rate to the desired level without requiring a corresponding increase in the number of contacts. The point is not to simply make more contacts but to make *better* contacts. ■■■

Producing a Project Plan

At this point, you have all the pieces necessary to construct a plan for your data mining project. This is the last task in developing your business understanding for the data mining project, and it provides the context for the rest of the work in your project.

Project Plan

Here, you will make a detailed road map for the project. The project plan should include all identified goals and selected techniques in a coherent procedure that directly addresses the business problem. The CRISP-DM process model provides a skeleton for this plan, but you will need to fill in the specifics at each point in the process, including duration, required resources, output, and dependencies. Also include details about where the risks and associated contingency plans fit into the process.

Example: **CRM.** The following table presents an outline of the project plan for the data mining project.

Phase	Time	Resources	Risks
Business understanding	1 week	All analysts	Economic change
Data understanding	3 weeks	All analysts	Data problems, technology problems
Data preparation	5 weeks	Data mining consultants, some database analyst time	Data problems, technology problems
Modeling	2 weeks	Data mining consultants, possibly some database analyst time	Technology problems, inability to find adequate model
Evaluation	1 week	All analysts	Economic change, inability to implement results
Deployment	1 week	Data mining consultants, database analyst	Economic change, inability to implement results

■■■

Initial Assessment of Tools and Techniques

At this planning stage, you also need to start thinking about what tools you will adopt for your data mining efforts. Your choice of tools will influence the rest of the data mining process, so it is important to choose a flexible suite of tools that provides the methods you need for the data preparation, modeling, evaluation, and deployment phases of the process. You will find a brief summary of data mining methods in Chapter 9.

For the examples this book, we will use Clementine from SPSS Inc., a comprehensive data mining workbench that provides data access and manipulation tools, a variety of modeling methods, and deployable model results that can be easily incorporated into regular business operations.

Summary

This chapter outlined the importance of establishing a solid business understanding of the data mining project. The critical tasks and associated results of this phase include:

Determining business objectives. Defining the goals from a business perspective.

Task results:

- Background
- Business objectives
- Business success criteria

Assessing the situation. Determining where things stand at the beginning of the project.

Task results:

- Inventory of resources
- Requirements, assumptions, and constraints
- Risks and contingencies
- Terminology
- Costs and benefits

Determining data mining goals. Translating business goals into terms that data mining can directly address.

Task results:

- Data mining goals
- Data mining success criteria

Producing a project plan. Creating a blueprint for the remainder of the project.

Task results:

- Project plan
- Initial assessment of tools and techniques

Chapter

4

Data Understanding

Collecting Initial Data

The second phase of the data mining process involves getting to know your primary asset—your data. Of course, the first step in getting to know your data is to *get* your data. This involves identifying the sources of data that you will use and then assembling the data and loading them into your data mining tool(s) for closer inspection.

In defining the data to be used, you need to keep in mind your data mining goals and the business objectives on which they are based. To the best of your ability, make sure that you can get all of the data that you need to achieve these goals. If you are lacking a critical piece of information to achieve a data mining goal, find out what it will take to get the information. For example, if you need measurements of customer satisfaction but do not have that kind of data, you will have to collect the information actively, probably with some kind of survey. E-commerce provides an excellent channel for surveys, since the deployment costs for Web surveys are quite low compared to traditional phone or mail surveys. If you need demographic data, you can also use survey methods, or you may be able to purchase the information from commercial data resellers. The main point is that you may have to seek out data actively if you don't have all of the data you need in-house.

Next, you will have to decide in detail what information you need. For example, you might have decided that you need account balances (among other things). You then have to decide which account balances to include, on what dates, for which customers, and so on. If you decide to use demographic data, which personal characteristics will you use? Are there characteristics that must be excluded because of legal or ethical constraints? You will have to assess your available data and decide which databases to use, what characteristics (columns) to take from each database, how to merge the various data sources together coherently, and how to get the final result into your data mining tool.

Example: **Web mining.** The company has three primary internal data sources: the Web logs containing details of individual Web events (page views, searches, and so on), customer registration data (from a form submitted on the Web site), and order transaction data. The analysts decide that the data mining project could benefit from more detailed demographic data than is available from the registration database, so they purchase demographic data from a data vendor, giving them a fourth data source. ■■■

Example: **Fraud detection.** The agency has a database of grant applications for the last year. The agency also determines that localized rainfall information is necessary to assess the potential productivity of each farm accurately for the time period covered by the grant. The rainfall data is available from another government agency and can be downloaded from the other agency's Web site. ■■■

Describing the Data

Once you have assembled the data, you need to look at the overall characteristics of the data. Characteristics such as amount of data, value types, and coding schemes have an impact on how you proceed with data mining. By getting a handle on these characteristics early in the data mining process, you can make the best use of your data and avoid being blindsided by problems.

In assessing the amount of data, there are two primary considerations: the number of items described (database records) and the number of characteristics used to describe them (database fields). For most data mining techniques, there are trade-offs involved with data size. In some cases, larger data sets—more records, more fields, or both—can produce more accurate models. On the other hand, larger data sets always require more time to process. Taking the time to get a good sense of the amount of data you have will help you make decisions about selecting and constructing data in the data preparation phase.

The value types and coding schemes of the data are equally important. These attributes determine how the information in your database maps onto the real-world entities that it describes. **Value types** describe what sort of values are legitimate for each field in the database. Some fields are **numeric**, such as age or account balance. Such fields can take numeric values within a reasonable range, and in most cases, the usual mathematical operations, such as addition and subtraction, can be applied to them. Others fields are **symbolic**, such as gender or account type. Such fields take values from a limited set of possibilities, and there is usually no particular ordering or numerical "meaning" to the values—you can't do arithmetic with them, for example. Others may be **Boolean**, which are true or false characteristics. There are additional value types but too many to discuss in detail here. The main point is that the types of fields in your data affect how your data mining tools work and your ability to build good, reliable models in a reasonable amount of time. In particular, symbolic fields with a large number of unique values can cause problems. (We will discuss this further in Chapter 5.)

Coding schemes refer to the correspondence between values stored in the database and the actual characteristics being measured. For numeric fields, the value in the database is simply a quantitative measurement of the characteristic of interest. However, there are almost always multiple ways of measuring any characteristic, and it is important to find out what measurement scheme is actually used. A recent example of the importance of this is the loss of a NASA Mars probe because of the confusion between English and metric measurements in the flight calculations.

For symbolic fields, values are typically represented by integers or character strings. In these cases, the coding scheme always has a certain arbitrariness to it. For example, you may have a database field that indicates customer gender—male or female. You can encode this kind of information in a number of ways, as shown in the following table:

Males	Females
0	1
1	0
1	2
'M'	'F'
"MALE"	"FEMALE"
"male"	"female"

Each row represents one possible coding scheme. Note that the last two rows are not equivalent; for many databases and analysis tools, "MALE" is not the same as "male". It is important to understand how your symbolic fields are coded. This is especially true if you are integrating data from multiple sources, which may use different coding schemes to represent the same information. For example, your in-house customer database may use a 0/1 coding scheme for gender, while a purchased mailing list database may use M/F. In such cases, you will need to decide on a common representation scheme and make whatever conversions are necessary to ensure that all of the data use the same representation.

At this point, you also need to be sure that you understand what each database field represents. Often, this can be more difficult than you might expect. For example, a field labeled *CC_BALANCE* seems simple enough—it is the credit card balance. However, there are a lot of details to be filled in. Is this an instantaneous "snapshot" balance or is it an average balance? If it is a snapshot, when was it recorded? If it is an average, what is the window of averaging? Does this amount include pending transactions? As you can see, different answers to these questions will lead to different interpretations of this field in the context of your data mining process.

This kind of information is often called **metadata**—that is, data about data. Once you get this information, you should document it formally and put it in a place where it is easy to find—ideally inside your data warehouse itself. Then it will be available for future projects, and the person using the data a year from now won't have to duplicate your efforts to track these details down.

Exploring the Data

This task involves looking at your data at a very fine level of detail. Now that you know how your data are measured and represented in the database, you will use querying, visualization, and reporting or OLAP tools to examine the characteristics of the data itself. (See Chapter 10 and Chapter 11 for an overview and examples of tools used for data exploration.) This gives you critical insight into your market and customer base and can provide important clues about how to best achieve your data mining goals.

A large part of this involves looking at subgroups in your data. For example, you may spend some time looking at how customers from different market areas differ on various characteristics or how customers who use one set of products compare to those who use a different set. This process should prove invaluable in generating hypotheses about interesting relationships that can be exploited to reach your objectives. It will also give you information that can be used in the next task, verifying data quality.

Example: **Fraud detection.** In exploring the data, the agency discovered something interesting. There were a few applicant names for which there were multiple records in the database. The agency recognized this as a problem, so this information was noted for further consideration during data quality verification (see "Verifying Data Quality" on p. 39).

Figure 4-1
Distribution graph of applicant names showing multiple entries

Distribution of name

Value	Proportion	%	Count
name618		1.33	4
name777		0.67	2
name601		0.33	1
name602		0.33	1
name603		0.33	1
name604		0.33	1
name605		0.33	1
name606		0.33	1
name607		0.33	1
name608		0.33	1

Table Annotations

Example: **Web mining.** One thing the analysts needed to understand immediately was the kinds of sessions they were seeing at their site. A **session** is defined as the series of consecutive Web hits from a single visitor, as tracked using cookies and/or IP addresses. The first thing they looked at was the number of individual page hits for the session. The distribution of number of hits per session is shown in Figure 4-2.

Figure 4-2
Distribution of number of hits in session

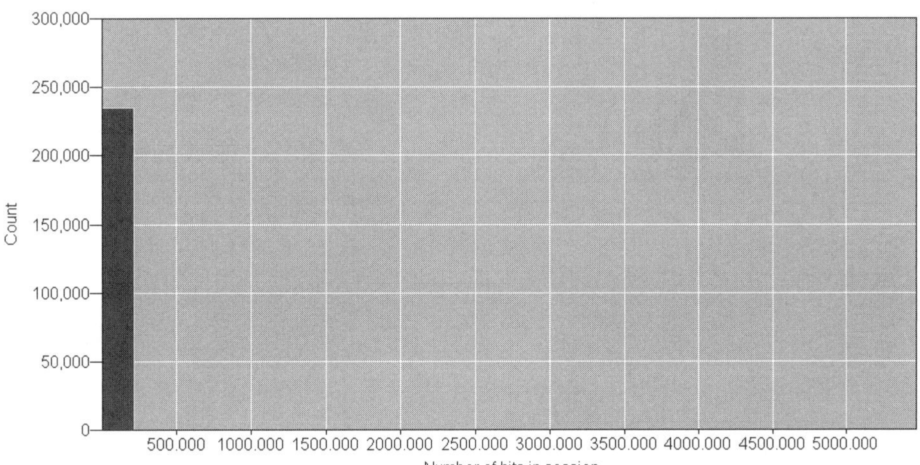

As you can see, a large majority of sessions had fewer than 100 hits, as you might expect. However, there are a handful of cases with hundreds or even thousands of hits. (You can't see the bars representing those sessions because there are so few of them relative to the number of shorter sessions. But the scale of the graph tells you that there is something out there at the high end.)

To get a better picture of these extreme cases, the analysts selected only those sessions with more than 200 hits and looked at their distribution, shown in Figure 4-3.

You can see that this is a relatively small number of sessions, but some of them have an extraordinarily high number of hits. Further investigation revealed that most of these high-hit-count sessions were generated by automatic Web crawlers, or "bots," crawling the site. We can eliminate these records from our analysis, since we are interested only in the Web-surfing behavior of actual people.

Figure 4-3
Distribution of number of hits for sessions with more than 200 hits

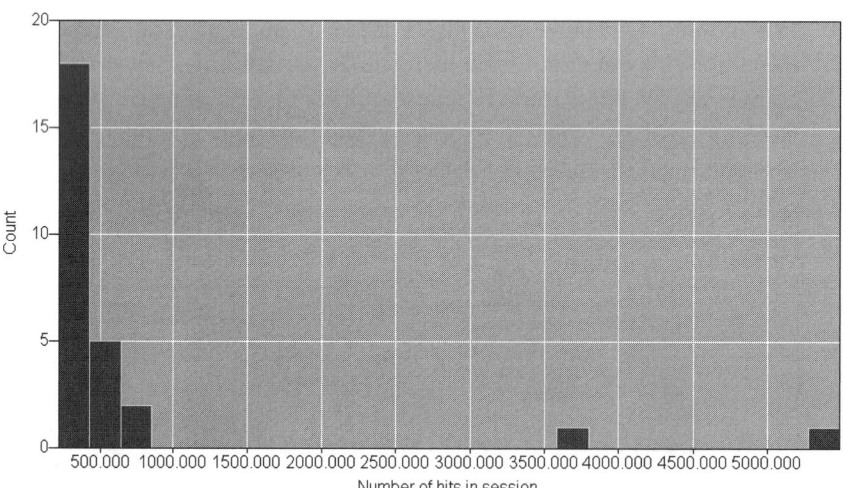

Verifying Data Quality

> Errors using inadequate data are much less than those using no data at all.
>
> —Charles Babbage

Unfortunately, virtually no database contains perfect data. Databases are maintained by fallible human beings, and data management is a complex, error-prone process. However, you needn't be discouraged by this fact. As Babbage pointed out, there is a great deal of value even in imperfect data. The trick is to know what kinds of problems exist in your data and, when possible, to correct those problems before you begin mining the data in earnest.

There are a number of ways that data can be "dirty," including:

- **Missing data.** This includes values that are not specified at all (blanks) or are entered as some noncontent value (for example, a category called "no response").
- **Data errors.** This includes values that are entered incorrectly in the database, such as typographical errors.
- **Measurement errors.** This includes values that are entered correctly but were erroneous to begin with, such as transaction counts that are based on the wrong time window.
- **Coding inconsistencies.** This includes values that are represented in a way that is confusing or inconsistent, such as using unusual units of measurement for numeric fields or having multiple synonymous categories for symbolic fields (for example, having values of both "male" and "M" in a gender field).
- **Bad metadata.** This includes mismatches between the stated meaning of a field and its apparent meaning, such as a field labeled *account balance* that contains only integers.

The same tools used in exploring your data can be used to help assess data quality. By examining OLAP reports and data visualizations, you should be able to spot the most troublesome data problems. The data quality report you create here will be indispensable during the data preparation phase and will allow you to maximize the value of your data.

Example: Fraud detection. As part of the data exploration process, the agency discovered that there were some applicant IDs with multiple records in the database.

At this point, the agency didn't really understand the reason for the multiple records but knew that these IDs should be unique. In the data quality report, the agency noted this problem and recommended that the records for these IDs be excluded from the analysis. In the long term, it would be worth investigating the cause of the multiple records to correct the problem in the database and prevent it from recurring. ■■■

Example: CRM. Using the Quality node in Clementine, the analysts discovered that the marital status field had a high proportion of missing values. This was noted in the data quality report, and the information will be used in the next phase in determining whether or not to use this field for modeling in this project.

Figure 4-4
Data quality results for CRM data

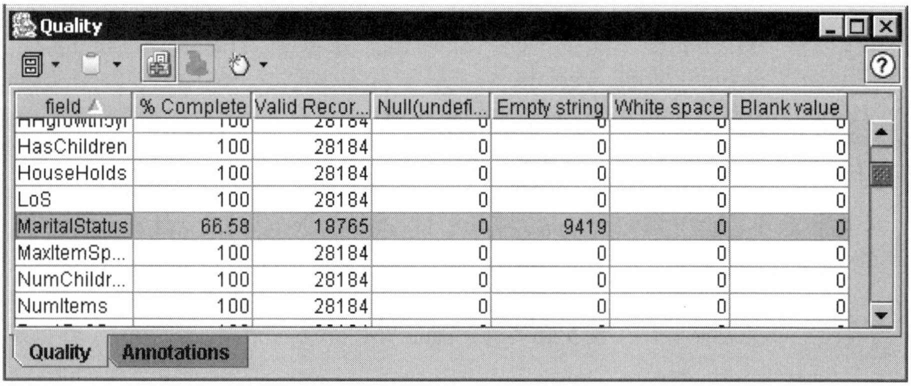

Quality

field	% Complete	Valid Recor...	Null(undefi...	Empty string	White space	Blank value
HasChildren	100	28184	0	0	0	0
HouseHolds	100	28184	0	0	0	0
LoS	100	28184	0	0	0	0
MaritalStatus	66.58	18765	0	9419	0	0
MaxItemSp...	100	28184	0	0	0	0
NumChildr...	100	28184	0	0	0	0
NumItems	100	28184	0	0	0	0

Quality | Annotations

■■■

Summary

This chapter outlined the steps in getting to know your data. The critical tasks and associated results of this phase include:

Collecting initial data. Finding out what you have to work with.

Task results:

- Initial data collection report

Describing the data. Understanding the basic structure of your data.

Task results:

- Data description report

Exploring the data. Digging into the details of your data.

Task results:

- Data exploration report

Verifying data quality. Assessing the usefulness and reliability of your data.

Task results:

- Data quality report

Chapter

5

Data Preparation

As a result of the data understanding phase, you have developed some working knowledge of your available data. The next step is to use that knowledge to assemble and package the data for mining.

How you go about preparing the data for mining will depend on several aspects of your project, including the business problem you're trying to solve, the data you have available, the tools you are using to prepare and mine the data, and other external factors, such as legal or ethical constraints or changes in business plan.

There are several things that need to be done in preparing the data. These include:

- Selecting the data to mine
- Cleaning the data to minimize the impact of data quality problems
- Constructing new data elements, such as derived attributes and generated records
- Integrating data from multiple data sources
- Reformatting data to suit the business problem and mining tool

Selecting Data

The first task is to decide what data to mine. Very rarely will you use all of the available data for data mining. There are almost certainly pieces of data in your database(s) that are not relevant to the business problem you are trying to solve. There may also be problems with data quality such that certain characteristics are measured so unreliably (or so rarely) that trying to include them would create more problems than they are worth.

If you are going to exclude some of your data from the analysis, you need to decide what parts of the data you will actually use. You will need to consider several factors in making this decision, including data mining goals, data quality, and technical constraints.

There are generally two ways you can select data: you can select which items (rows) to include, and you can select which characteristics or attributes (columns) to include. The criteria for each of these selections will be different. In most data mining situations, you will use both methods of selection—that is, you will use a subset of items and a subset of characteristics. This selection process allows you to focus your data mining resources on the heart of the business problem you are trying to solve.

The important thing in this task is to have a clear rationale for each data inclusion/exclusion decision. For each piece of data that you analyze, you should be able to explain exactly why you are using that bit of data. You don't need to know the precise value of each piece of data up front, but you should be able to articulate why you expect that data to have value. Conversely, for each portion of your data that is excluded, you should be able to describe why you didn't use it.

Selecting Rows

In preparing your data for data mining, you should already know what your fundamental units will be. They may be customers, accounts, business locations, products, or any other entity about which you have data and need to make business decisions. Each row in your mining data set should represent one of these units. You now need to decide which *specific* units to include in your mining data set. For example, if you are analyzing accounts, you will need to decide which accounts to use. Your decision will depend on the business problem and the availability of data. Some examples of selection criteria for accounts might be:

- **All accounts.** Include everything in your database.
- **Active accounts.** Include open accounts, but remove closed or inactive accounts from consideration.
- **Accounts in good standing.** Include only active accounts that are in good standing.
- **Profitable accounts.** Include only accounts with positive profitability estimates.
- **Accounts with complete data.** Exclude accounts with missing information in required fields.
- **Random sample.** Choose a subset of accounts at random to make the analysis more tractable.

Example: **Web mining.** In looking at the session data, the analysts discovered several high-hit-count sessions that were not actual human visitors but automatic Web indexing programs. Those rows were excluded from the final data set, since the analysts were interested in the behavior of real customers only. ■■■

Sampling

There is some debate among data mining experts about how many rows of data you should use. The basic choice is between using as much data as possible or using systematic sampling to select a subset of the data.

You Always Use a Sample (Whether You Want to or Not)

Sometimes the question about using all of the data is incorrectly framed as a choice between using a sample or not using a sample. The fact is that your data *always* represent a sample of some larger "virtual" pool of possible data. Even if you use every record in your data warehouse—even if that means millions of records—your goal will be to apply any information you gain to new situations. For example, you don't analyze all of the transactions from your online store just because you want to satisfy your intellectual curiosity. You do so because you want to use the resulting models to predict and optimize *future* transactions. The data in the database concern a limited duration of time, but you want to draw conclusions and make decisions that apply to a much larger time range, including the future, as shown in Figure 5-1. In that sense, the database represents a sample of transactions from all of the transactions in this larger time frame.

Figure 5-1
Time ranges for transaction data and for decisions based on data mining

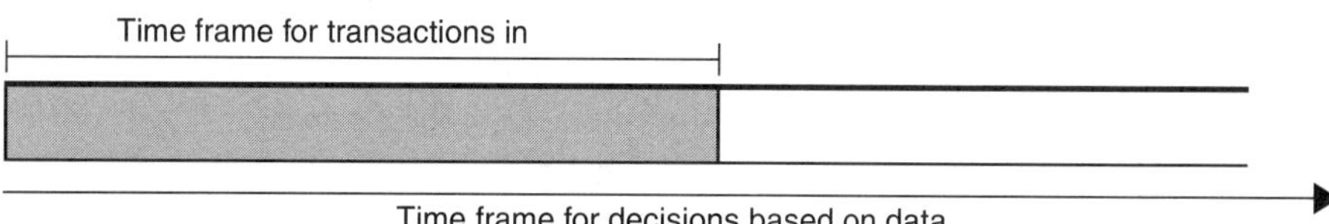

The bottom line is that your entire database itself is a sample. The choice is not *whether* to use a sample, but *how large* your sample should be.

Advantages of Sampling

The primary advantage of using a subsample of your data is efficiency. The time it takes to extract, process, clean, and analyze 1,000,000 records is longer than the time needed for 10,000 records. In some situations, the time needed to analyze the entire database will be prohibitive, requiring hours or days to perform each step in the analysis. This is a situation where sampling can really pay off. By using a smaller sample from your database, you can perform the analysis more quickly. With a reduced sample, you have more freedom to "play" with the data a bit—to try different approaches for analyzing the data to see what you discover. When you have decided on a model or an analysis, you can always go back and test it on the entire database to make sure it generalizes.

Disadvantages of Sampling

The primary disadvantage of sampling is that it reduces the precision of your estimates. For example, with a million records, you might be able to estimate the proportion of smokers in your customer base to within one-tenth of 1%, whereas you could estimate it to within only 1% with a smaller sample of 10,000 records. For some applications, you might actually need that extra digit of precision. In such situations, the additional cost of analyzing the entire database may be justified. However, a sample of several thousand records can give you precision that is good enough for most data mining applications.

A second drawback to using sampling is that there is always a chance of selecting a sample that doesn't really match the characteristics of the overall database. For example, if you select a sample of 100 customers, you might end up with 75 men and 25 women just by chance, even though the complete database has a more equal distribution of genders. The larger the sample, the less likely this is to happen. Additionally, use of proper sampling techniques can reduce the risk of getting such an unusual sample. Validation techniques give you added insurance against this problem—if your data work well on a test set, you can be fairly confident that your results will generalize to the rest of the data in the database.

Another concern with using a subsample is that you may have trouble identifying rare events. For example, in the CRM data, only about 8% of customers responded to the last marketing campaign. If you took a sample of 10,000 claims randomly, you would have about 800 fraudulent claims in that sample. This imbalance between fraudulent and valid claims can make it difficult for many data mining algorithms to find ways to separate them. Fortunately, you can get around this problem by using a special sampling method called **balancing,** or **stratified sampling**, discussed below.

Selecting a Sample

Several methods can be used for selecting sample records from a larger set of records. Some methods are quite complex and beyond the scope of this book; however, two basic methods should enable you to use sampling effectively in data mining.

The first method is **simple random sampling**, a straightforward technique in which you decide how many records you want to analyze and then randomly select that many records from the database. The key feature is that all of the records in the database have an equal chance of being selected for the sample. This means that the selected sample should end up being very similar to the overall database in terms of relationships in the data. The larger the sample, the more likely this is to be true. For example, if you select only 100 accounts from your database, you may end up with a sample that doesn't look very much like the entire database. However, if you randomly select 10,000 records, you can be fairly confident that the sample represents the characteristics of the larger database.

The second method is **stratified random sampling,** also known as **balancing**. This method should be used when you want to control the proportions of certain types of records in the sample. An example was given earlier—when you are trying to predict a rare event, it sometimes helps the data mining algorithms to find patterns if there are approximately equal numbers of records with and without the event. For example, when analyzing customer response to a marketing campaign, you might choose 1000 customers who responded and 1000 customers who did not respond. This will help your data mining software identify the characteristics that distinguish between the two types of customers.

Some data mining tools, including Clementine, have built-in balancing functions. If your tool does not have this feature, you can still use stratified sampling, by first splitting your data into subgroups based on the characteristics you want to balance. These groups are called the **strata**. Then, for each subgroup, you use simple random sampling to select the number of records you want. Once you have selected a subsample from each stratum, you append the subsets to create the data set you will analyze.

Example: **Web mining.** After excluding the sessions generated by bots and crawlers, there were 48,715 records representing individual sessions in the database. The analysts selected a sample of 10,000 records for modeling, to allow faster building of models and consequently more freedom to adjust parameters and try different approaches. ■■■

Example: **CRM.** Since the analysts were trying to predict a relatively rare event (response to a marketing promotion), the analysts decided to balance the data using stratified sampling. The analysts used Clementine's ability to automatically balance skewed data such as this, so they didn't have go through the explicit steps of calculating the exact proportions of each category and devising a sampling scheme to select records from each category. The resulting data set contained all responder records, and approximately the same number of non-responder records (selected randomly from all non-responders), to provide an even split. ■■■

Selecting Columns

You will also need to make decisions about which characteristics you are going to use in your analysis. You already made some decisions about this in the data understanding phase. Now it's time to reassess those decisions in light of what you learned in exploring and quality checking. Possible reasons for excluding characteristics that you previously thought important include:

- **Lack of usefulness.** In exploring your data, it may become clear that a characteristic is not really associated with much of anything else, so it won't add anything to a data mining solution.
- **Poor data quality.** If the characteristic is poorly measured, contains a lot of errors, or has many blanks or missing values, it may be best to exclude it from your analysis. You can often salvage some fields in the cleaning process (see "Cleaning Data" on p. 49), but other fields may have problems that are severe enough to make them beyond recovery.
- **Redundancy.** If there is a set of characteristics that all tend to measure the same thing in slightly different ways, it may only be worth keeping one or two characteristics from that set in your data analysis. Adding additional characteristics from such a closely-related set often adds very little to the data mining solution.
- **Complexity.** Some characteristics, such as categorical characteristics with a large number of categories, can increase the complexity of models without increasing the ultimate value of those models. For example, if you have postal (ZIP) code information for customers, you probably shouldn't include postal code among your predictors. In such cases, you may be able to capture much of the information from this kind of complex characteristic in a set of simpler characteristics derived from the original. For example, you might get more value from replacing postal code with a few aggregated demographic fields such as average income, household size, and so on, for the area. (For more information on this process, see "Derived Attributes" on p. 54.)

Conversely, you may discover in exploring your data that you have left out something important. In that case, you will need to revise your initial decision and add the missing characteristic(s) to your list. Keep in mind that this may involve locating and accessing that data or perhaps even collecting fresh data. As always, you will need to balance the potential value that the new data could add with the cost of getting the data.

Example: **CRM.** Recall that in studying data quality during the data preparation phase, the analysts discovered that the *marital status* field contained a high proportion of blanks or missing values. For this reason they excluded it from further analyses. ■■■

Fine-Tuning Data Selection Criteria

These explicitly defined selection criteria are important, but they shouldn't be written in stone. As you go through the modeling process, you will probably need to adjust your selection criteria as you gain new insights into the data. In your first approach to selecting data, being wrong is not such a bad thing. Your modeling efforts will help you identify and fix any data selection problems. This is the primary reason for documenting your selection process: the feedback process between modeling and data selection is made much easier by explicitly spelling out your selection criteria.

Example: **Web mining.** On closer examination of the session-length data, it also turned out that there were a large number of one-hit sessions (approximately 60% of all sessions were one-hit sessions). Many of these, like the very long sessions found earlier, were indexing agents or "bots." The rest presumably were users who somehow mistakenly ended up at the site, perhaps expecting something else, and left immediately. Neither of those groups were relevant to the question at hand, so these sessions were also excluded from the final data set. ■■■

Cleaning Data

No matter how careful your data entry staff and database managers are, it is very likely that there are some problems in your data. You will want to fix as many of those problems as possible before you mine the data. As you learned in Chapter 4, there are several kinds of data quality problems. Different problems require different approaches to cleaning.

Missing Data

Sometimes you don't have all of the data for a particular person or account. Perhaps the person never returned the product registration card, or perhaps the purchased demographic data doesn't include records for all of your customers. It's important to understand where your data have missing values and, whenever possible, *why* those values are missing.

There are several ways to handle missing values. The ideal solution is to go out and find those values. Unfortunately, in many cases, this is very difficult or impossible to do. When you can't get the actual values, you will have to use another method to work with the missing data. One method is simply to exclude rows that contain missing values from the analysis. The primary drawback of this approach is that it reduces the number of valid records for your analysis. A related method is to exclude characteristics (columns) that contain a lot of missing values. The downside here is that you may end up excluding important information and reducing the value of your results. Another approach is to replace missing values with some estimated value, a process called **imputation**. For example, if you have a record with a missing value for income, you could replace the missing value with the average income. This method keeps you from having to throw away some records, but it also tends to make the variability seem smaller than it really is for the characteristics in question, and thus can make fields seem less important for modeling than they really are.

Missing values are especially troublesome when they are systematic (that is, when the probability of a particular value being missing depends on some important characteristic in the record). For example, if people who are relatively affluent are more likely to skip certain questions about income on a questionnaire, then you have to question the validity of any analysis involving those questions. There may be a strong relationship between wealth and those questionnaire items, but you won't see the relationship because the customers at one end of the income scale didn't respond. In a situation like this, you need to be careful about using characteristics with a lot of missing values. Consider using related characteristics that have more complete data in place of the troublesome characteristic.

Example: **Web mining.** In the order (purchase) data, the analysts discovered that there were a small number of records with missing values for the field *order discount amount*. They were able to replace these values by comparing the amounts charged to the customers' credit cards against the prices listed in the catalog as of the order date to compute the actual discount given to the customer. ■■■

Data Errors

The best way to avoid data errors is by using robust data entry procedures to prevent them from happening in the first place. Unfortunately, when you're using stored data for data mining, the data have already been entered, the damage has been done, and you have to work with what's available.

If you've discovered data errors in your data, you can often use the information that alerted you to the error in the first place to correct the problem. For example, if your demographic data tell you that a middle-income family has 22 cars in the household, you can probably assume that the data entry person accidently hit the 2 key twice. You would then replace the 22 with a 2.

You can also use logical dependencies in your data to uncover and correct errors. For example, if you find a record for a customer containing information about an active auto loan but it also claims that the customer doesn't own a vehicle, you know that there's a problem. In this case, assuming that you perform careful verification on your account data, it's probably safe to assume that this customer does indeed own a vehicle of some kind, and you can change the data to reflect this.

In some cases, this process can be automated. In other cases, you will have to investigate ambiguous records manually. For such cases, you will have to decide how much effort to spend on investigating problem records in cleaning the data. If there are certain characteristics that contain consistent errors, you may be better off simply omitting those characteristics from the analysis rather than making a Herculean effort to repair the errors.

Example: **Web mining.** In examining the data on customer orders, the analysts discovered inconsistencies between the gender values reported by customers during registration and the gender values found in the purchased demographic data.

Figure 5-2

Matrix of self-reported gender (rows) by demographic record of gender (columns)

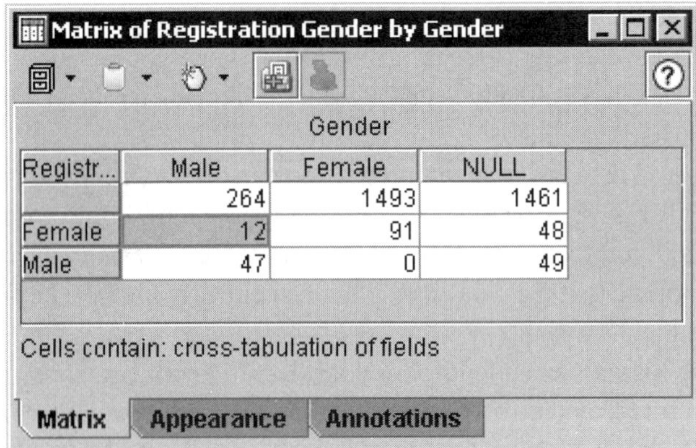

Since the number of inconsistent cases was small, the analysts decided to dig further into the data and try to determine the true gender for each customer. It turns out that these 12 orders belonged to just four customers, and over half of them belonged to a single customer. Unfortunately, the available data did not provide enough detail to disambiguate the gender of these four customers. So, for these four customers (and their 12 orders), both gender fields were set to null, to indicate the absence of reliable gender information. ■■■

Coding Inconsistencies

In "Describing the Data" on p. 34 in Chapter 4, you read about the importance of understanding how values are represented in the database. There will almost certainly be cases where you are integrating data from multiple sources, and you have redundant information that is coded differently. For example, your customer database may have names separated into two columns, one for last name and one for first name, whereas the demographic data you purchased has a single field for the full name. In such situations, you will need to choose a coding scheme for your mining data set and convert values to that coding scheme where necessary.

Another source of difficulty with coding schemes is the use of "special" values to denote missing or invalid values. It is common, especially with numerically coded characteristics, to code missing values as a specific value or range of values. For example, your database might contain information on questionnaire responses.

Suppose that each answer is a rating from 1 to 5. You may discover that whenever a customer refused to respond to a question, the answer was coded as 99. Make sure that such coding conventions are taken into account when you analyze the data. Otherwise, as you can imagine, all of those 99s in the database will make your data mining results meaningless.

Bad or Missing Metadata

You can also have problems in which the data you want to analyze doesn't really mean what you think it does. For example, if you have a characteristic called *gender* but the data take values between one and ten, you can be pretty sure that the characteristic is mislabeled. In that case, you will have to do some detective work and try to learn what this characteristic *really* represents. A more subtle example is this: suppose you have a characteristic called *income* that takes integer values between 1 and 7. This is most likely some categorized measurement of income, in which each value indicates a range of incomes—for example, "1" indicates an annual income of between 0 and $20,000, "2" indicates an income of between $20,001 and $40,000, and so on. However, if you don't know what the relationship is between values in the database and actual income ranges, you may have a problem making use of this information.

To make the most of your data mining efforts, you will need complete, accurate metadata. This may mean interviewing various colleagues and staff who have worked with the data, tracking down and sifting through dusty documents, contacting outside sources (such as former employees or outsourcing firms), and perhaps even some trial-and-error experimentation to discover the answers.

Example: **Web mining.** Some of the data provided in the original Web logs was a bit esoteric, and the labels in the data warehouse did not provide enough information to clarify the nature of the fields' contents. The analysts had to consult the documentation for the Web server software in use at the site to get the details of what was being written to the logs (and hence what was appearing in the data warehouse). ■■■

Constructing Data

There will also be situations where you need to construct new data. As with selecting data, there are two basic ways to construct data: you can create new characteristics (columns), or you can create new items (rows).

Derived Attributes

It is often useful to combine existing attributes to create new characteristics. For example, there are often ways of combining information to create useful indexes, such as a debt-to-equity ratio or a change in monthly transaction volume. Such derived attributes often convey information more concisely than the original separate attributes.

There are also situations where transforming the data, or using a formula to change the way a measurement is expressed, can lead to better data mining results. An example of this is Web page processing time. Web page processing times often follow a skewed distribution, with most values clustering around a small to moderate value but with a few very large times. One way to help data mining tools handle such data better is to transform it so that the values are more symmetrically distributed. Using a logarithmic transformation changes the distribution on the left in Figure 5-3 to the distribution on the right. The distribution on the right can provide better results with many data mining algorithms. The drawback is that transformed attributes can sometimes be difficult to interpret. You have to transform them back to the original scale to understand the full implications of the results. For more information about interpreting histograms, see “Histograms” on p. 109 in Chapter 11.

Figure 5-3
Distribution of last request processing times (left) and derived processing times (right)

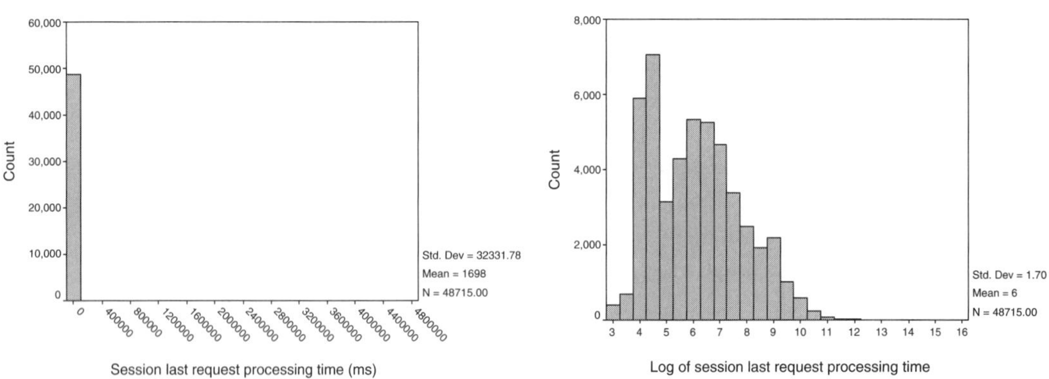

You can also apply this process to categorical (set) characteristics. An example of this would be combining similar categories to create a simplified categorization scheme. For instance, you might want to derive a field for product categories, each of which contains several related products. This field can be much easier to use in modeling than a field that lists all of the specific products available for sale. This approach can also be useful in reformatting data for specific data mining tools (see "Formatting Data" on p. 58).

Example: **Fraud detection.** A key piece of information that was not included in the original data was the potential income one would expect from each farm, if all conditions were normal. However, the analysts were able to calculate an estimate of this, based on the values of *farm size*, *rainfall*, and *land quality*, which were present for each application. ■■■

Data Reduction

Derived attributes can also be useful for summarizing a group of related fields into one or two fields that capture the most important information from the original group of fields. The idea of using a few derived attributes to represent information from a large number of attributes in the original data is called **data reduction**.

There are a number of ways to used derived attributes for data reduction. One is to simply identify a group of related attributes and choose the one that is the "best" representation of what all of those attributes are trying to measure. For example, if you have fields for monthly income, annual income, and economic level, you might choose annual income as the best representative of the group and omit the other two fields.

There are also modeling methods that can be used to distill a number of attributes down to their essence. Factor analysis is one modeling method that takes a set of numeric attributes and tries to find the common threads between them. This is often useful with surveys, where there may be several questions that all get at the same underlying "theme," or **factor**. For example, you might have the following questions on a customer satisfaction survey:

- How satisfied were you with your shopping experience?
- How would you rate the service and value you received?
- How likely are you to shop here again?

You can tell from the questions that the analysts are all basically trying to assess customer satisfaction. Building a factor analysis model from these attributes would give you a derived attribute that measures the common trait in those questions.

Another way to perform data reduction is to group cases based on similar patterns of values for a set of attributes and then use the group membership in lieu of those attributes. A classic example of this is the use of market segmentation schemes, such as PRIZM codes (Claritas, 2000), that classify customers according to various economic and demographic characteristics. One can often use such segment information in place of a large set of personal characteristics. This kind of grouping of similar records is usually done by applying some type of clustering model, such as a hierarchical clustering model or a Kohonen model.

One word of caution about data reduction: it is easy to be overly aggressive with data reduction. Data reduction techniques work well only when the derived attributes do a good job of summarizing the original attributes. When you use something like factor analysis or clustering to summarize attributes, check your models to be sure they are really capturing all of the useful information in the original attributes before you consider excluding those original attributes from your mining data set.

Example: **CRM.** In order to help understand each customer's relationship with the company, the analysts decided to summarize past purchase information into Recency, Frequency, and Monetary scores and then to combine these into a single index (known as an **RFM score**) of customer activity. This single field could then take the place of several raw data fields in model building. ■■■

Generated Records

There are situations in which you will probably want to be able to generate new records as well. New records represent items (rows) that are derived from your data or from prior knowledge about the business domain. For example, if you perform a cluster analysis on your customers, you might add a record representing each cluster's profile to the database.

There may also be cases where you need to generate records that represent averages or sums for particular groups. This process, called **aggregation,** computes the appropriate information across the original item-level records to form group-level records. One of the main uses of this technique is to create group averages, which you can then merge back into the main data set (see "Integrating Data" on p. 57) and use to calculate derived attributes that describe how each item compares to its group average. For example, you could compute average purchase amount data by zip code, and then merge that zip code-level data back into the purchase data. You would then have the actual purchase amount and group average purchase amount for each account. By subtracting the group average from the actual purchase amount, you get an indication of how each account compares to the other accounts in its zip code.

Example: **Web mining.** The data warehouse contained records for each Web page hit, but the analysts were more interested in Web sessions, from the time a user first visits a page on their site until the user leaves the site. The hit-level data were aggregated to the session level by combining multiple hit records based on a session ID (tracked using cookies during the user's visit). These session-level records were then merged with customer data to provide more complete session information. ■■■

Integrating Data

In most data mining situations, you will be using data from multiple data sources. You will need to plan out the process of bringing the data from multiple sources together to facilitate data mining.

There are two basic ways to integrate data from multiple sources:

- **Merging.** Merging involves combining data from two different sources on the same items. In other words, you have two data sets with the same *records* but different *fields*, and you want to combine them so that each record has fields from both data sets. For example, you may have internal customer data that you want to integrate with purchased demographic data. By merging the two data sources based on a unique identifier for each record (for example, a social security number), you create a data set that includes both customer database characteristics and demographic characteristics—a data set that can be mined. Note that the records in the separate databases need not match up in a one-to-one manner. For example, you could integrate customer-level data from your internal database with census-tract-level data from an external data source. Each customer record is matched with the corresponding census tract record, in a **many-to-one** manner. For example, if two of your customers happen to be next door neighbors, they will very likely belong to the same census tract. Thus their records in the database would both be matched to the same record in the tract-level database.

  When merging data sets, there are usually items (records) that appear in one data set but not the other. You can decide how those cases are handled during the merge operation. If you want to include all records, even if they don't appear in both data sets, this is called an **outer join**. If you decide to include only records that appear in both data sets, it is called an **inner join**.

- **Appending.** Appending involves combining two or more sets of items from different data sets. In other words, you have two data sets with the same *fields* but different *records*, and you want a combined data set of records from both data sets.

For example, to mine data for a new marketing campaign, you may want to combine a database of Web customers with a separate database for phone customers. In doing so, you'll have to check that the characteristics (fields or columns) in the databases are similar. You'll also have to decide how to reconcile any differences in fields across databases. For example, if your Web customer database includes a *session time elapsed* characteristic and your phone customer database includes a *call duration* characteristic, you could either treat them as separate characteristics or combine them into a *transaction duration* characteristic in the combined data set.

Formatting Data

The last task in data preparation is making sure you have satisfied all of the data format requirements of your data mining tool(s). For example, some tools expect the first column of the data set to be a row identifier with a unique value for each row. Some tools also expect the target characteristic (the thing you want to predict) to be the last column of the data set. Still other tools expect the rows to be sorted based on values of predictor or target characteristics. Finally, some tools restrict the way you can code certain characteristics, such as requiring numeric codes for categorical data.

To be sure that your data is ready for your mining tools, you may need to rearrange the order of characteristics (fields) in the data set, and you may also have to derive "new" attributes to recode some problematic characteristics. For example, if your data set contains a *gender* characteristic that takes the values "MALE" and "FEMALE" but your data mining tool can work only with numeric values, you could derive a new attribute, *gender_n*, that takes values 0 (for males) and 1 (for females).

The Data Set

After you have gone through all of these tasks, you should have in hand a data set suitable for mining. Before you jump into mining the data, take the time to write a detailed description of the data set you intend to mine, including what it contains and how it was constructed. This data set description will be an important resource for the modeling, evaluation, and deployment phases of the data mining cycle.

Summary

This chapter covered how to get your data ready for mining. The critical tasks and associated results of this phase include:

Selecting data. Making a decision about which data to use and which not to use.

Task results:

- Rationale for inclusion/exclusion

Cleaning the data. Doing what you can to repair mistakes and omissions in the data.

Task results:

- Data cleaning report

Constructing data. Creating new fields or records to supplement those already in your data set.

Task results:

- Derived attributes
- Generated records

Integrating the data. Combining your multiple sources of data into a single data set suitable for mining.

Task results:

- Merged data

Formatting the data. Modifying the representation of the data so that it is internally consistent and facilitates mining.

Task results:

- Reformatted data

There are also two general results from the data preparation phase that are not associated with specific tasks:

- Data set
- Data set description

Chapter 6

Modeling

Now that your data are ready, you've come to the heart of data mining—analysis. In this stage, you apply reporting, visualization, statistical, and artificial intelligence techniques to find meaningful and useful patterns in your data. These powerful techniques will help you discover new things about your business process, confirm suspected relationships, and estimate how potential changes in your business practice will impact the bottom line.

You will need to do several things in the modeling phase, including:

- Select a modeling technique.
- Generate a test design.
- Build a model.
- Assess the model.

Selecting a Modeling Technique

The first step is to determine which modeling technique(s) you will use. Most data mining tools provide a variety of modeling techniques, appropriate for different situations. The choice you make will depend on:

- The set of techniques offered by your data mining tool(s)
- The nature of the business problem
- The kind of data you have
- Your data mining goals
- Other practical considerations, such as time required for model building, level of data mining or statistical expertise required, etc.

You can find more details about different modeling techniques in Chapter 9 through Chapter 13. The information in these chapters should help you choose techniques that are suitable for your particular data mining needs.

Example: **Fraud detection.** Since the data mining goal here is to identify unusual applications that may be suspicious, the analysts decided to approach the problem by first building a model that predicts the amount of the claim based on the other information in the data set. The predicted claim amount can then be compared to the actual claim amount, and applications with large discrepancies between the two values can be flagged for closer investigation.

To do this modeling, the analysts were more interested in accuracy than in explanatory ability. Thus, they decided to use a neural network for the prediction task, since neural networks tend to have very good accuracy. A variety of approaches to neural network modeling is supported in Clementine, so the analysts had the means to perform the modeling task using the technique they wanted. ■■■

Example: **Web mining.** In this case, the analysts were interested as much in explanation as in accuracy. They wanted to understand exactly which factors were causing people to leave their Web site so they could take action to correct these problems. Because of this, they decided to try some decision tree approaches to the problem. Decision trees usually have good accuracy, and they are relatively easy to understand as well. Clementine supports two popular decision tree algorithms: C5.0 and C&RT. The analysts decided to try both algorithms and decide how to use the resulting models after assessing them. ■■■

Example: **CRM.** The company was most interested in getting an accurate model of customer response; explanatory considerations were secondary. Company analysts decided to try several modeling methods to determine which one provided the most accurate and most general model. They chose to build models using C5.0, logistic regression, and a neural network. ■■■

Modeling Assumptions

Remember that the purpose of data mining is to abstract useful information from a mountain of data. Most data mining techniques do this by making simplifying assumptions about the data and the processes that are measured by the data. For example, discriminant analysis is a commonly used data mining technique that relies on assumptions about how the values of predictors are distributed to work properly. To ensure that your modeling technique is really appropriate, you should be able to state the assumptions of the technique explicitly and, ideally, evaluate these assumptions to be sure that they are reasonable in the context of your problem.

In many cases, the assumptions that underlie the various data mining techniques are subtle, and they often involve mathematical technicalities that are beyond the scope of this book. Chapter 9 through Chapter 13 contain references to more in-depth descriptions of each modeling technique, where you can find discussions of the assumptions required.

If you discover that the assumptions of your first-choice modeling technique aren't reasonable for your data, you may be able to address the problem by returning to the data preparation phase. You can often construct derived attributes or reformat the data so they are more compatible with the assumptions of your chosen technique. However, sometimes you will find that more basic assumptions are violated in ways that can't be addressed by transforming the data. In that case, you may need to choose a different modeling technique that doesn't rely on the problematic assumption(s).

Example: **Web mining.** For predicting whether a session will continue after the current page view, the analysts speculated that processing time for the last page would be an important predictor. However, as you saw in "Derived Attributes" on p. 54 in Chapter 5, the values for this field are highly skewed—that is, most of the values are pushed to the low end of the distribution, with a few values trailing off toward the high end. However, by using a logarithmic transformation, the analysts altered the shape of the data to make it easier for their modeling techniques to use that information effectively. ■■■

Generating a Test Design

Modeling is an iterative process. You can't simply dump your data into a machine learning algorithm and wait for the answer to pop out. Most modeling techniques have a wide variety of settings and configurations, and these settings can have a dramatic effect on the value of the resulting model. Because of this, you will almost always need to build several models, using different settings and often different algorithms, to find the best model for your problem.

The next question is, how will you know when you have a good model, or which model of several is the "best"? The answer is that you will need to test your models. The test design is a description of the steps you will take in testing your model. It typically includes describing the criteria for model "goodness" and defining the data on which those criteria will be measured.

Measuring "Goodness" of a Model

There are many ways to define "goodness" in a model. Usually, the primary criterion will be how well the model summarizes the data. For **supervised models** (models in which you have information on the outcome for some past data and you can compare the model's predictions to the observed outcomes), this can be an estimate of the accuracy of the model, or more commonly, the converse, an estimate of the error rate. In a sense, the error rate is actually measuring the "badness" of the model rather than the "goodness," but it is easy to see that these are related ideas. The model with the smallest error rate is also the model with the highest accuracy.

Model Accuracy

When the outcome or prediction is a category, such as *buy/don't buy*, the error rate can be calculated as simply the percentage of records for which the model makes the right prediction. In some situations, this simple error rate may be adjusted for various factors, such as small data sets or a large number of categories for the outcome field.

When the outcome or prediction is numeric, such as "net profit of sale," the calculation becomes a bit more complex. For such problems, a model will very rarely get the prediction *exactly* right, but a good model will make predictions that are usually *very close* to the observed outcome value. The error measurement in this case is usually based on the difference between the prediction and the observed value for each record, summarized across all records.

Keep in mind that in some situations, there are important differences among the kinds of errors that a model can make. For example, the cost of extending credit to a customer who eventually defaults on a large debt may be much higher than the lost profit from a customer whose credit request is declined. In such cases, you would want to favor models that were good at identifying high-risk customers even if that meant also labeling some customers as "high risk" who would have turned out to be creditworthy.

Your data mining tool should perform all of the error rate calculations for you. But you still need to understand how your tool calculates error rates for different kinds of models so that you know what the results mean when you see them.

Example: **Fraud detection.** The analysts decided to use a neural network model to predict claim value. In this case, the neural network was a standard multilayer perceptron with a numeric output unit. (See "Neural Networks for Prediction" on p. 163 in Chapter 13 for more information about neural networks.) To measure the accuracy of the network, the analysts planned to plot predicted values versus actual values to quickly see how well the network predicted claim value. The correlation between predicted and actual values would be used to provide a more objective measure of agreement between the values. ■■■

Example: **Web mining.** In this project, the goal is to predict whether a session will continue after each event during the session. Since the outcome is categorical (session continues versus session ends), accuracy can be described using a simple classification table showing how often the predicted category matches the actual category. ■■■

Other Criteria

Sometimes accuracy of the model is really the only criterion that counts. You don't care about understanding the model or how long it takes to build or apply to new data; you just want the best predictions you can possibly get. In this case, selecting a model is easy—choose the model with the lowest overall error rate.

More commonly, however, there are other important considerations in assessing a model, including ease of interpretation, speed of model building, effort required to deploy the model, and so on. In addition, there are some model types, such as some cluster models, that don't have any external value they are trying to match. For such models (commonly called **unsupervised models**), the idea of accuracy doesn't really apply; you can't measure accuracy if there's no "gold standard" with which to compare the model's classifications.

When generating your test design, make a list of all the important technical criteria, rank them based on importance, and develop concrete ways to measure each one. Note that some of these "other criteria" are at least partially subjective in nature. For example, "ease of interpretation" is not necessarily something you can quantify and calculate. It is an impression you formulate based on your reaction as you view the model structure and what it tells you about the patterns in the data. For these subjective criteria, you will need to decide who will rate the models for these characteristics and how to handle disagreements if participants in the process have different ideas about how models should be ranked on these criteria.

Example: **Web mining.** For this project, it isn't enough to generate an accurate model. The model must also be interpretable and lead to insight into what makes site visitors more likely to leave the site. Thus, the model generated will be judged both on accuracy and insight. The data mining consultants will work closely with the business analysts at the company to determine whether the models meet the "insight" criterion. ■■■

Defining Test Data

At first glance, it may seem reasonable simply to test each model on the data that were used in building the model. This is one way to obtain an estimate of the accuracy of the model. Unfortunately, there is a problem with this approach—it tends to make the model look better than it really is. As you already know, the modeling techniques used in data mining are very powerful pattern recognition algorithms. Sometimes these algorithms can misconstrue quirks or random variations of the training data as part of the pattern. This problem of models fitting "noise" as well as the "real" pattern is called **overfitting**. Testing the model on training data tends to overestimate accuracy because you are presenting the same random variations back to the model, which dutifully predicts them in addition to the true underlying pattern in the data.

The best way to get a realistic estimate of the accuracy of a model is by testing it against a different set of data than you used to build it in the first place. A new set of data will have the same underlying patterns as the training data, but the random variations will be different, so you will get a better sense of how well the model is able to separate the real pattern from the noise. This will also give you a better estimate of how well the model will generalize to new data when you are ready to apply it in your business process.

In data mining, the one thing that's generally not a problem is quantity of data. You often have an embarrassment of riches when it comes to data volume. You can use this to your advantage when building models. You usually have only one set of data, but by **partitioning** your data you can create multiple sets—one for training and one for testing. In fact, many data miners prefer to partition their data into three data sets: one for training models, one for testing during the fine-tuning of model parameters, and one for validating the final model(s). The primary questions here are how large each partition should be and how to decide which records go into which partition. There are no hard and fast rules for making these determinations, but keep in mind that you will need enough data in the training set to build good, solid models, and the data sets should be as similar as possible to the new data to which the model will eventually be applied.

Example: **Fraud detection.** Clementine's neural network algorithm has an automatic partitioning feature that trains the neural network on one portion of the data and tests its accuracy on the remaining data. This feature was used in place of explicitly defining test data outside the algorithm. ■■■

Example: **CRM.** Because the company planned to build several different types of models for this project, its analysts decided to use an explicit partitioning of data to provide training and test data. The data were split into two partitions, each with approximately 50% of the records in the data set. The same partitioning was used for all models built. ■■■

Building the Models

Now that you know what kinds of models are appropriate for your data mining goals and what criteria you will use to judge the models, it's time to build them.

Your data mining tool will handle all of the calculations in building models. It should also make it easy to see the characteristics of each model you build, and it should be easy to build several different models to find the best combination of model type and parameter settings for your particular data mining goal(s).

Model building can be a complex process. It is important to keep track of what you are doing and how you are doing it so that you can retrace your steps if necessary and be sure that everyone understands the process during both the assessment task and the evaluation phase. (For more information about the evaluation phase, see Chapter 7.)

When you are done modeling, you should have three things to show for your efforts: parameter settings, models, and model descriptions.

Parameter Settings

Most modeling techniques have a variety of parameters (or settings) that you can adjust to control details of the model building process. For example, with neural networks, you can typically change the architecture of the network, the number of hidden units, the learning rate, and other aspects of the modeling algorithm. (For more information, see "Neural Networks for Segmentation" on p. 134 and "Neural Networks for Clustering" on p. 145 in Chapter 12 and "Neural Networks for Prediction" on p. 163 in Chapter 13.) With a decision tree, you can control the depth of the tree, set the minimum number of records required for a node to be split, and so on. (For more information, see "Tree-Based Methods" on p. 132 in Chapter 12.)

For each model you build, you will need to decide what values to use for these parameters. Many data mining tools are designed with very general default settings, which can result in adequate models for a wide variety of data sets and data mining goals. However, it is often possible to measurably improve the accuracy or other characteristics of the model by adjusting these parameters to suit your particular situation.

There are no hard and fast rules about selecting values for your parameter settings, but the more you know about the modeling technique and your problem domain, the more able you'll be to make informed decisions about these settings. In many instances, it makes sense to build multiple models using a variety of parameter settings. This will give you insight into how the parameter settings affect the resulting models' characteristics and can help you home in on the optimal settings for your data mining goal.

Whether you use your data mining tool's default parameter settings or specify your own, keep careful notes on the settings you used and why you chose them. This information will be important for the model assessment task (see "Model Assessment" on p. 70) and for the iterative process of improving your models.

Example: **CRM.** For this project, the analysts decided to stick with the default Clementine settings for each of the three models built (C5.0, logistic regression, and neural network) except for the C5.0 model, where they requested a ruleset rather than a tree model. If the models performed well enough, they would use them as is. If not, they would revise the parameter settings to try to improve the models. ■■■

Models

When you've selected your desired parameter settings, your data mining tool will process the data and return a representation of the resulting model. You should be able to examine the model to see the kinds of patterns it reveals in the data as well as aspects of the model's performance, including accuracy (for supervised models), time taken to build the model, and so on. Finally, each model should give you a means of applying the model to new data, both for testing and eventual deployment. Once you have built the model(s), save them for future examination and use.

Example: **Fraud detection.** The neural network model was built with 4 units in the hidden layer. Accuracy of the model was quite good, with a correlation between predicted and actual claim values of 0.975. (Recall that 1.0 represents a perfect correlation between two sets of values.) Sensitivity analysis revealed that the two primary determinants of the network's predictions were *main crop* and *estimated income.* ■■■

Example: **CRM.** The three models revealed the following:
The C5.0 model performed adequately, with a list of 90 rules. It was correct for about 69% of records in the test data.

The neural network model had 83 input units and 8 hidden units and was correct for 70.7% of records in the test data. Sensitivity analysis revealed that there were several important predictor fields for the model, including RFM, whether the customer bought a hi-fi system, maximum amount spent, whether the customer bought a personal sound system, and the total amount spent.

The logistic regression model was correct for 74.7% of records overall. Important predictors identified by the model included whether they were having a white-collar worker in the household (according to the demographic data), the average amount spent per item, and whether the customer purchased cables, cassette tapes, and videotapes. Surprisingly, this model did not depend significantly on RFM scores. ■■■

Example: **Web mining.** The two models revealed the following:
The C5.0 ruleset model resulted in 31 rules for determining whether the session continued. Some of the rules were quite complicated, but many were easy to understand. Accuracy for this model was 72.6%.

The C&RT model had a similar accuracy, 72.4%, but the structure of the tree was very simple, with only three splits, and was easily understood. ■■■

Model Descriptions

In addition to the software representation of the model created by your data mining tool, you will want to create some descriptive information about each model. This should include your interpretations of the model results—both the structure and performance of the model. It should also include information about any difficulties encountered in building the model (such as extremely long build times, model-specific data quality issues, or tool-specific calculation problems).

Assessing the Models

Now that you have built some models, you need to look at them and determine which one(s) are good enough to consider final. This is the point at which you apply the test plan that you generated earlier to rank the models according to the criteria you specified.

Model Assessment

For each model you created, you will need to assess the model on each criterion that you included in your test plan. Some of these criteria will be objective, such as model accuracy. Others will be subjective and will be rated by the individuals specified in the test plan.

Once you have assessed each model on all criteria, rank them based on the criteria, keeping in mind the relative importance of each criterion. For example, if accuracy is your primary criterion and interpretability is a secondary criterion, then a model that is much more accurate than another model should probably be ranked higher than that model, even if it is somewhat less interpretable.

Various types of charts can be very helpful in assessing and comparing models based on accuracy. Gain charts show you how much of an improvement the model gives over naive "guessing," where you assume that the most common outcome is the probable value for all records.

Figure 6-1
Gain chart for several models predicting the same outcome

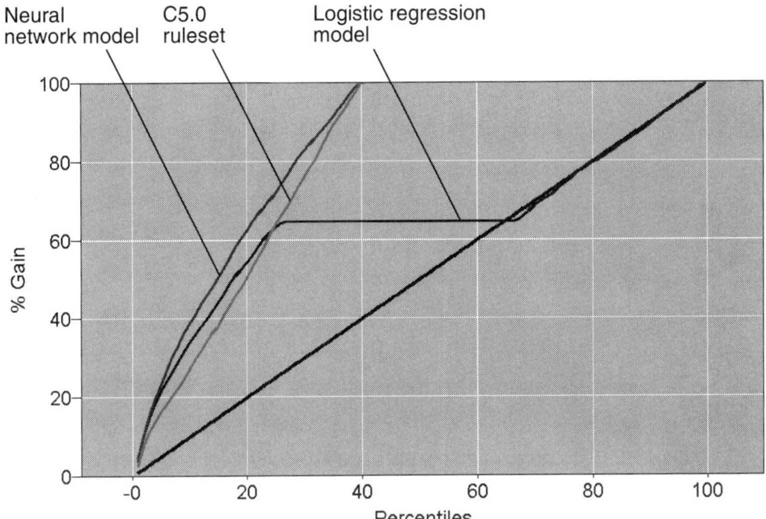

By plotting gain curves for multiple models on the same chart, you can get a sense of how the models compare on accuracy. Note that the comparison depends on where the "sweet spot" for your data mining problem is. For example, consider the gain chart shown in Figure 6-1. For the top 20% of records, the logistic regression model performs better than the C5.0 ruleset; however, for the top 30%, the C5.0 ruleset outperforms the logistic regression model. (The extraordinary difference here is due to the C5.0 ruleset's more sophisticated handling of missing values.)

Example: **Fraud detection.** Plotting predicted claim amounts versus actual amounts showed that the predictions were generally quite good. The correlation of 0.975 confirms that the model is effectively capturing the relationships between the application characteristics and the claim amount.

Figure 6-2
Plot of predicted (neural network) versus actual claim amounts

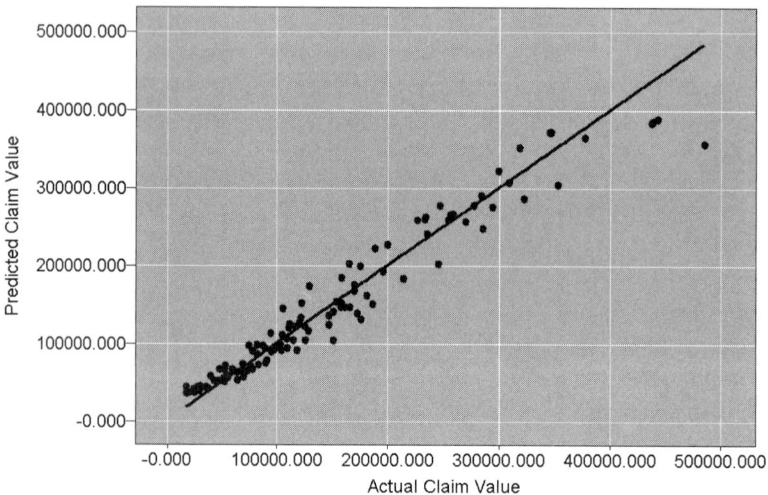

■■■

Example: Web mining. The classification tables for the two models on the test data are shown in Figure 6-3. You can see that the two models have very similar accuracy overall—72.6% for the C5.0 model versus 72.4% for the C&RT model.

Figure 6-3
Classification tables for Web mining models: C5.0 ruleset (left) and C&RT tree (right)

		Session Continues		
$C-Se...		False	True	Total
False	Count	9314	3440	12754
	Total %	66.495	24.559	91.054
True	Count	398	855	1253
	Total %	2.841	6.104	8.946
Total	Count	9712	4295	14007
	Total %	69.337	30.663	100

		Session Continues		
$R-Se...		False	True	Total
False	Count	9232	3387	12619
	Total %	65.910	24.181	90.091
True	Count	480	908	1388
	Total %	3.427	6.482	9.909
Total	Count	9712	4295	14007
	Total %	69.337	30.663	100

The two tree models were also compared using a gain chart, shown in Figure 6-4.

Figure 6-4
Gain chart for Web mining models

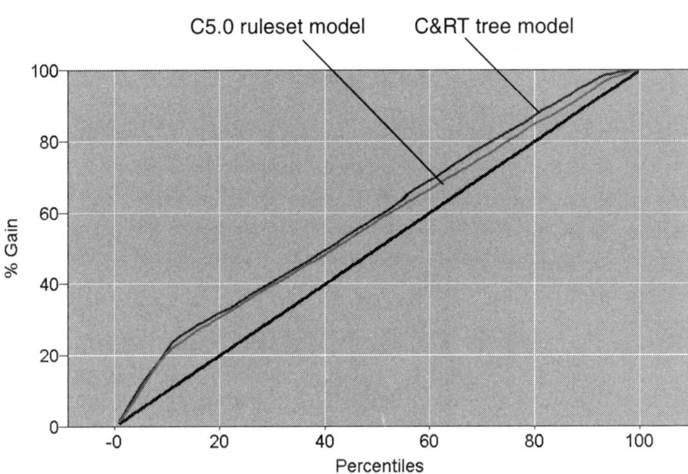

The chart shows that the C5.0 model has a slight advantage over the C&RT model across the range of percentiles.

In considering the insight criterion, the C5.0 model has a large advantage over the C&RT model. The rules found in the C5.0 ruleset identified specific Web site features that were associated with abandonment so that these features could be modified or eliminated to reduce abandonment. The C&RT tree was parsimonious and easy to read, but it did not give many hints about improving the Web site. Because of this, the C&RT model was discarded and the C5.0 ruleset was used as the final model. ■■■

Revised Parameter Settings

Part of the process of assessing models is determining ways to improve them. One way that you might be able to improve a model is to adjust the parameter settings to better suit your problem and your data set. This is where the value of multiple models can really become apparent.

For example, suppose you build a neural network with a single hidden layer of 20 units and another with a hidden layer of 16 units. You may find that while the network with 20 hidden units performs better on the training data, the one with 16 hidden units is more accurate on the testing data, indicating that it will generalize better. On the basis of this, you may find it worthwhile to build some further models with smaller hidden layers to find the optimal trade-off between the predictive accuracy you get from large hidden layers and the generalizability you get from smaller ones.

As you gain experience in data mining, you will find that model building, as with the rest of the data mining process, can benefit from an iterative approach. After you build a first wave of models, you gain insight into the patterns in your data and into how to adapt the models to your specific data mining goals. By using these insights to build subsequent models, you can often improve your data mining results significantly.

As you use this iterative approach, however, always be sure to carefully document any changes you make and the results of those changes. It does no good to document your initial models if you've changed everything by the time you're done and you haven't documented the changes. This documentation is the key to understanding your data mining results and making the most of what you learn during the modeling phase.

Example: **CRM.** The analysts wanted to see if it would be possible to improve the models' performance by adjusting some of the parameters. Specifically, they decided to see if they could simplify the models in order to make them generalize better.

For the C5.0 model, they switched the algorithm mode from *favor accuracy* to *favor generality.* This resulted in a model with fewer rules (44 rules versus 90 for the *favor accuracy* model), and slightly better accuracy on the test data (69.5% correct).

For the neural network model, the training method was changed from *quick* to *prune.* This method begins with a large network structure and during training gradually removes unneeded connections and nodes to simplify the resulting model. The resulting model had 23 input units and 2 hidden units and was much smaller than the unpruned network. The accuracy was about 70.6%, virtually identical to that for the original model.

For the logistic regression model, the set of predictors was restricted to those selected by the pruned neural network. This produced a model with accuracy of 74.1%, slightly lower than the original model with all predictors. ■■■

Summary

This chapter discussed how to apply data mining algorithms to your data to generate models. The critical tasks and associated results of this phase include:

Selecting a modeling technique. Deciding which algorithm(s) are likely to give the best results for your problem.

Task results:

- Modeling technique
- Modeling assumptions

Generating a test design. Specifying how you will assess the utility of each generated model.

Task results:

- Test designs

Building the models. Applying the selected modeling technique(s) to your data set.

Task results:

- Parameter settings
- Models
- Model descriptions

Assessing the models. Applying the tests describe in the test plan to determine which of the generated models are most useful.

Task results:

- Model assessment
- Revised parameter settings

Chapter 7

Evaluation

At the beginning of the evaluation phase, you have data mining results, which you have assessed in technical terms. It's now time to step back and put those data mining results in the larger context of your business goals to determine whether they will help your organization get to where you want it to go.

Remember that the models that you built during the modeling phase are not the only results of your data mining project. There are also conclusions and inferences that may be derived from the models or from any of the other steps in the data mining process. We refer to these conclusions and inferences as **findings**. The results of your data mining process include both models and findings. The evaluation phase helps you integrate all of your results—both models and findings—to see what you've gained from the data mining process.

There are three primary tasks in the evaluation stage:

- Evaluating model results
- Reviewing the data mining process
- Determining next steps

Evaluating Model Results

There is some overlap between model assessment (performed as part of the modeling phase) and evaluating model results. The main difference is that model assessment focuses on the technical aspects of the model: accuracy, interpretability, and so on. Evaluation, on the other hand, focuses on the substantive business implications of the model: how well the model helps you achieve your business objective(s).

Evaluating model results requires a good understanding of each model and the original business objectives that you defined in the *business understanding* phase. You need to interpret the results of each model in the context of the relevant business goal. This calls for interpreting the substantive content of the models, including the meaning of predictors selected by the model, what the structure of the model (rules, clusters, trees, etc.) tells you about your business process, and how well the predictions of the model would help you address the business issue at hand. It also means considering the findings from all of the data mining phases that you've completed so far and whether there are implications for your business objectives that you hadn't considered previously.

When you have evaluated the models, you should have a set of approved models that can be applied to your business process. These are the models that satisfy both technical and practical criteria.

Example: **Fraud detection.** The model to predict claim amount was more than satisfactory in providing an accurate baseline for identifying unusual claim amounts. After evaluating the results, the agency approved the model and deployed it. ■■■

Example: **CRM.** Because there was no appreciable difference in accuracy between the original set of models and the revised models, the company decided to use the simpler revised models. Simple models tend to be more robust toward subtle changes in the data than intricate models.

For the three models, company analysts plotted the total profit (excluding fixed costs) against the proportion of customers contacted.

Figure 7-1
Expected profit based on portion of customer base contacted

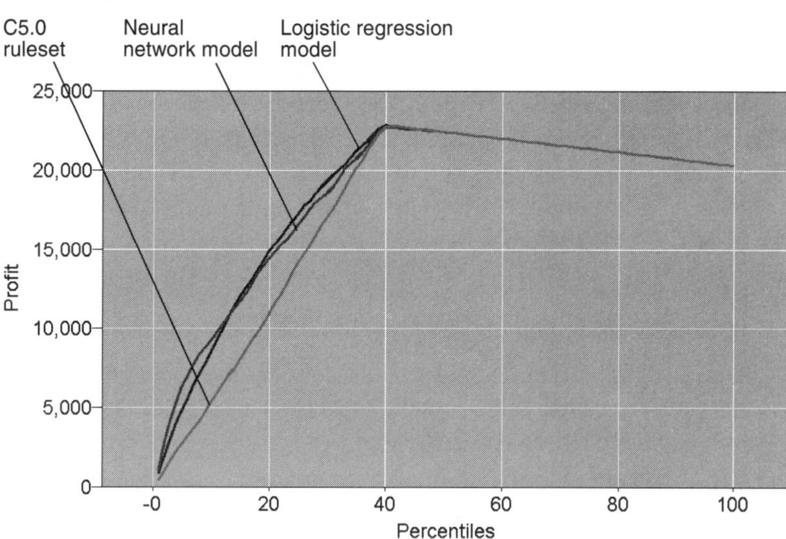

Remember that the fixed costs for the promotion totaled approximately $20,000. You can see that contacting more than about 35% of customers will lead to a profitable campaign, with the peak profit at about 40%. The logistic regression model does slightly better than the other models, so the company decided to use that model to build the customer list for the promotion. ■■■

Example: **Web mining.** The accuracy of the C5.0 model was adequate for the task. However, in this case, evaluation is more complex. Because the company was looking for insight into what makes customers leave the Web site, the analysts had to look into the details of the model to see what it was telling them about their customers' behavior.

Examining the rules in the C5.0 ruleset revealed several factors that seemed related to probability of abandonment. One event that commonly appeared in the rules predicting abandonment was a hit on one of the "replenishment" pages. Hits on leg-care pages also signaled a tendency to leave the site. And, as suspected, long page processing times tended to lead to abandonment. These are all useful observations that identify opportunities for improvement in the site.

The rules also contained some obvious information that was not useful. For example, the rules dutifully reported that viewing the checkout pages indicated that the visitor was probably going to leave the site. ■■■

Reviewing the Data Mining Process

An important part of evaluating your results is to review the process that you used to generate those results. The first step is to summarize the process—what decisions were made at each stage in the process, and how were those decisions made? There are two reasons for this retrospective examination: to determine if you need to refine or revise some of your previous activities and to learn what to do (and what *not* to do) during your next data mining project. Here are some specific points to consider:

- For each stage in the process, did the stage contribute to the value of the results that you generated?
- How could the handling of each stage have been improved or streamlined?
- If there were failures during the process, consider them carefully. Try to determine if there is any way the failures could have been avoided or if there were ways the impact could have been reduced.
- If there were activities that led to dead ends, think of ways that you might have been able to predict that result. This will help you direct your resources more productively in the future.
- For each decision that you made, consider alternatives in light of what you have learned. Would you have made different decisions anywhere in the process?
- Were there surprises (either good or bad) during the process? If so, can you identify any signs that might have allowed you to foresee them?

After considering these points, you should have a pretty good idea where you stand, and you should be prepared to make a more efficient, more focused effort in the next iteration of this project (if required) and in future projects.

Determining Next Steps

You know what you have. You know how you got it. Now, you are ready to decide what to do next. There are three basic alternatives:

- **Continue to deployment phase.** If you are satisfied with your models, and you don't think you can significantly improve your results with further iterations (or you don't have the resources for further iterations), you can move on to the deployment phase.
- **Go back and refine or replace your models.** If you think that you are on the right track, but haven't generated the best possible results, you might want to go through another iteration of modeling and evaluation. Take what you have learned so far and use it to make your next round of modeling more productive and on-target.
- **Wrap up the project and work on something more promising.** Sometimes, the data mining process reveals that there is nothing to be gained by applying models to a particular business process. Other times, you may discover that the required kind of data simply aren't available or are too expensive. In either case, you have learned something important, but you do not have any specific models that can be applied directly to the business objective. If you find yourself in this situation, make careful notes of what you have discovered, so others can benefit from your knowledge and avoid duplicating your efforts. Next, try a completely new approach to the current business problem or move on to a more tractable problem.

In deciding on the next step, consider each of the approved models in terms of accuracy, ability to address the business goals, and potential for deployment. For each option, weight its advantages and disadvantages. For example, there is a trade-off between continuing to the deployment phase and going through another modeling iteration. More iterations may result in better models but may also incur costs. Eventually, you will reach a point where your models are good, and the costs of refining them further will outweigh the benefits of those refinements. The better you understand your models and your process, the better you'll be able to judge when you've reached that point of diminishing returns.

Regardless of your choice, be sure to document your decision thoroughly, including the reasoning behind it. This documentation will be invaluable in presenting your decision to others in your organization and in helping you and your colleagues learn from your experience and become adept at data mining.

Examples: Fraud detection, CRM, Web mining. For all three examples, suitable models were found, and the projects proceeded to the deployment phase. ■■■

Summary

This chapter presented issues in evaluating your data mining results in a business context. The critical tasks and associated results of this phase include:

Evaluating results. Deciding what's worth implementing and what's not.

Task results:

- Assessment of data mining results
- Approved models

Reviewing the process. Thinking about what you did and how well it worked (or didn't work).

Task results:

- Review of process

Determining next steps. Deciding how to proceed from here.

Task results:

- List of possible actions
- Decisions

Chapter

8

Deployment

> Whoever acquires knowledge but does not practice it, is as one who ploughs but does not sow.
>
> —Saadi, Persian poet

After evaluating your data mining results, you are ready to act on what you've learned. Deployment is the process of using your new insights to improve the way you do business. In this phase, you will prepare to make real changes to your business practice based on what you have learned from data mining.

Integrating data mining results into your business processes can be complex. It requires careful planning and consideration. There are four primary tasks involved in the deployment phase:

- Planning the deployment
- Planning monitoring and maintenance
- Producing the final report
- Reviewing the project

Planning the Deployment

The first step in planning your deployment is to summarize your deployable results. Think about each of the approved models that you identified in the evaluation phase. Don't forget that results can include other kinds of information gained in addition to formal data mining models. For example, in the Web mining project, the tangible results of the data mining process are the insights gained from the rules, rather than the ruleset *per se*.

For each distinct model or finding in your results, consider the following questions:

- How will the knowledge or information be propagated to its users?
- How will the use of the result be monitored or its benefits measured (where applicable)?

For each deployable model or software result, consider the following questions:

- How will the model or software result be deployed in the organization's systems?
- How will its use be monitored and its benefits measured?

Also keep in mind that there may be a number of pitfalls on the way to deployment. Identify possible problems that may crop up as you prepare to act on your results. For each potential problem, make sure that you think about how the contingency could be handled, either by rectifying the problem or by taking an alternate approach to deployment that avoids the problem.

Example: **Fraud detection.** The software model created here will be deployed in conjunction with the agency's application database to score new applications for suspicious claim amounts. The neural network model will be deployed using Clementine Solution Publisher. This Clementine option allows the agency to encapsulate or *publish* the entire data stream, including reading the data from the database, executing any data preparation steps required (such as calculating derived fields), applying the neural network model, performing post-processing on the results, and writing the results back to the database. The published stream can then be run automatically at regular intervals, such as once a month, to extract newly entered applications, score them, and add notes to the database about unusual claim amounts.

Figure 8-1
Stream for scoring new application records in the database

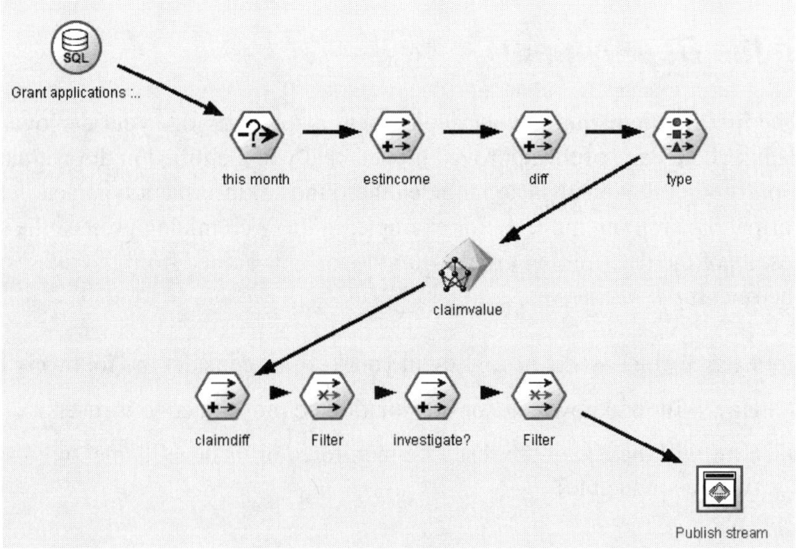

■■■

Example: **CRM.** The deployment of the model in this project consists of generating a list of targeted customers for the mailing. The list will be generated by scoring the customer database, selecting the customers that are predicted to respond, sorting them by confidence of prediction, and selecting the highest 40% of customers. If the model is accurate, this mailing list will maximize the profit for the marketing campaign.

Once the list is generated, it will be given to the marketing manager in charge of the campaign to be used for the mailing. ■■■

Example: **Web mining.** Deployment for this project equates with communication. The company takes advantage of the data mining results obtained by sharing new insights with those who can use them—the Web team. The Web team will implement changes to the Web site based on the patterns revealed in the research. The analysts will meet with the Web developers to go over the findings and discuss their implications and how to use them to improve the site. ■■■

Planning Monitoring and Maintenance

Deployment of data mining results is never a "set it and forget it" endeavor. Important aspects of your enterprise are changing all the time, and you will need to track how well your deployed results are keeping up with those changes. Eventually, nearly all data mining results will become dated due to changes in your business goals, your target market, the general economic climate, or any number of other dynamic aspects of your organization. It's important to monitor your results so you know when change affects them, and you can respond accordingly.

When planning your monitoring and maintenance program, consider the following points for each deployable result:

- What changing influences do you need to track that may affect the validity of the results?
- How will accuracy or validity of the result be measured and monitored?
- How will you determine when the data mining result or model should not be used any longer? Identify criteria (validity, threshold of accuracy, new data, change in application domain, etc.) that determine the "expiration" of the model or result.
- What should happen when the result or model expires? Is it sufficient to update or rebuild the model (or reconstruct the result) with newer data? Are the changes pervasive enough to require a completely new data mining project?

- If the original problem that was the impetus for this project changes or goes away, can the result be useful for other purposes? By documenting the original business problem, you make it easier to recognize when the model no longer serves its original purpose. In that case, you can then decide whether the result can be applied to a different, perhaps related, problem.

Once you have a grasp of these issues, develop and document your monitoring and maintenance plan. Make sure to include all of the details (or at least as many of them as you can identify during the planning stage) so everyone knows what to do and how to do it.

Example: **Fraud detection.** The agency's investigation unit will begin integrating its data on fraud with the agency's primary database to facilitate monitoring of the data mining results. Specifically, having data on successfully detected fraudulent applications will let the analysts evaluate the current strategy of identifying anomalous cases and investigating them. It will also allow a more direct approach in the future, where models are used to directly predict validity status of claims.

In the meantime, however, the analysts will need to use some caution in interpreting detection rates based on the deployed model. This is because the model is being used to flag applications for closer inspection; if the investigators are spending most of their time looking into the flagged cases, then naturally the bulk of the fraudulent claims they find will be in that group. To adequately monitor the effectiveness of the model, there should be routine investigation of some nonflagged cases. This will make it possible to compare the hit rate for the flagged applications to the hit rate for nonflagged applications. ■■■

Example: **CRM.** Monitoring CRM deployment will be made via the store's loyalty card program. Targeted customers will have a special note added to their card database record. That will make it possible for the company to track purchases by those customers to see if they meet the expectations set by the data mining results. It will also make it possible to compare the targeted group with the general customer pool to determine the exact effect of the marketing campaign on purchasing behavior.

This particular data mining model will expire when the promotion ends. However, if the company can demonstrate the positive impact of data mining on the promotion, similar data mining projects can be run in conjunction with future promotions. ■■■

Producing the Final Report

A significant part of deployment is simply getting the word out about what you've done and how it will benefit your organization. There are probably several key stakeholders who will need to be briefed on your results and how you got them. The final report (and final presentation, if necessary) conveys this information to the people who need it.

The first step in this task is to decide what reports are needed. Begin by determining who your target audiences will be. For example, suppose you need to communicate your results to two specific audiences:

- Database and Web administrators who will deploy your data mining models on the Web server
- Management sponsors of the project

These audiences are quite different, and you will probably need a separate document for each of these audiences.

This won't always be the case. Sometimes, you can serve more than one audience with a single report. The important point is that the report should provide the necessary information for its specific audience in a way that is easy for that audience to understand and use. A dense report full of technical specifications may be exactly what the database administrator needs, but such a report may be inappropriate for data entry operators. Identify key audience(s), determine each audience's needs, and make sure you meet those needs.

Although the content of the report will vary with the audience, most reports should contain at least the following basics:

- Description of the original business problem
- Process used for the data mining project
- Costs of the project
- Information about any deviations from the original project plan
- Summary of the data mining results (models and findings)
- Overview of the deployment plan, including expected benefits of deployment
- Recommendations for future work

More technically oriented audiences will typically need more details about the data mining results and deployment plans, whereas management or end-user audiences usually are more interested in the business problem, costs, and expected benefits.

For some audiences, the report may take the form of a presentation rather than a written document. Generally, this kind of presentation will contain information similar to the written report but described at a different level of detail and structured differently. Such presentations often take the form of an overview, highlighting key points without a lot of detail. This kind of presentation can be useful for people such as busy executives who simply need to understand the basic concepts. It can also be useful for people who are slated to get a written report, giving them a high-level context for the details that they will read about (or have already read) in the report.

Example: **Web mining.** To convey the findings of the data mining project to the Web team, the analysts prepared a document summarizing the findings with easy-to-understand charts and tables. Some examples from the report are shown below.

Figure 8-2
Excerpts from Web mining report

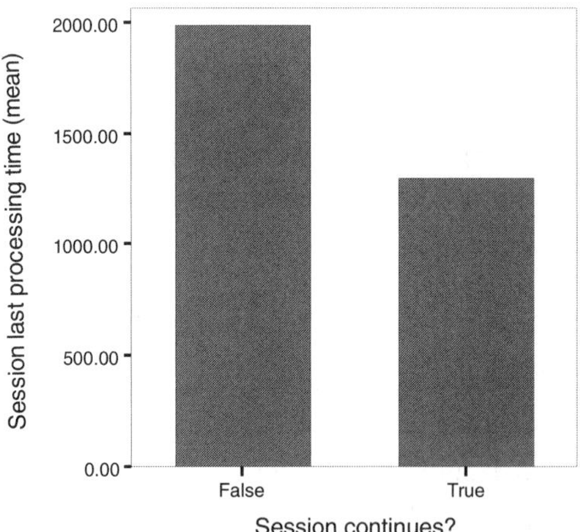

This chart shows the effect of processing time on propensity to leave the site. Sessions with longer processing times are more likely to end than those with shorter processing times. If we want to keep people at our site, we can't make them wait for page downloads!

Variables: AVTIMPAG
BRANDNAM: Total

	Session continues?			
	False		True	
Session Last Template	N	% of N in CONTINUE	N	% of N in CONTINUE
account/address\.jhtml	8	72.7%	3	27.3%
account/billing_info\.jhtml	2	66.7%	1	33.3%
account/change_password\.jhtml	2	66.7%	1	33.3%
account/create_address\.jhtml			2	100.0%
account/credit_info\.jhtml	21	63.6%	12	36.4%
account/edit_address\.jhtml	1	33.3%	2	66.7%
account/past_orders\.jhtml	24	77.4%	7	22.6%
account/past_orders_details\.jhtml	32	86.5%	5	13.5%
account/shipping_info\.jhtml	4	57.1%	3	42.9%
account/your_account\.jhtml	81	59.1%	56	40.9%
articles/dpt_about\.jhtml	130	67.7%	62	32.3%
articles/dpt_about_AdvisoryBoard\.jhtml	62	66.7%	31	33.3%
articles/dpt_about_BoardOfDirectors\.jht	41	60.3%	27	39.7%
articles/dpt_about_Careers\.jhtml	117	76.0%	37	24.0%
articles/dpt_about_HealthWellness\.jhtml	19	42.2%	26	57.8%
articles/dpt_about_Investor\.jhtml	34	53.1%	30	46.9%
articles/dpt_about_MgmtTeam\.jhtml	186	84.9%	33	15.1%
articles/dpt_about_PressReleases\.jhtml	43	53.1%	38	46.9%
articles/dpt_about_advisoryboard\.jhtml	1	100.0%		
articles/dpt_about_boardofdirectors\.jht			3	100.0%
articles/dpt_about_healthwellness\.jhtml	1	100.0%		
articles/dpt_about_investor\.jhtml			2	100.0%
articles/dpt_about_mgmtteam\.jhtml	7	70.0%	3	30.0%
articles/dpt_about_pressreleases\.jhtml	3	100.0%		
articles/dpt_about_the_press\.jhtml	84	85.7%	14	14.3%
articles/dpt_affiliate\.jhtml	57	67.1%	28	32.9%
articles/dpt_contact\.jhtml	71	92.2%	6	7.8%
articles/dpt_faqs\.jhtml	152	95.0%	8	5.0%
articles/dpt_payment\.jhtml	5	50.0%	5	50.0%
articles/dpt_privacy\.jhtml	9	25.0%	27	75.0%
articles/dpt_refer\.jhtml	34	70.8%	14	29.2%
articles/dpt_returns\.jhtml	6	26.1%	17	73.9%
articles/dpt_shipping\.jhtml	25	59.5%	17	40.5%
articles/dpt_terms\.jhtml	151	95.6%	7	4.4%
articles/new_returns\.jhtml	30	69.8%	13	30.2%
articles/new_security\.jhtml	20	66.7%	10	33.3%
articles/new_shipping\.jhtml	101	80.2%	25	19.8%
checkout/Billing\.jhtml	17	89.5%	2	10.5%
checkout/confirm_order\.jhtml	327	81.8%	73	18.3%
checkout/creditcard\.jhtml	4	44.4%	5	55.6%
checkout/expressCheckout\.jhtml	209	61.5%	131	38.5%
checkout/expresscheckout\.jhtml	11	73.3%	4	26.7%
checkout/shipping\.jhtml	2	33.3%	4	66.7%
checkout/thankyou\.jhtml	686	98.6%	10	1.4%
main/assortment2\.jhtml	135	60.3%	89	39.7%
main/assortment\.jhtml	2096	66.8%	1041	33.2%
main/boutique\.jhtml	1412	65.6%	739	34.4%
main/cust_serv\.jhtml	133	78.2%	37	21.8%
main/departments\.jhtml	1151	61.9%	709	38.1%
main/freegift\.jhtml	164	90.6%	17	9.4%
main/freeshipping\.jhtml	7	70.0%	3	30.0%
main/home\.jhtml	1618	75.7%	518	24.3%
main/leg_news\.jhtml	67	60.9%	43	39.1%
main/leg_news_fashion_word\.jhtml	59	81.9%	13	18.1%
main/leg_news_healthwellness\.jhtml	91	88.3%	12	11.7%
main/leg_news_legkicks\.jhtml	106	79.7%	27	20.3%
main/legcare_vendor\.jhtml	133	65.8%	69	34.2%
main/lifestyles\.jhtml	368	67.4%	178	32.6%
main/login2\.jhtml	213	58.4%	152	41.6%
main/login\.jhtml	17	47.2%	19	52.8%
main/loign2\.jhtml	1	100.0%		
main/newproducts\.jhtml	2	66.7%	1	33.3%
main/order_closed\.jhtml			1	100.0%
main/registration\.jhtml	494	79.9%	124	20.1%
main/registration_shipaddress\.jhtml	2	22.2%	7	77.8%
main/replenishment\.jhtml	241	75.8%	77	24.2%
main/sales_assortment\.jhtml	26	72.2%	10	27.8%
main/search_results\.jhtml	1837	68.1%	860	31.9%
main/seasonal_assortment\.jhtml	4	80.0%	1	20.0%
main/shopping_cart\.jhtml	351	46.5%	404	53.5%
main/theme_assortment\.jhtml			2	100.0%
main/vendor2\.jhtml	116	57.7%	85	42.3%
main/vendor\.jhtml	1145	67.7%	547	32.3%
main/welcome\.jhtml	55	33.3%	110	66.7%
products/productDetailLegcare\.jhtml	442	74.7%	150	25.3%
products/productDetailLegwear\.jhtml	3935	69.7%	1708	30.3%
replenish/create_replenish\.jhtml	8	100.0%		
replenish/view_replenish\.jhtml	7	87.5%	1	12.5%
Total	19256	69.2%	8558	30.8%

This table shows the breakdown of whether the session continues or not based on the last template viewed. Problem templates are highlighted. Note that some high-abandonment pages such as the checkout pages are not highlighted, because there are specific reasons for those pages to appear at the end of a session.

Each of the highlighted templates will have to be examined individually to determine why it seems to be driving traffic away from the site. In some cases, there may be minor formatting issues that users find irritating. In other cases, we may have to perform some significant site restructuring to adequately address the problem.

Reviewing the Project

As the final step in your data mining project, you will want to review the project. This involves finding out what you learned about data mining itself (as opposed to what you learned about your business or your data) and using that knowledge to improve your future data mining efforts. There are two perspectives that are particularly important to this review: the participants in the data mining process and its beneficiaries.

To get the participants' perspective, interview all the significant people involved with the project. What are their impressions of the project? What did they learn? What parts of the project did they think went well, and where did unexpected problems arise? Was there any information that would have made their part of the project go more smoothly?

The beneficiaries of the project can be a large and diverse group, so think carefully about this before setting out to get their perspective. There are obvious beneficiaries, such as the management sponsor(s) and any rank-and-file workers who will be responsible for implementing and using the results. But there are often other, less obvious constituencies that belong in this group as well—for example:

- Customers, if their interactions with your organization will be affected by the data mining results
- Business partners and other external organizations whose interactions with you will be affected
- Workers in your organization who may not be directly involved in everyday use of the data mining results, but who will be affected by them in other ways
- Management executives who may need to adjust their short-term or long-term plans based on the deployment of data mining results in your day-to-day operations

From each of the beneficiaries, find out whether the data mining results offer them noticeable improvements over conditions prior to deployment. Also find out if they are having trouble with the data mining results that might lessen their positive impact, such as confusion over new procedures or lack of confidence in the results.

After getting this kind of information from both participants and beneficiaries, you should be able to integrate it into a comprehensive view of the data mining process. Take the time to find patterns that can be generalized into nuggets of wisdom that you (or others) can apply to future data mining projects. In writing the review, try to focus on the important lessons that you learned.

Summary

This chapter outlined the steps for bringing your newly acquired knowledge into your daily business practices. The critical tasks and associated results of this phase include:

Planning deployment. Deciding how to use the data mining results.

Task results:

- Deployment plan

Planning monitoring and maintenance. Determining how to keep track of the effects of the deployment and make adjustments as necessary.

Task results:

- Monitoring and maintenance plan

Producing the final report. Getting the whole project down on paper.

Task results:

- Final report
- Final presentation

Reviewing the project. Considering what you learned and how it can be applied to future data mining projects.

Task results:

- Experience documentation

Chapter

9

Methods

Chapter 9 through Chapter 13 describe many of the methods used in data mining and include examples for most methods. These methods can be categorized as follows:

Online Analytical Processing (OLAP). These methods enable you to explore the current state of the data. They give you the power to summarize existing data simultaneously at various levels of aggregation. Different views of the same OLAP cube can provide different perspectives on the data, revealing patterns that would have been difficult to spot otherwise.

Exploratory graphics. Graphics put the data in a format that is accessible to the eye and brain, making patterns easy to grasp. Graphics can also help you identify unusual records and trouble spots.

Models for identifying groups. These methods are used when the goal is to identify records based on a certain set of characteristics. Segmentation (classification) models give you a way to predict categories for new records. Clustering models enable you to identify groups of similar cases where no external classification exists.

Modeling for numeric outcomes. These methods give you the power to make quantitative (numeric) predictions and forecasts for new records based on patterns in your current data. They help you to understand the relationships among the fields in your data set.

Chapter

10

Online Analytical Processing (OLAP)

Online analytical processing (OLAP) is a powerful tool for examining your data at any point in the data mining process, especially in the data understanding and data preparation phases. It consists mainly of generating **multidimensional tables**, or tables of results summarized across several fields or dimensions. These tables, sometimes called OLAP cubes, can usually be manipulated or rearranged interactively to view different breakdowns of the data "on the fly." OLAP uses multidimensional tables to provide easy accessibility to complex data. For example, you may have agricultural claim value figures summarized by geographic region, crop, and claim type. In a multidimensional table, each of these grouping characteristics becomes a **dimension** defining how the claim value figures, called **measures** or **variables**, are broken down. Multidimensional tables in this context are often called **OLAP cubes**.

The power of multidimensional tables lies in three characteristics:

Ease of use. You don't need specialized training to read a table of numbers. This makes multidimensional tables ideal for disseminating results to people who need information but are not data analysts.

Insight. The right table can give penetrating insight into your business process. The ability to manipulate multidimensional tables allows you to gain different perspectives on the patterns you see and allows you to "drill down" to examine patterns in more detail. It also provides a good way to check for potential data quality problems.

Flexibility. The structure of the table is general, and you can include whatever you want in the table cells. You can use counts, percentages, sums, averages, other summary statistics, or any combination of these to fill your table. This allows you to focus on the most important data aspects.

Figure 10-1
A multidimensional table (OLAP cube)

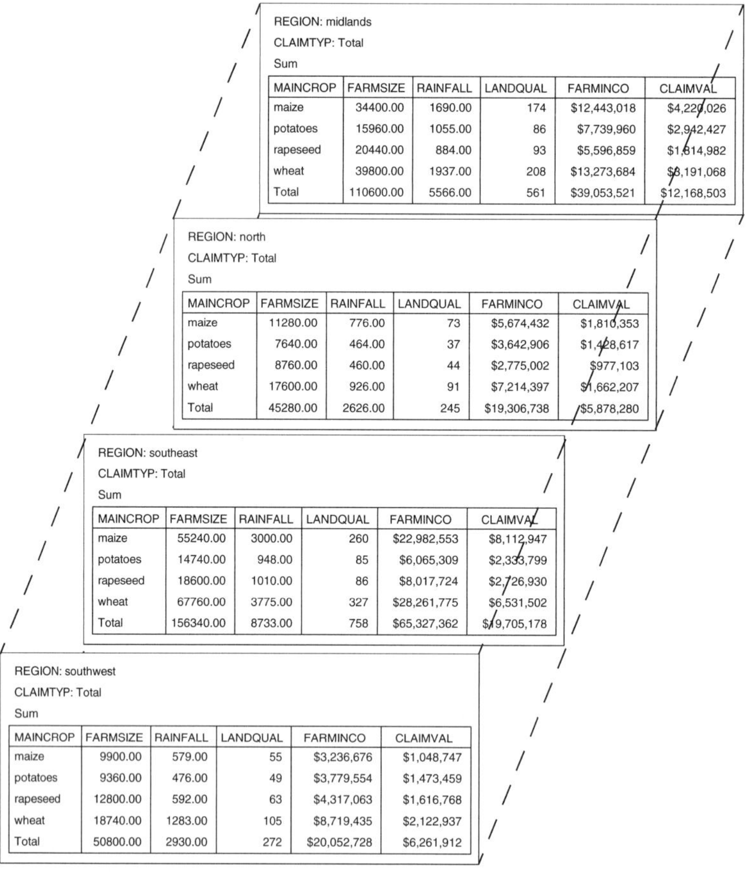

REGION: midlands
CLAIMTYP: Total
Sum

MAINCROP	FARMSIZE	RAINFALL	LANDQUAL	FARMINCO	CLAIMVAL
maize	34400.00	1690.00	174	$12,443,018	$4,220,026
potatoes	15960.00	1055.00	86	$7,739,960	$2,942,427
rapeseed	20440.00	884.00	93	$5,596,859	$1,814,982
wheat	39800.00	1937.00	208	$13,273,684	$3,191,068
Total	110600.00	5566.00	561	$39,053,521	$12,168,503

REGION: north
CLAIMTYP: Total
Sum

MAINCROP	FARMSIZE	RAINFALL	LANDQUAL	FARMINCO	CLAIMVAL
maize	11280.00	776.00	73	$5,674,432	$1,810,353
potatoes	7640.00	464.00	37	$3,642,906	$1,428,617
rapeseed	8760.00	460.00	44	$2,775,002	$977,103
wheat	17600.00	926.00	91	$7,214,397	$1,662,207
Total	45280.00	2626.00	245	$19,306,738	$5,878,280

REGION: southeast
CLAIMTYP: Total
Sum

MAINCROP	FARMSIZE	RAINFALL	LANDQUAL	FARMINCO	CLAIMVAL
maize	55240.00	3000.00	260	$22,982,553	$8,112,947
potatoes	14740.00	948.00	85	$6,065,309	$2,333,799
rapeseed	18600.00	1010.00	86	$8,017,724	$2,726,930
wheat	67760.00	3775.00	327	$28,261,775	$6,531,502
Total	156340.00	8733.00	758	$65,327,362	$19,705,178

REGION: southwest
CLAIMTYP: Total
Sum

MAINCROP	FARMSIZE	RAINFALL	LANDQUAL	FARMINCO	CLAIMVAL
maize	9900.00	579.00	55	$3,236,676	$1,048,747
potatoes	9360.00	476.00	49	$3,779,554	$1,473,459
rapeseed	12800.00	592.00	63	$4,317,063	$1,616,768
wheat	18740.00	1283.00	105	$8,719,435	$2,122,937
Total	50800.00	2930.00	272	$20,052,728	$6,261,912

Note: The examples in this chapter were created with SPSS software.

What to Include in the Table

Traditionally, the body of a table contains counts, percentages, sums, and averages, displayed in the table cells. These values often reveal important and interesting information. However, you can expand your table by using other summary statistics to gain insights that are not obvious in traditional tables.

Counts and Percentages

Tables based on counts and percentages show you how units (customers, transactions, accounts, etc.) are distributed across groups of interest. For example, you might want to look at the pattern of grant applications across regions and crop type. Counts give absolute numbers in each subgroup, while percentages describe the distribution of applicants within certain subgroups. Counts are most useful when you want to compare actual sizes of groups. Percentages are better when you want to compare patterns of values across groups. Look at the tables in Figure 10-2. The table on the left shows counts, and the table on the right shows percentages. The table on the left shows that the number of maize growers from the midlands region who filed for arable land development grants was about twice the number from the north region. On the other hand, *patterns* within groups are easier to see in the table on the right because everything is rescaled to 0–100%. For example, the *proportion* of applications by midlands maize growers for arable land development grants (as opposed to decommission land grants) is actually a bit less than that of their north region counterparts. The difference is due to the fact that the north region had fewer applicants overall than did the midlands region.

Figure 10-2
Tables with counts and percentages

FARMSIZE
N

REGION	MAINCROP	CLAIMTYP arable_dev	decommission_land	Total
midlands	maize	13	15	28
	potatoes	5	9	14
	rapeseed	8	9	17
	wheat	12	22	34
north	maize	6	5	11
	potatoes	1	5	6
	rapeseed	3	5	8
	wheat	6	8	14
southeast	maize	20	23	43
	potatoes	6	8	14
	rapeseed	7	7	14
	wheat	22	32	54
southwest	maize	5	4	9
	potatoes	1	6	7
	rapeseed	2	8	10
	wheat	6	11	17

FARMSIZE
% of N in CLAIMTYP

REGION	MAINCROP	CLAIMTYP arable_dev	decommission_land	Total
midlands	maize	46.4%	53.6%	100.0%
	potatoes	35.7%	64.3%	100.0%
	rapeseed	47.1%	52.9%	100.0%
	wheat	35.3%	64.7%	100.0%
north	maize	54.5%	45.5%	100.0%
	potatoes	16.7%	83.3%	100.0%
	rapeseed	37.5%	62.5%	100.0%
	wheat	42.9%	57.1%	100.0%
southeast	maize	46.5%	53.5%	100.0%
	potatoes	42.9%	57.1%	100.0%
	rapeseed	50.0%	50.0%	100.0%
	wheat	40.7%	59.3%	100.0%
southwest	maize	55.6%	44.4%	100.0%
	potatoes	14.3%	85.7%	100.0%
	rapeseed	20.0%	80.0%	100.0%
	wheat	35.3%	64.7%	100.0%

Sums and Averages

Often, you need to know more than the number of cases in a certain category. You need a summary of some quantitative variable. The most common summary statistics are the **sum** and the **average**. The sum is the total value across all records in a particular subgroup. The average (also known as the **mean**) is the sum divided by the number of records in the subgroup. It is the value you would expect for a new record if you know only that the record falls into the given subgroup. For example, if the average arable land development claim value for midlands maize farmers is $141,575, then in the absence of other information, $141,575 would be your best estimate of any new midlands maize farmer's claim amount for the same type of grant.

Figure 10-3

Mean (average) claim value by region, main crop, and claim type

CLAIMVAL
Mean

		CLAIMTYP		
REGION	MAINCROP	arable_dev	decommission_land	Total
midlands	maize	$141,575	$158,637	$150,715
	potatoes	$114,629	$263,254	$210,173
	rapeseed	$127,255	$88,549	$106,764
	wheat	$124,439	$77,173	$93,855
north	maize	$195,991	$126,882	$164,578
	potatoes	$437,473	$198,229	$238,103
	rapeseed	$77,672	$148,817	$122,138
	wheat	$116,210	$120,618	$118,729
southeast	maize	$152,051	$220,518	$188,673
	potatoes	$112,667	$207,224	$166,700
	rapeseed	$173,785	$215,776	$194,781
	wheat	$126,076	$117,432	$120,954
southwest	maize	$121,465	$110,356	$116,527
	potatoes	$258,536	$202,487	$210,494
	rapeseed	$214,936	$148,362	$161,677
	wheat	$173,805	$98,192	$124,879

Remember that sums and averages, though related, measure fundamentally different conditions. Use sums when you want to know the total value of the variable *across* items. Use averages when you want to know the value for the *typical* case. Figure 10-4 illustrates the difference. The group with the highest *total* claim values (measured by the sum) is land decommission grants to maize farmers, with a total of $8,527,301. In contrast, the group with the highest *average* claim value is land decommission grants to potato farmers, with a mean of $222,612. While the average potato farmer files for a larger grant, maize farmers outnumber potato farmers, so as a group they receive more grant funds.

Figure 10-4

Claim value statistics by claim type and main crop

CLAIMVAL
REGION: Total

	CLAIMTYP			
	arable_dev		decommission_land	
MAINCROP	Sum	Mean	Sum	Mean
maize	$6,664,772	$151,472	$8,527,301	$181,432
potatoes	$1,945,159	$149,628	$6,233,144	$222,612
rapeseed	$2,897,427	$144,871	$4,238,356	$146,150
wheat	$6,007,036	$130,588	$7,500,678	$102,749

Measures of Variability

Counts, percentages, sums, and averages all convey important information about your data. But there are important aspects of the data that are difficult or impossible to see with these statistics. One important characteristic of any field is the **variability** in the values. In other words, it's just as important to know how much values vary from record to record as it is to know the sum or the average value. There are several ways to measure variability:

Range. This is the highest value minus the lowest value. It indicates how large the range of values is in your data.

Variance. This is a statistic that summarizes the variability in the values. It is based on all of the values in the data, not just the most extreme values. The variance gives higher weight to values that are farther from the mean.

Standard deviation. This statistic is the square root of the variance. It is a similar index based on all of the values, but it is measured in the same units as the original field (for example, dollars or accounts).

Minimum and maximum values. By examining the smallest and largest values explicitly, you can see what the most extreme values are. Often, extreme values represent interesting cases that warrant further study.

These different approaches to measuring variability lead to different conclusions because they measure different aspects of variability. For example, Figure 10-5 shows variability statistics for claim value broken down by main crop for the southeast region. Notice that the group with the largest *range* is maize farmers, but the group with the largest *standard deviation* is potato farmers. This apparent discrepancy is due to the fact that the range considers only two values, the minimum and the maximum, whereas the standard deviation considers the distance of every value from the mean.

Figure 10-5
OLAP cube of claim values by main crop for the southeast region

REGION: southeast
CLAIMTYP: Total
CLAIMVAL

MAINCROP	N	Mean	Std. Deviation	Range	Minimum	Maximum
maize	43	$188,673	$141,860	$576,570	$29,811	$606,381
potatoes	14	$166,700	$144,211	$424,001	$30,377	$454,378
rapeseed	14	$194,781	$111,898	$412,144	$30,272	$442,416
wheat	54	$120,954	$84,365	$428,030	$10,647	$438,677
Total	125	$157,641	$120,152	$595,734	$10,647	$606,381

In Figure 10-6, you see two hypothetical distributions of field values. Both distributions have the same minimum and maximum values and thus the same range of values. However, the distribution on the left has all of the other points piled up in the center, whereas the distribution on the right has the other points evenly spread out between the extreme values. The standard deviation, by taking into account *all* values, reveals the difference in the two distributions.

Figure 10-6
Two hypothetical distributions with equal ranges but different standard deviations

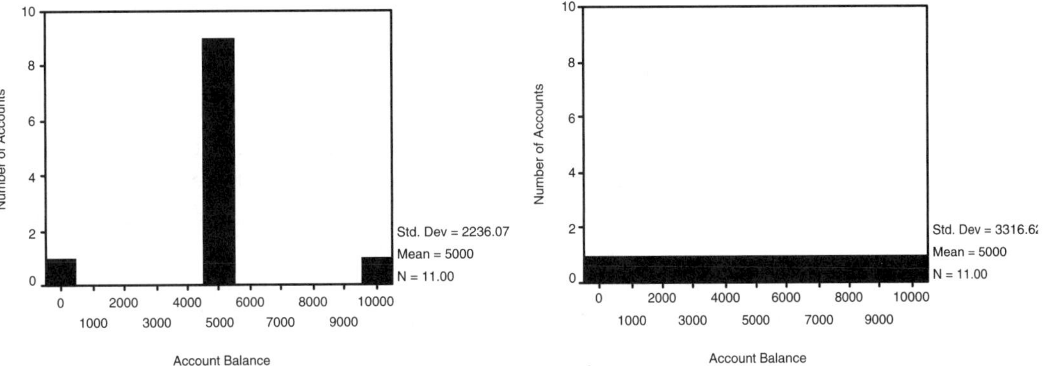

Getting the Most from OLAP

Selecting summary statistics for an OLAP cube and generating the cube are the first steps to knowledge. You must also be able to view, manipulate, and disseminate the table to make the best use of the data. The advantage of OLAP cubes over traditional static reports is that the person reading the table can arrange the data to display different patterns of interest. With an OLAP cube, you aren't stuck with whatever you get in the initial report—you can explore the data to find the answers *you* need.

There are three main characteristics of an OLAP cube that determine its usefulness: structure, contents, and format. The **structure** of the table refers to how the dimensions "slice and dice" the data. OLAP cubes have three ways of slicing data—rows, columns, and layers. Rows and columns should be familiar. **Layers** represent an additional way to slice data. Imagine that your table is a book; the rows represent lines on a page, the columns represent words, and the layers represent separate pages. Refer to Figure 10-1, which illustrates a simple OLAP cube. In this table, rows represent main crops, columns represent distinct measures (summary variables), and layers represent regions. (Each value for the layer dimension is shown as a separate table in the figure, but in the actual OLAP cube, the layers are all part of the same table.)

Your table should include all of the relevant fields as dimensions and the appropriate statistics to answer the question at hand. A dimension can define rows, columns, or layers in a table. Dimensions can also be nested. For example, you could subdivide each region by main crop to define a row for each region/main crop combination, as shown in Figure 10-3. This kind of nesting allows you to examine data in three, four, or more dimensions without resorting to layers. Unfortunately, nesting multiple dimensions quickly leads to large, unwieldy tables. In such cases, an interactive table with layers is often clearer than a huge table without layers. With today's powerful report OLAP tools, you can go back and forth between nested and layered dimensions easily.

You will also need to pay careful attention to the **contents** of the table. In general, when generating the table, the rule is to include anything you think you might need to see in the table, even if you're not sure you'll actually use it. It's easier to hide something temporarily than to regenerate the entire table because something important was left out. For example, suppose you want to compare average claim values and claim value variability between the midlands region and the north region, broken down by main crop. All of the information you need appears in Figure 10-7. Unfortunately, there is also extraneous data for other regions, as well as several irrelevant (for this query) statistical summaries.

Figure 10-7
OLAP cube with extraneous information

CLAIMVAL

		CLAIMTYP											
		arable_dev						decommission_land					
REGION	MAINCROP	Sum	N	Mean	Std. Deviation	% of Total Sum	% of Total N	Sum	N	Mean	Std. Deviation	% of Total Sum	% of Total N
midlands	maize	1840472.70	13	141574.8231	83621.21769	4.2%	4.3%	2379553.40	15	158636.8933	126226.74368	5.4%	5.0%
	potatoes	573145.90	5	114629.1800	62334.39853	1.3%	1.7%	2369281.50	9	263253.5000	193986.35880	5.4%	3.0%
	rapeseed	1018040.20	8	127255.0250	73599.75717	2.3%	2.7%	796941.30	9	88549.0333	46526.30772	1.8%	3.0%
	wheat	1493272.40	12	124439.3667	95669.55356	3.4%	4.0%	1697795.24	22	77172.5109	52487.74277	3.9%	7.3%
	Total	4924931.20	38	129603.4526	80773.04379	11.2%	12.7%	7243571.44	55	131701.2989	125321.25218	16.5%	18.3%
north	maize	1175944.90	6	195990.8167	101973.11147	2.7%	2.0%	634407.70	5	126881.5400	113299.52054	1.4%	1.7%
	potatoes	437473.00	1	437473.0000	.	1.0%	.3%	991144.20	5	198228.8400	113992.29281	2.3%	1.7%
	rapeseed	233017.40	3	77672.4667	48158.20700	.5%	1.0%	744085.30	5	148817.0600	97939.20058	1.7%	1.7%
	wheat	697260.90	6	116210.1500	97517.26569	1.6%	2.0%	964946.50	8	120618.3125	63356.90361	2.2%	2.7%
	Total	2543696.20	16	158981.0125	121316.26666	5.8%	5.3%	3334583.70	23	144981.9000	93036.56199	7.6%	7.7%
southeast	maize	3041029.20	20	152051.4600	118411.18455	6.9%	6.7%	5071917.80	23	220518.1652	155017.88830	11.5%	7.7%
	potatoes	676004.10	6	112667.3500	90570.33972	1.5%	2.0%	1657794.70	8	207224.3375	168476.57932	3.8%	2.7%
	rapeseed	1216497.10	7	173785.3000	151177.48500	2.8%	2.3%	1510433.00	7	215776.1429	56971.72285	3.4%	2.3%
	wheat	2773672.40	22	126076.0182	106233.27201	6.3%	7.3%	3757829.40	32	117432.1688	67022.74988	8.5%	10.7%
	Total	7707202.80	55	140130.9600	113951.17831	17.5%	18.3%	11997974.90	70	171399.6414	123876.57339	27.3%	23.3%
southwest	maize	607324.90	5	121464.9800	85153.92296	1.4%	1.7%	441422.30	4	110355.5750	30901.40067	1.0%	1.3%
	potatoes	258536.00	1	258536.0000	.	.6%	.3%	1214923.30	6	202487.2167	97267.58034	2.8%	2.0%
	rapeseed	429872.00	2	214936.0000	55649.30368	1.0%	.7%	1186896.30	8	148362.0375	63480.71177	2.7%	2.7%
	wheat	1042830.60	6	173805.1000	114968.26853	2.4%	2.0%	1080106.50	11	98191.5000	78199.43937	2.5%	3.7%
	Total	2338563.50	14	167040.2500	96798.64294	5.3%	4.7%	3923348.40	29	135287.8759	81419.49087	8.9%	9.7%
Total	maize	6664771.70	44	151472.0841	102183.62127	15.1%	14.7%	8527301.20	47	181431.9404	138624.19424	19.4%	15.7%
	potatoes	1945159.00	13	149627.6154	117471.29526	4.4%	4.3%	6233143.70	28	222612.2750	151679.56047	14.2%	9.3%
	rapeseed	2897426.70	20	144871.3350	106247.35472	6.6%	6.7%	4238355.90	29	146150.2034	77284.11098	9.6%	9.7%
	wheat	6007036.30	46	130587.7457	101615.80728	13.6%	15.3%	7500677.64	73	102749.0088	65662.37613	17.0%	24.3%
	Total	17514393.70	123	142393.4447	103407.53421	39.8%	41.0%	26499478.44	177	149714.5675	115312.88941	60.2%	59.0%

Wading through the extraneous data can be an arduous and error-prone task. Notice in Figure 10-8 how much easier it is to make direct comparisons between the two relevant regions after the unneeded material has been removed (hidden).

Figure 10-8
OLAP cube with relevant information only

CLAIMVAL

		CLAIMTYP					
		arable_dev			decommission_land		
REGION	MAINCROP	Sum	Mean	Std. Deviation	Sum	Mean	Std. Deviation
midlands	maize	$1,840,473	$141,575	$83,621	$2,379,553	$158,637	$126,227
	potatoes	$573,146	$114,629	$62,334	$2,369,282	$263,254	$193,986
	rapeseed	$1,018,040	$127,255	$73,600	$796,941	$88,549	$46,526
	wheat	$1,493,272	$124,439	$95,670	$1,697,795	$77,173	$52,488
	Total	$4,924,931	$129,603	$80,773	$7,243,571	$131,701	$125,321
north	maize	$1,175,945	$195,991	$101,973	$634,408	$126,882	$113,300
	potatoes	$437,473	$437,473	.	$991,144	$198,229	$113,992
	rapeseed	$233,017	$77,672	$48,158	$744,085	$148,817	$97,939
	wheat	$697,261	$116,210	$97,517	$964,947	$120,618	$63,357
	Total	$2,543,696	$158,981	$121,316	$3,334,584	$144,982	$93,037
Total	maize	$6,664,772	$151,472	$102,184	$8,527,301	$181,432	$138,624
	potatoes	$1,945,159	$149,628	$117,471	$6,233,144	$222,612	$151,680
	rapeseed	$2,897,427	$144,871	$106,247	$4,238,356	$146,150	$77,284
	wheat	$6,007,036	$130,588	$101,616	$7,500,678	$102,749	$65,662
	Total	$17,514,394	$142,393	$103,408	$26,499,478	$149,715	$115,313

Summary

OLAP cubes can give insight into your data that is difficult or impossible to obtain from static tables or reports. Active OLAP cubes make it easy to explore your data. Modern OLAP tools allow you to interact with the data in a cube to examine many different patterns quickly and to disseminate your results to the employees who can make the most of them.

Chapter

11

Exploratory Graphics

Un croquis vaut mieux qu'un long discours. (A sketch is better than a long speech.)

—Napoleon

You have no doubt heard the saying, "A picture is worth a thousand words." Nowhere is this more true than in data mining. Often, information that would take hours to decipher from tables or complex mathematical models is easily identified in the right chart. Modern data mining techniques are getting better and better at recognizing patterns, but the human brain is still the best pattern-recognition system available. Exploratory graphics can structure the information in your data so that you can readily perceive those patterns. This allows you to pinpoint the relationships that can help you build satisfaction and loyalty in your customers.

Types of Charts

This chapter describes several of the most useful and widely used chart types, each suitable for displaying certain kinds of information.

Bar Charts

In a nutshell

Purpose: to display quantitative or count values by groups or categories

Typical application: showing average customer sales by region

Strengths: easy to construct and interpret

Weaknesses: limited ability to show relationships among multiple characteristics or variability of estimates

Anyone who reads newspapers or magazines has seen examples of bar charts. Bar charts are useful when you want to compare values, counts, or proportions between groups. A bar chart shows at a glance how the groups compare to each other based on the characteristic of interest.

Figure 11-1
Example of a bar chart

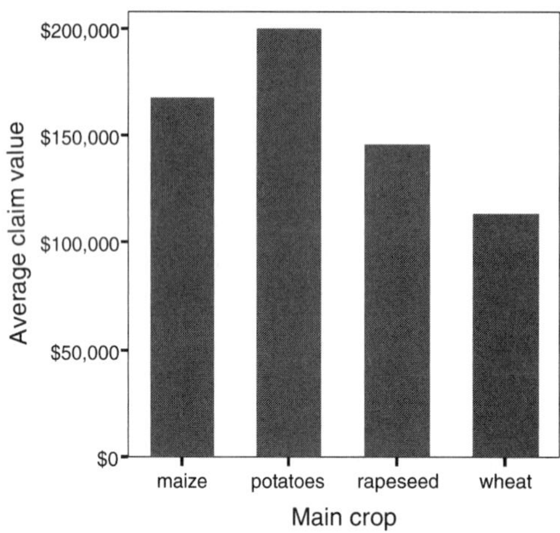

Figure 11-1 shows a bar chart of average grant claim value by main crop. The chart reveals at a glance that, on average, potato farmers file larger claims than farmers growing other crops. If you want to see something more detailed, you can use a clustered bar chart, where categories of one field are nested within those of another. Figure 11-2 shows a **clustered bar chart**, allowing quick comparisons between claim types within main crop groups.

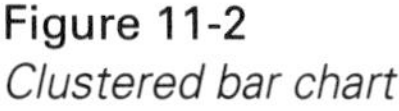
Figure 11-2
Clustered bar chart

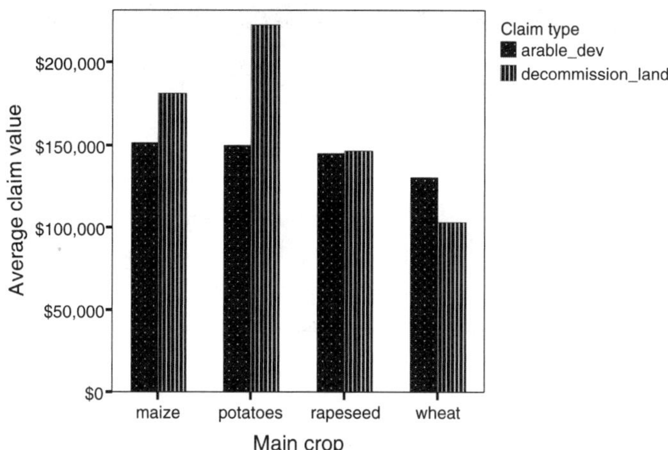

This graph shows that there seems to be more variability in decommission land claims than in arable land development claims, and while potato farms have the highest average value for decommission land claims, maize farmers have a slightly higher average for arable land development claims.

Distribution Charts

Distribution charts are specialized bar charts that show the number of records for each category in a set of categories. Such charts are useful for getting to know your data and for finding data quality problems.

For example, the distribution chart in Figure 11-3 shows that customers who buy for themselves form the largest group, and the number of customers who buy for their family is about the same as the number who buy for their friends.

Figure 11-3
Example of a distribution chart

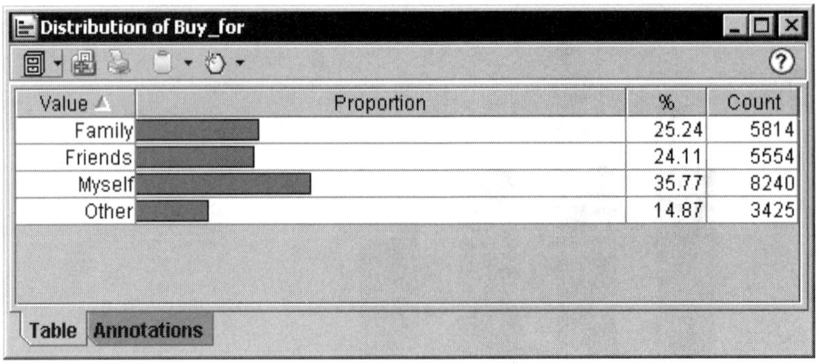

Distribution of Buy_for

Value	Proportion	%	Count
Family		25.24	5814
Friends		24.11	5554
Myself		35.77	8240
Other		14.87	3425

Table | Annotations

Pareto Charts

In a nutshell

Purpose: to display quantitative or count values by groups or categories, where the categories are ranked based on the values

Typical application: ranking film categories based on popularity

Strengths: easy to construct and interpret

Weaknesses: limited ability to show relationships among multiple characteristics or variability of estimates

When you want to find the important categories for a certain result, you can use another specialized kind of bar chart, a **Pareto chart**. A Pareto chart is basically a bar chart with the bars ordered by length. (In some software packages, including Clementine, you create this chart by creating a basic bar chart and then sorting the bars in the chart.) This sorting allows you to easily see the rank ordering of the categories in terms of the measured characteristic. Figure 11-4 shows a Pareto chart for a customer's self-reported favorite film category.

Figure 11-4
Example Pareto chart

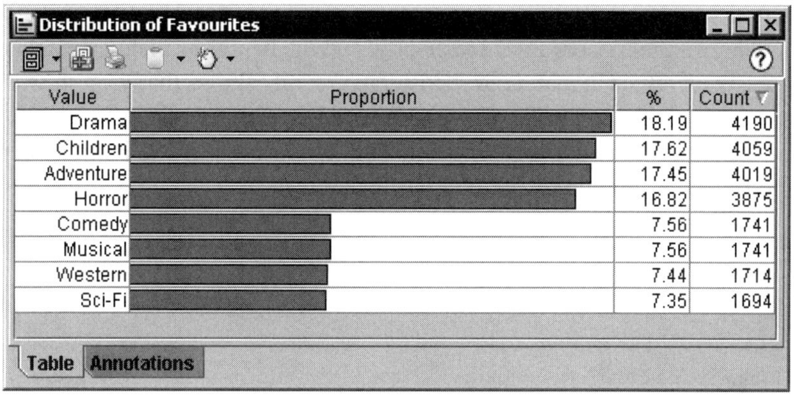

Distribution of Favourites

Value	Proportion	%	Count
Drama		18.19	4190
Children		17.62	4059
Adventure		17.45	4019
Horror		16.82	3875
Comedy		7.56	1741
Musical		7.56	1741
Western		7.44	1714
Sci-Fi		7.35	1694

Table Annotations

You can easily see that *Drama* is the most popular category, followed by *Children*, and so on. This information can help you allocate resources—in this instance, you might use such a graph to help decide how a Web server should respond when new customers log on, in the absence of direct, individual-level preference information.

Histograms

In a nutshell

Purpose: to graphically display the distribution of values for a quantitative characteristic

Typical application: showing the distribution of revenues across individual transactions

Strengths: easy to construct and interpret

Weaknesses: limited ability to show relationships among multiple characteristics; limited ability to make comparisons across groups

A **histogram** is a special kind of bar chart. It shows how the values of a numeric or quantitative characteristic are distributed. The range of values for the characteristic is split into evenly spaced smaller ranges (sometimes called **bins**), and the height of each bar corresponds to the number of cases with a value in that subrange. For example, Figure 11-5 shows a histogram of number of actions (page clicks, search form submissions, etc.) during a single Web site visit. The tallest bar represents the range of action counts that occurs most frequently, and the height of that bar indicates the frequency of values in that range. This graph readily shows that Web site visits consist of one or two actions. The heavily skewed pattern revealed here indicates that you may want to perform a transformation on this field before using it in building certain types of models. (For more information, see Chapter 5.)

Figure 11-5
Histogram of number of user actions per visit

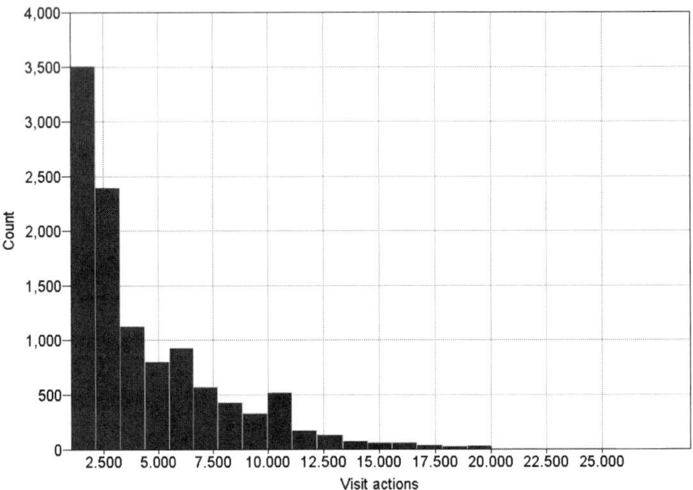

Line Charts

In a nutshell

Purpose: to graphically summarize a series of values for a numeric attribute

Typical application: showing changes in number of accounts opened per month across time

Strengths: good for showing change over time

Weaknesses: can lead to focusing on minor variations, ignoring overall trends

In some analyses, you want to tie certain points together. **Time series data**, in which the same thing is measured over and over again to note changes across time, provide a good example of this. Figure 11-6 shows a plot of time series data for sales at a retail store across 52 weeks. There is clear variability here, with peaks near the end of the cycle (perhaps representing holiday purchases).

Figure 11-6
Line chart of sales data

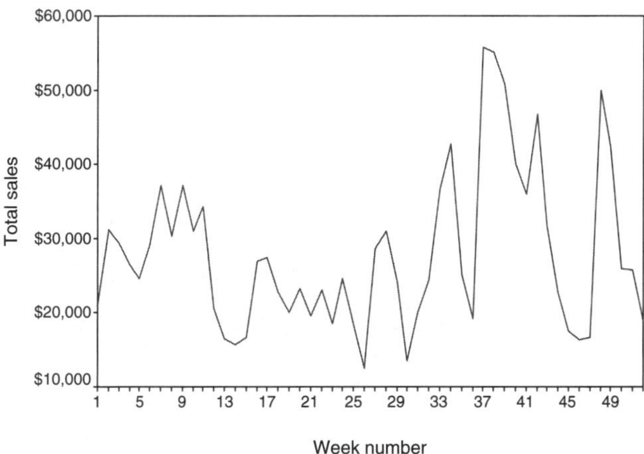

You can also make comparisons across store locations by plotting multiple lines in the same chart. For example, Figure 11-7 shows a line chart for sales of the original store

and two other locations. Stores 1 and 2 show similar patterns, but store 3 shows a much weaker pattern, with lower peaks in sales, even relative to the lower overall volume of sales at that store.

Figure 11-7
Line chart of sales data for three stores

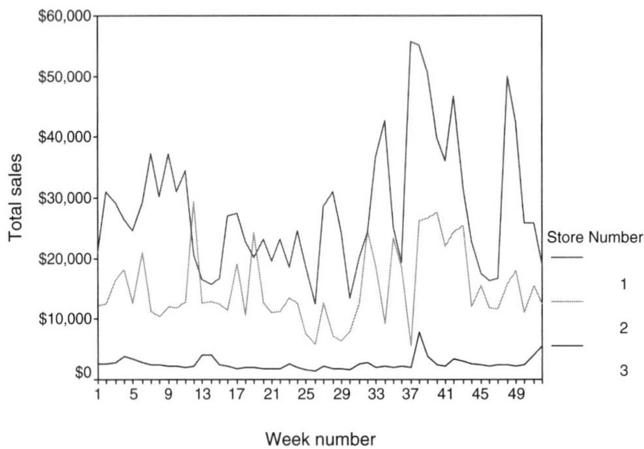

Pie Charts

In a nutshell

Purpose: to graphically summarize the breakdown of a total by groups or categories

Typical application: seeing how total sales are distributed across regions

Strengths: intuitively appealing; well known and understood

Weaknesses: limited ability to show relationships among multiple characteristics; can make distinguishing values difficult

Pie charts are sometimes useful for illustrating proportional relationships—for showing how much of the total comes from each of several groups. Figure 11-8 shows registered Web visitors broken down by whom they buy for.

Figure 11-8
Pie chart of customers for each category of "buy for"

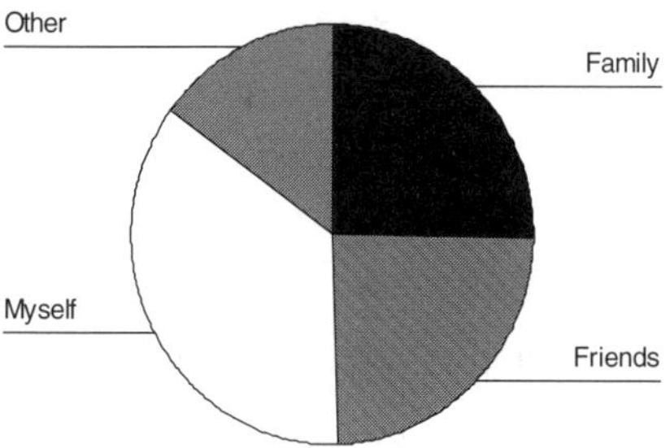

Unfortunately, pie charts are better at illustrating things that are well understood than they are for exploring new relationships. It's difficult in many circumstances to see the subtleties in your data with a pie chart. In Figure 11-8, it's hard to see exactly how the sales split between regions. For example, it's difficult to tell from the pie chart whether there are more *Family* buyers or *Friends* buyers. Now, compare the pie chart display to the corresponding bar chart in Figure 11-9. The bar chart quickly reveals which of the groups is larger, whereas you have to look closely to get the same information from the pie chart. Thus, while you might use pie charts for illustrating relationships, their role in discovering new information tends to be relatively limited.

Figure 11-9
Bar chart corresponding to pie chart in Figure 11-8

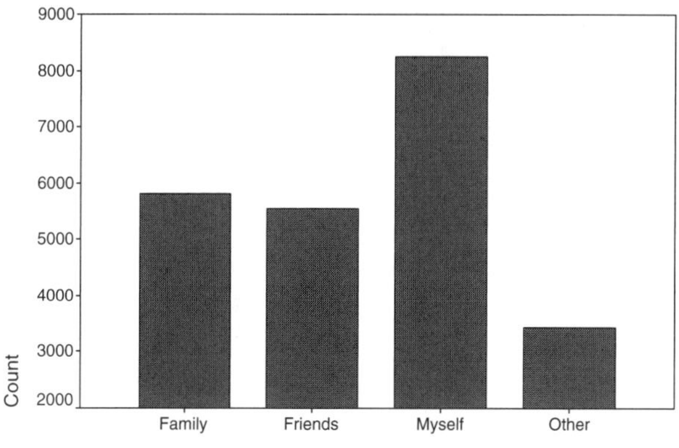

Web Graphs

In a nutshell

Purpose: to graphically show relationships between two or more characteristics

Typical application: checking the relationship between region, grant type, and main crop for grant applicants

Strengths: make multi-field relationship patterns stand out

Weaknesses: can be complicated, especially with many fields included

Sometimes it helps to be able to visualize the strength of relationships among several fields simultaneously. A Web graph can help you do that. A **Web graph** represents each field (or each value of a categorical field) as a dot, and lines connect each dot with every other dot. The weight or thickness of each line indicates the strength of the relationship between each pair of items.

Figure 11-10
Web graph of fields in agricultural grant application data

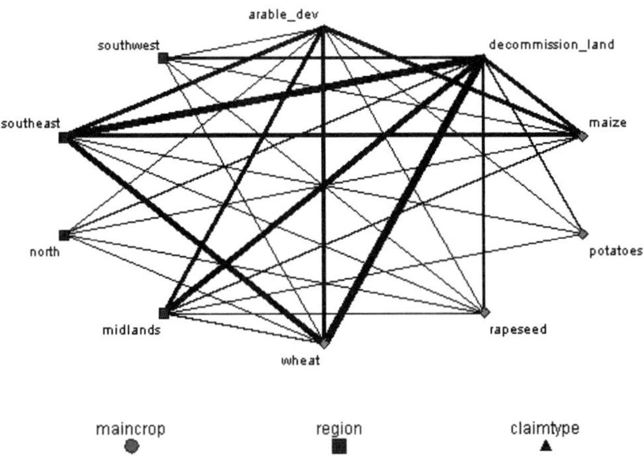

In this example, the strongest links are between the southwest region and land decommission grants and between wheat growers and those grants, indicated by thick

lines connecting the corresponding points in the graph. There are also moderately strong links between the southeast region and maize growers, and between arable land development grants and maize growers.

To tame some of the complexity of Web graphs, you can set a threshold to hide the weaker links. For example, Figure 11-11 shows the same graph with weaker links suppressed. This can often make the important patterns easier to see in the graph.

Figure 11-11
Web graph with weak links suppressed

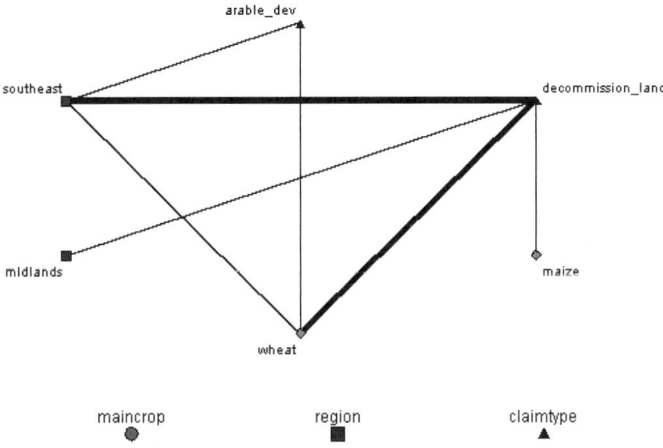

Point Charts

In a nutshell

Purpose: to graphically show relationships between two or more quantitative characteristics

Typical application: checking the relationship between rainfall and farm income for grant applicants

Strengths: make relationship patterns stand out

Weaknesses: somewhat less intuitive than some other chart types; 3-D scatterplots require (online) interactivity for full benefit

In some situations, you want to display points in a chart. Points are used to indicate individual records or to represent groups of records. Each point's location in the chart is based on values of one or more fields of interest. One of the most common point-oriented charts is the **scatterplot**, which locates points based on values of two numerical fields. Figure 11-12 shows a scatterplot of farm income versus rainfall for grant applicants. Each point in the chart represents one applicant. The location in the graph indicates the values for the two characteristics of interest for that applicant—the further to the right, the higher the rainfall at that applicant's location; the further toward the top, the higher the farm income reported by the applicant. If there is no relationship, you will see the points evenly distributed in the plot. If there is a pattern, the points will tend to cluster unevenly, revealing the pattern. You can clearly see a trend in this chart—rainfall has a strong limiting effect on income. Applicants with high rainfall don't necessarily have high income, but those with low rainfall almost always report low income.

Figure 11-12
Scatterplot of farm income versus rainfall

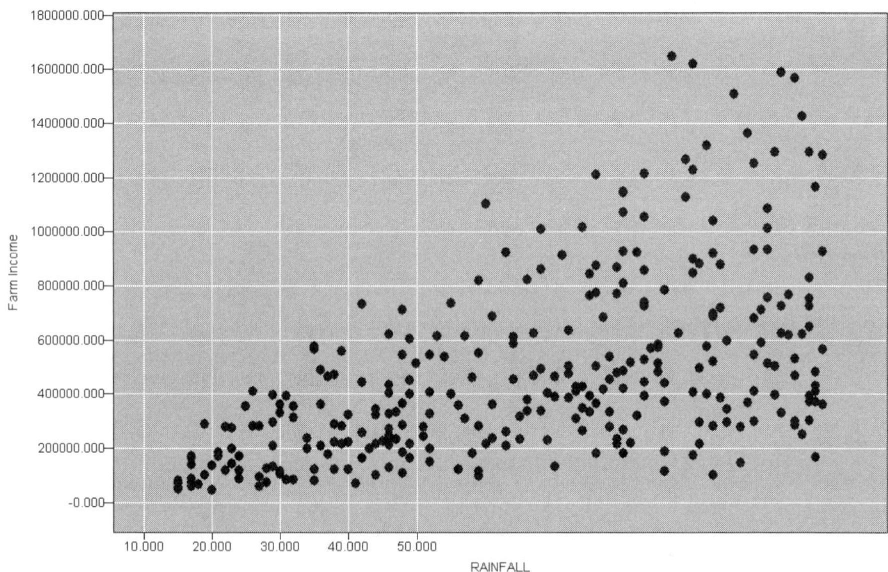

However, some cases defy this trend. You can examine such unexpected cases to learn what makes them unique. For example, consider the point indicated in Figure 11-13. This case is unique because this customer has a surprisingly high income for a location with only moderate rainfall. You can define the graph so that customer IDs are embedded as labels for the points. Of course, to show the label for every point would clutter up the chart and reduce its usefulness. However, by selectively displaying labels, you can identify the unique cases so that you can investigate them more closely. In this example, perhaps you would look up historical data for customer number 1501 to gain insight into what makes this customer unusual. Or perhaps you would invite this customer to complete a survey the next time he or she logged on to your Web site.

Figure 11-13
Selecting a unique point for further study

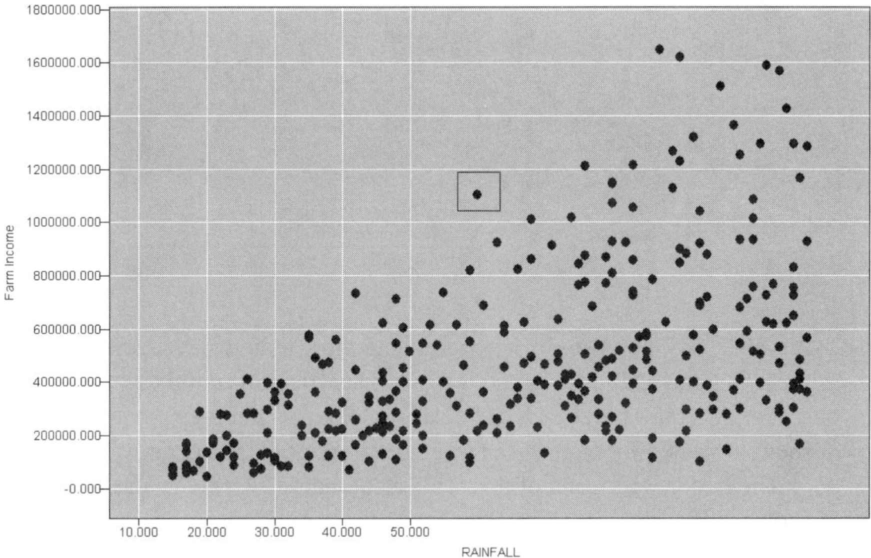

Sometimes you may find it useful to compare the patterns of separate groups. You can do this in a single scatterplot by assigning a different symbol to each group. For example, Figure 11-14 shows a scatterplot that is similar to the previous plot except that different symbols are used to represent different claim types. This graph shows that the relationship between rainfall and income appears to be similar for the two claim types.

Figure 11-14
Scatterplot for different claim types

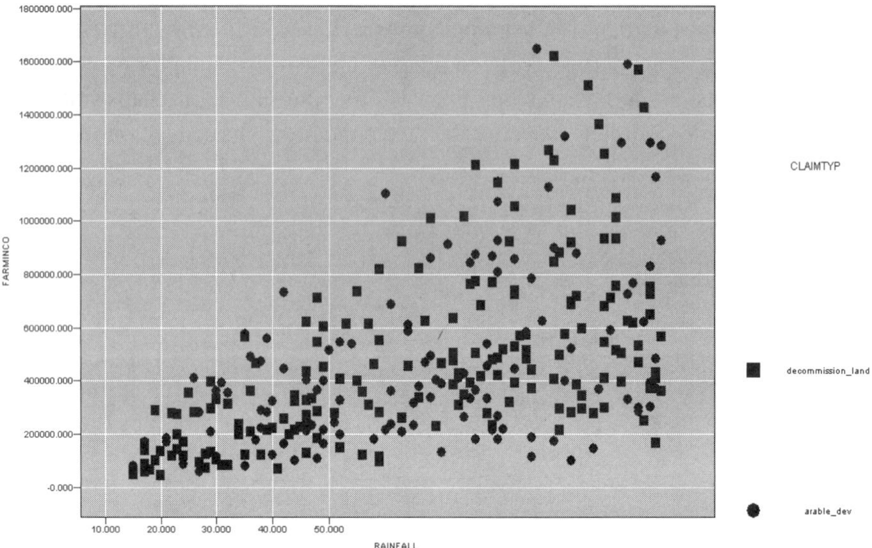

It is also possible to study patterns among more than two characteristics at the same time. One method for doing so is to use a **scatterplot matrix**, which is a table of scatterplots that shows each characteristic plotted against every other one. Figure 11-15 shows a scatterplot matrix for farm income, rainfall, and claim value.

The middle left panel of this scatterplot matrix represents the same information shown in Figure 11-14. The other panels show relationships between all other pairwise combinations of the three characteristics. In this scatterplot matrix, there appear to be relationships between all three fields. Unfortunately, it is hard to see exactly what form these relationships take.

Figure 11-15
Scatterplot matrix for three fields in fraud data

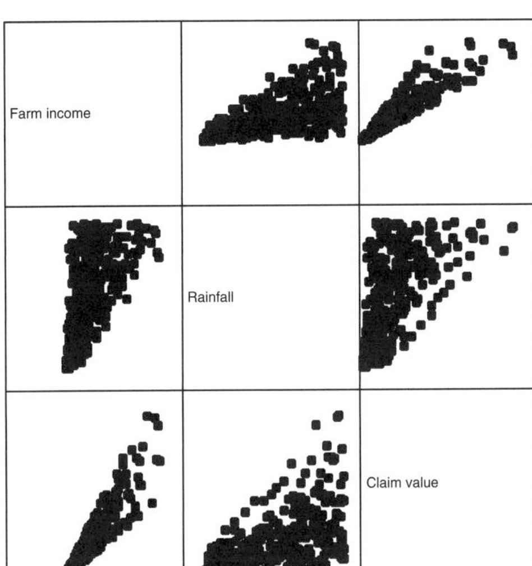

To visualize more complex relationships, you may need to use a **three-dimensional scatterplot**. This is simply a scatterplot with a third dimension added for another characteristic. If you think of a 2-D scatterplot as a slice of swiss cheese, with the holes representing points, then a 3-D scatterplot is like a solid chunk of swiss cheese, with the bubbles in the cheese representing the points.

A 3-D scatterplot can reveal subtleties of relationships that are difficult to see in a traditional 2-D plot. However, 3-D scatterplots do rely heavily on interactivity for their value. It is sometimes difficult to gain much information from a static 2-D representation (such as a printed version) of a 3-D scatterplot. In such cases, adding a **smoother** can help. A smoother is an enhancement to the plot that summarizes the relationships among the variables. Smoothers attempt to separate the basic trend in the graph from the random *noise*, making it easier to identify the larger pattern. Metaphorically speaking, the smoother hides the trees so that you can see the forest. In a 3-D scatterplot, the smoother appears as a surface in the graph. This surface flexes and bends to fit the data, but it has a certain amount of *stiffness*. This stiffness allows the surface to approximate the *overall* pattern rather than contorting to touch every point in the graph.

Figure 11-16 shows the relationship among loan balance, deposit balance, and tenure, using a scatterplot with a smoother to highlight the pattern in the data.

Figure 11-16
Three-dimensional scatterplot with a smoother

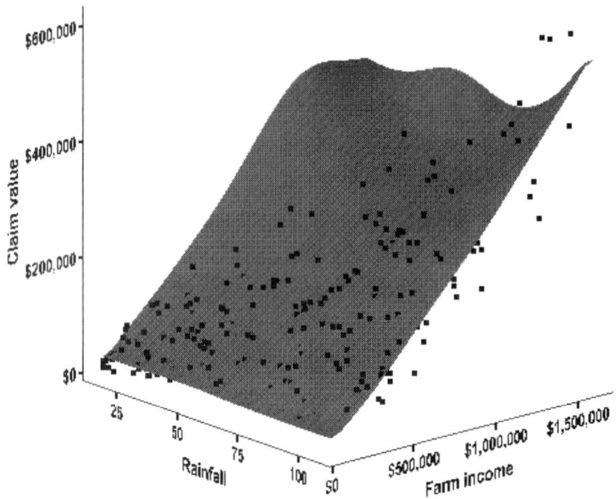

Chart Enhancements

You can make your charts even more informative by enhancing them. You've already seen how a smoother can be used to enhance a 3-D scatterplot. Other enhancements can show variability of numbers, confidence in plotted estimates, or relationships with additional fields.

Error bars can be used to show variability of values within groups or confidence of estimates. Figure 11-17 shows a bar chart with error bars that indicate the confidence interval for the mean within each group. (When you estimate a value such as a mean, there is a chance that your estimate won't be exactly right, although it's usually close to the true value. A confidence interval shows you a range of values in which the true value is likely to lie. This is analogous to the ubiquitous "plus-or-minus 4%" range given in political polling results.) Notice that the confidence intervals for the southeast and north regions overlap. This indicates that the apparent difference in means may be due to error in the estimate rather than a true difference.

Figure 11-17
Bar chart with error bars

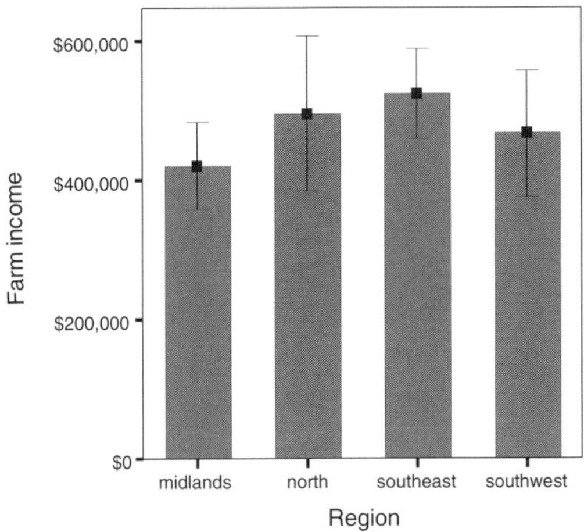

Symbols, **shapes**, and **colors** can all be used to display additional information in a plot. Figure 11-18 shows a scatterplot with rainfall and farm income plotted on the axes, shape defined by the region, and size of the points defined by claim value. Of course, there is a potential drawback of chart enhancements: if you try to add too many enhancements to a single chart, you can make it overly complex and difficult to interpret, reducing its value.

Figure 11-18
Scatterplot using shape and size to display additional information

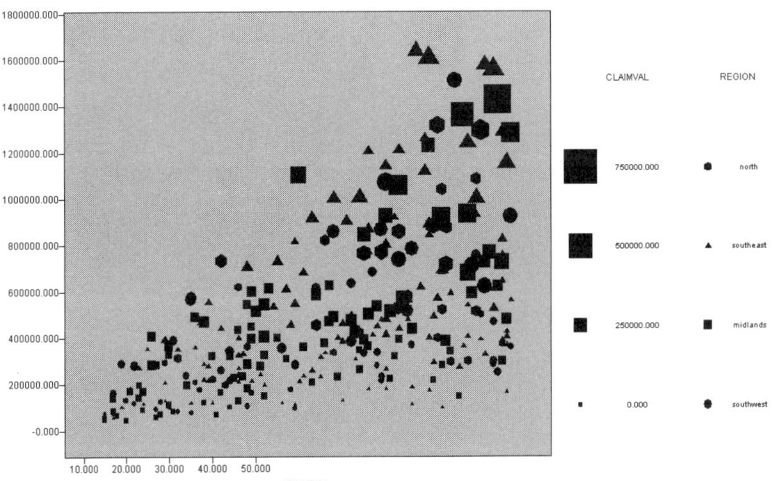

Reference lines can make charts more interpretable by adding context. A reference line is simply a line in a chart that indicates some particular value of interest. Figure 11-19 shows a bar chart with a reference line for the overall average (mean). This makes it easy to see which groups are above average and which are below average.

Figure 11-19
Bar chart with reference line for overall mean

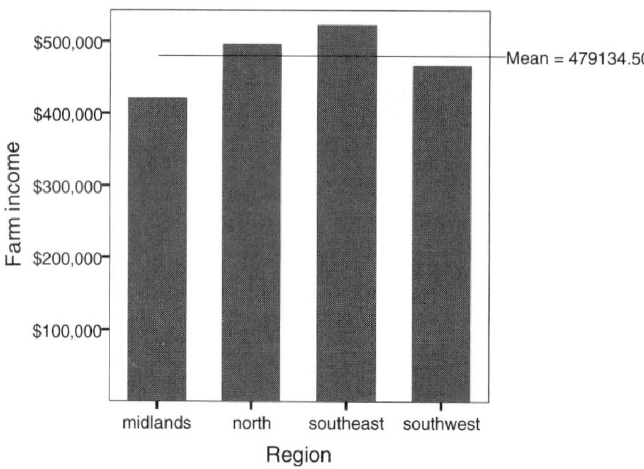

Selecting the Right Chart

To provide the information you want, a chart and its features must be appropriate for the analysis. Here are some guidelines for selecting the right chart.

Match the Chart to the Data

Different charts are appropriate for different data. If your chart is ill-matched to your data, you will get a chart that is difficult to interpret and that could even be misleading.

The table below serves as a quick reference for selecting an appropriate graph for your purpose.

If you want to...	Use this graph:
Check the distribution of values for a numeric (continuous) field	Histogram
Check the distribution of values for a symbolic (categorical) field	Distribution
Display a sum, average, or some other computed statistic for a set of categories	Bar
Rank categories based on a sum, average, or other computed statistic	Pareto (sorted bar)
Look for a pattern in values across time	Line
Find relationships between several fields or between categories of fields	Web
See the relationship between two (or more) numeric fields	Scatterplot (or scatterplot matrix)

Show the Relationship of Interest

There is no advantage to plotting data if they don't have any real bearing on the question at hand. Make sure that the characteristics you are using in your plots are relevant and that the information given by the plot can lead to a plan of action for checking data quality or improving the process you are examining.

Maximize the Information in Your Chart

Take advantage of all of the options that are available for generating informative plots. Use smoothers, error bars, reference lines, colors, shapes, or other graphic enhancements to get the most out of your plots.

Scaling is another important consideration. Pay close attention to the scaling of your chart (the range of values included on each axis), especially if you intend to make comparisons between charts. Such comparisons are much easier if the charts to be compared are all plotted on the same scale.

Resist the temptation to add "razzle dazzle" to your chart. Unnecessary decorations or special effects (such as 3-D effect for what is really a 2-D chart) can make it much more difficult to read a chart correctly. For example, in Figure 11-20, the first chart might look impressive in a presentation, but the second one is much easier to read and more useful in a data mining setting.

Figure 11-20
Fancy and plain charts for the same data

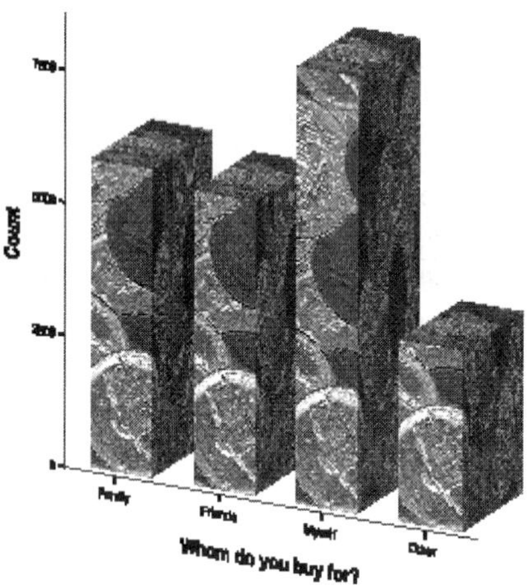

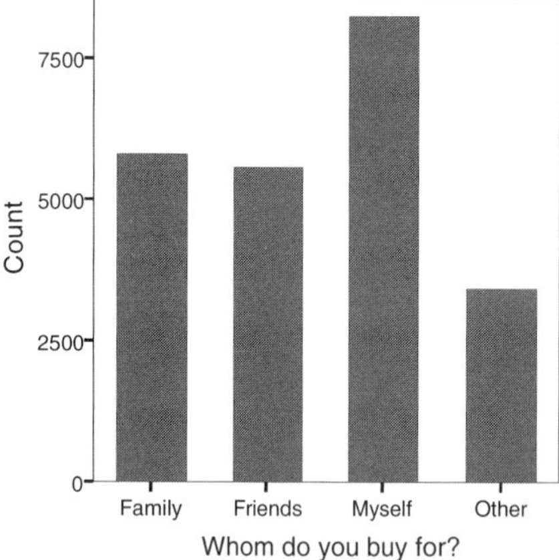

Summary

This chapter described the power of exploratory graphics. You know the basic chart types, and you know the advantages of interactive graphics over static graphics. Now you are ready to integrate exploratory graphics into your data mining process.

Chapter 12

Models for Identifying Groups

One of the fundamental tasks in data mining is to identify groups of records that are, in some important sense, similar to each other. You might want to identify groups of similar customers to help you decide who to target in your next marketing campaign, you might want to identify similar account histories to help you decide whose credit limit you should increase, or you might want to isolate certain transaction profiles to help you detect fraudulent transactions. This kind of information helps you run your organization more efficiently and serve your customers better. To do this, we use models. In data mining, a **model** is a special kind of mathematical summary of data that allows you to make estimates or predictions for new situations that are similar to those found in the original data.

Modeling refers to the process of using algorithms to derive a model for a particular set of data. The basic idea is to examine the relationship between known characteristics (represented in the data as a set of predictor fields) and the outcome or result of interest (represented by a target field) and to try to construct a model that will give you a predicted value for the target based on particular values of the predictors. For example, if you're trying to predict whether auditing a particular taxpayer's return will reveal errors or fraud (the target field), you might use information such as demographics, income, or differences between this year's return and last year's (the predictor fields) to help make the best prediction possible.

There are a number of ways to build a model for a set of data. The methods differ in the types of assumptions they make, how well they deal with noisy or incomplete data, how much time they take to estimate the model, and how interpretable the results are. There are several broad categories of model-building methods, which you will read more about in this chapter and the next.

This chapter will discuss models that are specifically designed for identifying groups. There is also another class of models that is used to forecast or predict numeric values, such as monthly revenue or number of hits on a Web server. Those models will be discussed in Chapter 13.

For identifying groups, the two main approaches to modeling are segmentation and clustering. **Segmentation**, also known as **classification,** is the process of examining known groups to determine which characteristics can be used to identify (or predict) group membership. An example would be a credit scoring application, where you have a set of accounts for which the default status is known and you want to predict defaults based on other account information, such as balance, payment history, other debt, and so on. **Clustering** is the process of identifying groups based on the similarity of some characteristics but without reference to any predefined group information. An example would be a crime investigator clustering financial transactions to help identify unusual transactions that may be evidence of money laundering or other irregularities. There may be no external criterion for categorizing transactions, but by identifying naturally existing similarities among transactions, it becomes easier to pinpoint transactions that don't fit any of the common profiles. The investigation could focus on those suspicious cases.

This chapter will describe some of the most commonly used models for identifying groups. Because most of these techniques are mathematically sophisticated, it is not possible to give in-depth coverage to each. Instead, we provide a brief introduction to each technique and then list references at the end of the chapter for further reading on the specific methods.

Segmentation Methods

Several segmentation or classification methods are commonly used in data mining. Each of these methods tries to find a relationship between some known characteristics (predictor fields) and an outcome of interest (a target field). For example, suppose you have some information about a customer from past transactions and purchased demographics, and you want to predict their response to a particular product promotion. In this case, the information in your database provides the predictor values and information about how the customer has responded to similar promotions in the past. After you have built a good model, you will be able to apply it to the new campaign to predict how customers will respond.

Segmentation models can also help you to determine which predictive information is crucial to making good predictions and which is extraneous. It may be that past purchase information is critical for predicting response, but family size information is not helpful in predicting response. This result would imply that your customer list for the promotion should be based on past purchases rather than family demographics.

There are several methods available for segmentation problems. They include discriminant analysis, logistic regression, tree-based methods, certain types of neural networks, and association rules. Each of these methods is described below.

Discriminant Analysis

In a nutshell

Purpose: to find relationships between a set of characteristics and a categorical outcome

Typical application: predicting the creditworthiness of a new credit card applicant based on application information

Strengths: quick to calculate; easy to interpret

Weaknesses: limited ability to capture complex (nonlinear) relationships; depends on certain assumptions about the nature of the data being analyzed

Discriminant analysis is based on the notion of drawing straight lines that separate groups from each other. The computer uses a mathematical algorithm to find the best separators for the target groups and then derives a set of equations that can be used to score (classify) future cases. Ultimately, the process for using discriminant analysis is straightforward—select a set of predictors and a target field and then run the analysis; the results tell you each predictor's role in generating the predictions, the overall value of the predictions, and the coefficients for equations that can be used to classify new cases.

For example, suppose that you have some credit data and you want to use only the information on a typical credit application to determine how an account will perform. The idea, of course, is that you want to be able to predict whether future applicants are likely to fall behind or default on payments. In your data, you have predictors such as duration of loan, number of other credit accounts, and length of employment, as well as a target variable that summarizes the status (current, delinquent, or default) of the corresponding account. Based on the results of the model, you will be able to identify which predictors are the most important for making accurate predictions, a set of discriminant functions (prediction equations) that will allow you to classify new records, and how well your predictions from the discriminant analysis match the actual outcomes for the accounts in your data set.

In this example, two discriminant functions are derived to separate the three target groups from one another. By looking at the values of these discriminant functions for your cases, you can determine what each discriminant function is accomplishing. The plot of values by discriminant functions is shown in Figure 12-1.

Figure 12-1
Plot of cases indicating how they are grouped by the discriminant functions

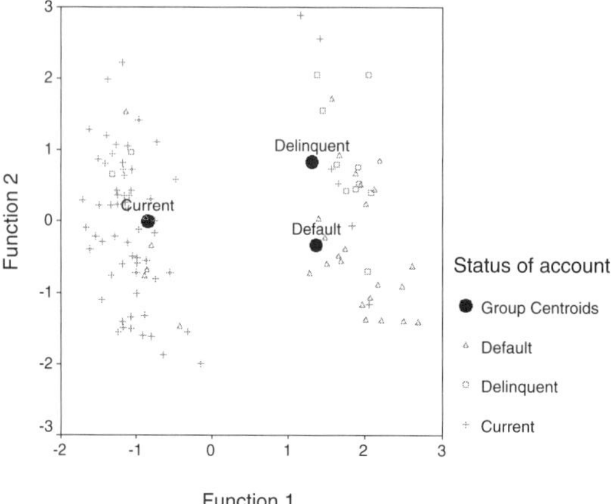

This chart shows variability in where cases fall along the two dimensions. There are also markers in the figure for **group centroids**, which represent the prototypical values for each category. You can see that function 1 seems to be trying to separate current accounts from other accounts and seems to be doing at least an adequate job. Function 2 seems to be trying to identify the delinquent cases, but there is much more overlap between delinquent and default cases. This indicates that those accounts tend to be harder to distinguish from one another. Ideally, the group centroid for the delinquent accounts would be further from the other two centroids along the second discriminant function (the vertical axis in the plot) so that there would be a clear separation of the three groups.

One of the things that you will find in the results for a discriminant analysis is a set of coefficients that provide a way of calculating three discriminant scores, one for each category of account status. Each case is then classified based on the highest of the three discriminant scores. Software can compute these scores for you and classify cases automatically—a process commonly known as **scoring**. This is a key feature for deployment, because it allows you to set up a system that can make on-the-spot decisions for your customers. For example, using a discriminant model to score credit application data could enable you to implement online credit applications from your Web site with instant approval or denial for the applicant.

You can evaluate the performance of your model by looking at the classification results table, shown in Figure 12-2. (This table is sometimes called a **misclassification table** or a **confusion matrix**.) This table is a summary of how well the predictions match the actual values for the target variable.

The table shows the actual account status values in the rows and the predicted status in the columns. Each cell shows the number of cases with the corresponding status and predicted status values. For example, in the test sample (under *Cases Not Selected*), there were 373 cases that were current and for which the discriminant analysis predicted current status. There were also 23 cases that actually were delinquent but that the analysis still predicted would be current, and there were 52 default accounts that were predicted to be current. By looking at this table closely, you can see the types of prediction mistakes that the discriminant model is making so that you can make the appropriate adjustments based on your domain knowledge. In this case, it seems to do a good job of separating the current accounts from the default accounts, but it seems to have trouble separating the delinquent accounts from the others. In thinking about this, you might decide that what is really important is finding the least risky accounts, so you might combine the delinquent and default categories into one high-risk category and rerun the analysis.

Figure 12-2
Classification results table (confusion matrix)

Count
Original

		Predicted Group Membership			
	Status of account	Current	Delinquent	Default	Total
Cases Selected	Current	152	4	23	179
	Delinquent	8	5	16	29
	Default	24	2	64	90
Cases Not Selected	Current	373	14	53	440
	Delinquent	23	2	34	59
	Default	52	8	143	203

Notice that there are two parts to the table, *Cases Selected* and *Cases Not Selected*. In this example, some of the data have been held out as a **test set**. The analysis was performed on the rest of the data (the **training set**), and then the results were tested on the test sample to see how well they generalize to new data. The *Cases Selected* section reports results for the cases that were used for the analysis. The *Cases Not Selected* section reports results for the cases that were held out. The footnotes indicate that the predictions are not bad overall—74.2% correct for the training sample and 73.8% correct for the test sample. Notice that prediction accuracy for the test sample is a little lower than that for the training sample. This happens because the model is derived from the training data, so, in effect, it has an "advantage" in classifying these data versus classifying new data. However, the reason for developing a model like this is usually to be able to make predictions about new cases, so the test sample results give a better measure of the goodness of the model.

Logistic Regression

In a nutshell

Purpose: to find relationships between a set of characteristics (fields) and a categorical outcome

Typical application: predicting the creditworthiness of a new credit card applicant based on application information

Strengths: quick to calculate; provides predicted probabilities as well as a single predicted category

Weaknesses: can be difficult to interpret; requires some statistical knowledge to execute properly

Logistic regression is another method that is similar in many respects to discriminant analysis. However, rather than drawing a straight line to separate groups, logistic regression calculates the probability of a particular record being a member of the target group, based on the values of the predictor fields. Because of certain mathematical aspects of probability, the model doesn't predict the probability directly. Instead, it predicts a value, called a **logit**, that is derived from the probability. The logit can easily be converted to a probability and vice versa, but using logits helps to ensure that you get reasonable models in a wide variety of situations. Traditional logistic regression focuses on questions where there are only two possible outcomes (target categories). However, models for outcomes with more than two categories can be built using an extension of logistic regression known as **multinomial logistic regression**.

Using logistic regression is similar to using discriminant analysis. You select a set of predictors and a target field and then run the analysis; the results tell you each predictor's role in generating the predictions, the overall value of the predictions, and the coefficients for equations that can be used to classify new cases.

Let's return to the credit example. You can use multinomial logistic regression to separate current, delinquent, and default status accounts. Classification results based on a model that uses the same predictors as the discriminant model used are shown in Figure 12-3 for both training (selected) and test (unselected) cases. You can see that the logistic regression model is doing a fairly good job of separating the high-risk accounts from the low-risk accounts. Its predictions are correct over 76% of the time for the test cases. Notice that in this analysis, the model actually shows slightly better accuracy on the test sample (76.6% correct) than it does on the training sample (74.8%). This is unusual, but it doesn't necessarily indicate a problem with the analysis. Remember that these classification results are *estimates* of the accuracy you would see if you could test all of the possible accounts, and they are subject to small amounts of error.

Figure 12-3
Classification results for the logistic regression model

Count

		Predicted Group Membership			
	Status of account	Current	Delinquent	Default	Total
Selected	Current	153	3	23	179
	Delinquent	9	2	18	29
	Default	22		68	90
Not Selected	Current	384	5	51	440
	Delinquent	22		37	59
	Default	48	1	154	203

Tree-Based Methods

In a nutshell

Purpose: to find relationships between a set of characteristics (fields) and a categorical outcome

Typical application: predicting customers' responses to a marketing campaign

Strengths: easy to interpret (for small trees); generally good predictive value

Weaknesses: subject to overfitting; large trees can be unwieldy, especially for interpretation

One of the most popular techniques in data mining is **tree-based segmentation**, also known as **decision trees**. This class of methods includes CHAID, classification and regression trees (C&RT), QUEST, and C5.0, among others. These methods start with all of the sample records and split them into two or more subgroups that tend to be more **homogeneous** than the original sample was—the cases in each subgroup are similar to each other in terms of the target characteristic. Each of these subgroups is then split again into even smaller subgroups, and so on, until either a good solution is found or it becomes clear that there is no point in going any further. Figure 12-4 shows an example of a decision tree for predicting customer response to a marketing campaign that was created using the C&RT method.

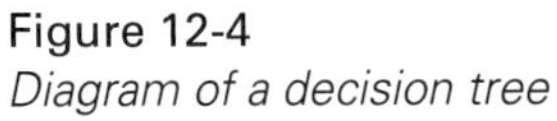

Figure 12-4
Diagram of a decision tree

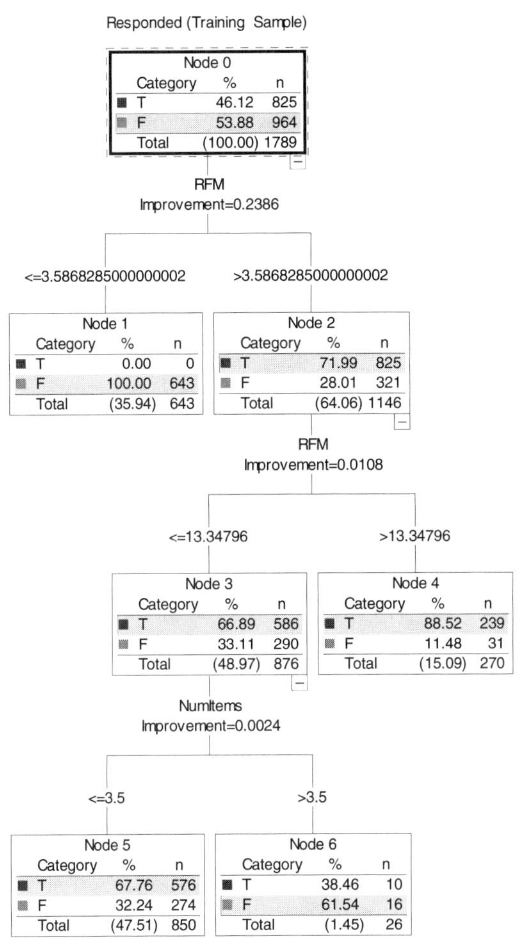

There are subtle differences in how each tree-based method makes decisions, such as which field to use for a particular split, how many splits to make, and what criterion to use for deciding when to split and when not to. The decision about which method to use depends on aspects of your data and the question you are trying to answer.

The main advantage of tree-based methods is that the results usually come in a form that almost anyone can understand. For each node in the tree, a straightforward rule can be derived for identifying cases that belong to that node. For example, in the tree shown in Figure 12-4, node 6 contains records in which the customer has a calculated RFM (recency/frequency/monetary) score greater than about 3.6 (top split) but less than about 13.3 (middle split), and number of items purchased greater than 3.5 (bottom split). Based on the results of the decision tree, members of this subgroup are expected to respond favorably to the promotion. These "rules" for identifying homogeneous subgroups in a database can be used to select cases that have desirable characteristics for further action—in this example, you might use your historical data on customers to target your marketing efforts to those who are most likely to respond.

Neural Networks for Segmentation

In a nutshell

Purpose: to build a mathematical model of general relationships between a set of characteristics and a categorical outcome

Typical application: identifying customers who are likely to purchase a new product or service

Strengths: can capture complex nonlinear relationships; usually produce good predictions

Weaknesses: can take a long time to estimate; often difficult to interpret

Neural networks are also a very popular class of methods in data mining. The concept of a neural network is based on a computer abstraction of the way your brain works. In your brain, information is processed by cells called neurons. Each neuron collects information from other neurons that are attached to it, and it aggregates and processes that information and passes it along to other neurons. In an artificial neural network (usually just called a neural network), elements called **nodes** function similarly to the neurons in your brain. Each node collects information from the nodes that connect to it, and it passes the processed information to the nodes that it connects to. When you put a number of nodes together, they process information in parallel, allowing the system to find complex relationships. Information in a neural network is encoded in the strengths (called **weights**) of the connections between nodes.

Figure 12-5
Example of a common type of neural network

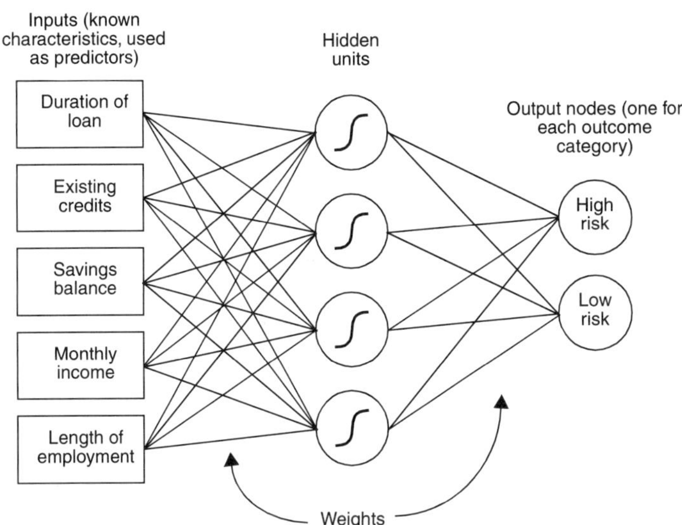

There are many different kinds of neural networks. The network illustrated in Figure 12-5 is an example of a common type—a **backpropagation network** (also known as a **multilayer perceptron**). Values for the known characteristics (the predictors) are presented to the input nodes, the information flows through the network and is processed by a set of internal nodes called **hidden units**, and the information from those hidden units then passes through to the output nodes, which generate a predicted outcome for the case in question.

Once you have set up the neural network by defining a set of nodes and how they are interconnected, the network has to be **trained**. The network trains itself by looking at one record at a time. For each record, it makes a prediction for the target value, based on what it knows so far, and then checks its guess against the actual value for that case (the **teaching** input). It then adjusts the weights so that its next guess will be better—in effect, it learns from its mistakes. The network then looks at the next case, learns what it can from it, and so on. As the network processes more and more data, it gets better and better at making predictions. Eventually, the network learns all that it can from the data; it then stops training and is ready for testing with new data.

The strength of neural networks is that for certain types of problems, they can make significantly better predictions than traditional statistical methods. They can learn arbitrary associations between predictors and targets, whereas many of the other techniques rely on certain assumptions about the relationship being linear or the values being distributed in a certain way. Unfortunately, neural networks also have some drawbacks in terms of interpretability. The results of a neural network are the weights of the connections between nodes. These weights can be used to derive complex equations for making predictions about new cases, but they don't give much insight into the nature of the associations between predictors and targets. Because of this, neural networks may not be the method of choice if you have to *explain* to someone how your predictive model works.

One way to get around this problem is by using a technique called **sensitivity analysis**. Sensitivity analysis can help you determine how important each predictor field is for the neural network model. It does this by generating a range of values for each predictor field, submitting them to the network as inputs, and measuring how much the output of the model changes for each change in the input. When you have an input field where a small to moderate change in the input value causes a large change in the output, that is evidence that the model is placing a large emphasis on that particular input field, usually because it is useful in predicting the outcome. Input fields that do not cause much change in the output no matter how much you change their input values are not as important to the model. With this approach, the exact nature of the relationship between inputs and outputs is still more obscure than for many other model types, but you can at least get a sense of which input fields are important for generating good predictions and which can probably be ignored.

Association Rules

In a nutshell

Purpose: to derive or induce if-then type rules that can be used to predict outcomes

Typical application: finding relationships among products that people tend to buy together on a shopping trip

Strengths: easy to understand; can identify multiple causes for particular outcomes

Weaknesses: can generate large lists of rules, only a few of which may be useful

Rule-based models are also popular in data mining. The basic idea behind association rules is to search the data for patterns of the following form:

if *(some condition is true)* **then** *(some other condition is probably true).*

Each such statement that is extracted from the data is called an **association rule**, or simply a **rule**. Association rules generally have two characteristics associated with them that measure their value: coverage and confidence.

Coverage describes how much evidence there is in the training data to back up the rule. It usually ranges between 0 and 1 (or between 0% and 100%) and is usually calculated as the number of records for which the **antecedents** (the *if* part of the rule) are true divided by the total number of records. In other words, it is the proportion (or percentage) of records in the training data for which the rule can make a prediction. Sometimes a related measure, called support, is reported instead of (or in addition to) coverage. **Support** is usually calculated as the proportion of records for which the *entire rule* is true.

Confidence describes how likely the rule is to give a correct prediction. Like coverage, it ranges between 0 and 1 (or 0% and 100%). It is usually calculated by the number of records for which the entire rule is true divided by the number of records in which the antecedents are true. The records where the antecedents (the *if* part of the rule) are true represent all the records for which the rule makes a prediction (correct or incorrect); the records where the rule is true represent the records for which the rule makes a correct prediction. So the confidence is just the proportion (or percentage) of predictions that are correct according to the training data.

In evaluating specific decision rules, you will want to consider both coverage (or support) and confidence. It's not enough to consider either one alone. For example, a rule with 100% confidence may not be worth very much if it is based only on two records. The rule may be highly accurate, but it applies so infrequently as to be useless. Conversely, a rule with high coverage but low accuracy may apply to a wide variety of situations, but the predictions are not reliable, so you may be better off basing your decisions on other criteria. Usually when you use association rules, you will be able to set some thresholds for both coverage and confidence, so you will see only the rules that are "interesting," at least in the sense of both being reasonably accurate and applying to a nontrivial subset of records.

Association rules can be found or induced through a variety of algorithms. Some algorithms, such as Apriori and Carma, scan the data looking for frequent items and build rules based on the items that occur frequently in the data. Other algorithms, such as C5.0, start by building a decision tree and then condensing the tree into a set of rules that captures the basic structure of the tree.

Sequential Association Rules

In many cases, your data will have a temporal aspect to it where transactions or some other events captured in the data occur over time, and you want to find patterns in the sequence of items over time. There are specialized association rule algorithms that are designed to handle this kind of sequential data.

When using rule induction with sequential data, it is important to distinguish items that occur at the same time from those that occur sequentially. For example, in a market basket analysis, the following two sequences are different:

- Milk and eggs, then bread
- Milk, then eggs, then bread

In the first sequence, milk and eggs are purchased together in a single transaction, and bread is purchased in a subsequent transaction. In the second sequence, milk is purchased in the first transaction, eggs are purchased in a subsequent transaction, followed by a third transaction where bread is purchased. The items in the first example that are purchased together (milk and eggs) are called an **itemset** and are considered a single event in the sequence. (Note that the last item in the sequence, bread, is also an itemset that happens to contain a single item.)

For some applications of sequential rule induction, you may want to treat items that occur close together in time—but not at the same time—as an itemset. You can often do this by setting a tolerance specifying the maximum time difference between items in an itemset. For example, in a market basket analysis, if a customer buys a set of items on a particular day and returns to the store an hour later to pick up a few things he forgot on the first trip, you may want to consider both transactions as a single transaction for the sake of data mining.

Clustering Methods

Clustering, like segmentation, identifies groups of similar cases. However, unlike segmentation methods, clustering methods don't attempt to predict outcomes or target categories. Instead, clustering tries to find groups of cases that have similar profiles, based on a set of known characteristics (clustering fields or variables). These methods try to maximize similarity between cases assigned to the same group and to maximize differences between the groups.

As an example of clustering, suppose you are trying to identify customers that would make good targets for a new product marketing campaign. Because this is a new product, you don't have any experience with marketing it, so you don't have any data on how customers have responded to such promotions in the past. However, you probably have some ideas about the customer attributes that might predict whether they will be interested in your product. You can take information from your customer base (including demographic data and purchase data on other products that you sell) and use clustering to identify homogeneous groups of customers. Each group can then be examined to derive a group profile, which describes typical customers in that group. By comparing the profiles that you get from the clustered groups to what you know about the product, you can identify segments that you expect to respond positively so that you can target them in your marketing efforts.

Hierarchical Clustering

In a nutshell

Purpose: to use similarities on a set of characteristics to identify homogeneous groups of cases

Typical application: grouping customers based on the services they use to identify distinct market segments

Strengths: can help determine how many clusters to define; shows graphically how cases are combined into clusters

Weaknesses: some algorithms are slow to compute and ill-suited to large data sets

Hierarchical clustering works by combining cases and clusters that are similar to each other, one pair at a time. You start with the same number of clusters as you have customers in your data set, with each customer in its own cluster. Then you start merging clusters, one pair at a time, and you keep merging them until you have one large cluster that contains all of the cases.

The method chooses which clusters to merge at each step by measuring the dissimilarity between clusters using a **distance score** and finding the two clusters that are closest (most similar) to each other. Those two clusters are then merged, and the process is repeated until all clusters have been merged. The distance between two clusters depends on how similar or dissimilar the profiles are for those clusters. There are many ways to calculate distance scores, depending on the types of fields that you are using to cluster, but in some sense, they all measure (dis)similarity between clusters, based on the profiles (as measured by the clustering fields in the database).

Of course, you don't really want all of the cases in one big cluster, but by continuing to merge clusters until all cases have been merged together, you can see the effect of your choice for number of clusters on your solution. For example, at the step *before* the final merge into one big category, there are two clusters. By looking at those clusters, you can see what a two-cluster solution looks like. By looking at the clusters a step before that, you can see what a three-cluster solution looks like, and so on.

One of the primary advantages of the hierarchical clustering method is that it doesn't require you to specify the number of clusters up front. Unfortunately, this method is not well suited to large data sets. With a large number of cases, calculations take a long time to compute, and the output quickly becomes unwieldy and difficult to interpret. For this reason, you will probably want to use small subsamples of data with hierarchical clustering, which you might then follow up by using *k*-means clustering on the full data set.

Figure 12-6 shows the results of a hierarchical cluster analysis (in the form of a special chart called a **dendrogram**) on a random subsample of 57 Web site movie buyers, based on categories of movies that they purchased. On the left, each case is listed. The dendrogram shows the pattern of merging cases and clusters until there is only one "branch" on the far right. By selecting a point somewhere between the two extremes, you get the set of clusters that have been merged up to that point. The decision about where to draw the line is subjective to some extent, and it relies on your use of domain knowledge to choose a clustering solution that makes conceptual sense. In this example, we've chosen the point indicated by the vertical dashed line. There are four tree branches (horizontal lines) that cross this point, which gives us four clusters, as indicated in the figure. The clusters can be profiled by generating a table of means for each cluster, as shown in Figure 12-7.

Figure 12-6
Dendrogram for hierarchical cluster analysis

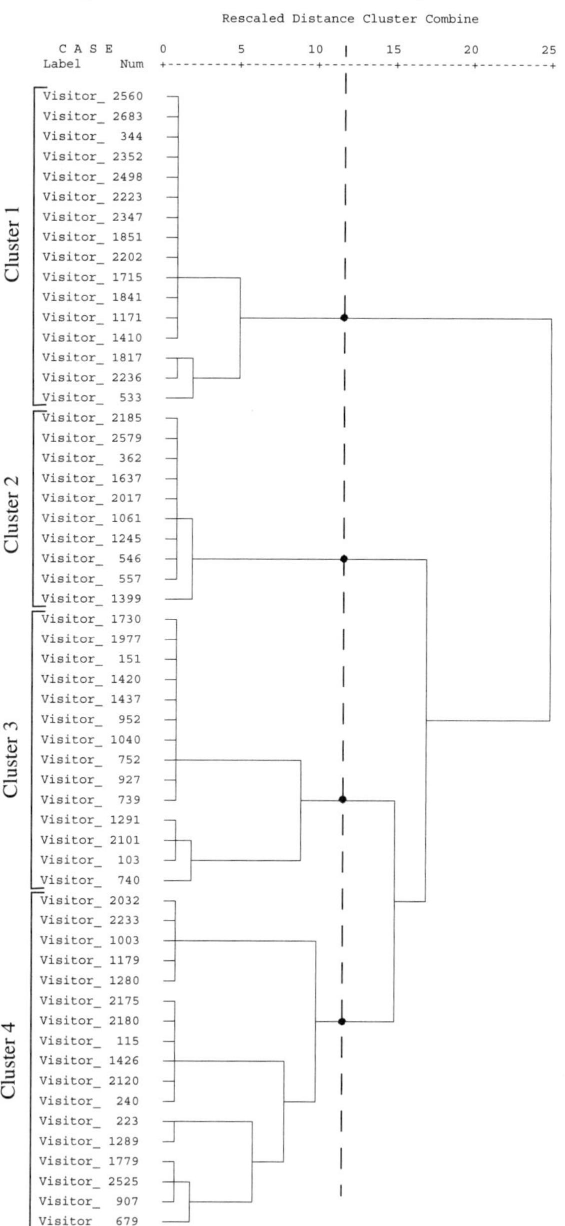

Figure 12-7
Means for clusters

Mean

Ward Method	num_Country_UK	num_Country_USA	num_Gender_F	num_Gender_M	num_Age_21-30	num_Age_31-40	num_Age_51-70	num_Age_71+	num_Buy_for_Family	num_Buy_for_Friends	num_Buy_for_Myself	num_Buy_for_Other	num_Style_Adventure	num_Style_Children	num_Style_Comedy	num_Style_Drama	num_Style_Horror	num_Style_Musical	num_Style_Sci-Fi	num_Style_Western
1	.36	.07	.07	.36	.00	.00	.43	.00	.00	.07	.36	.00	.00	.00	.00	.79	.29	.00	.00	.00
2	.06	.29	.12	.24	.06	.00	.35	.00	.00	.24	.18	.00	.12	.00	.00	.00	.00	.24	.29	.41
3	.50	.00	.31	.19	.00	.50	.00	.00	.50	.00	.00	.00	.00	1.00	.13	.00	.13	.00	.00	.00
4	.30	.10	.20	.20	.10	.20	.10	.00	.20	.00	.20	.00	.00	.00	1.00	.10	.00	.00	.00	.00

The means show that cluster 1 customers tend to purchase drama and horror movies, cluster 2 customers enjoy an eclectic mix of musicals, science fiction, and westerns, cluster 3 customers tend to buy children's movies, and cluster 4 customers like comedy movies. (Note that the demographic fields weren't used in the cluster analysis; they are included only to give a more complete profile of the clusters. In addition, values for these fields don't add up to 1.0 because the demographic information isn't available for all customers. For example, in cluster 1, we know that 7% of the customers are female, and 36% are male. For the other 57% of customers in that cluster, we don't have any information on gender.)

Remember that this analysis was based on a random subsample of respondents so that we could avoid producing an avalanche of output. The next logical step is to apply the *k*-means clustering method with four clusters to the entire set of customers to see how well the solution generalizes to the rest of the data.

K-Means Clustering

In a nutshell

Purpose: to use similarities on a set of characteristics to identify homogeneous groups of cases

Typical banking application: grouping customers based on the services that they use to identify distinct market segments

Strengths: relatively quick to compute; usable with large data sets

Weaknesses: must specify number of clusters ahead of time

***K*-means clustering** is more straightforward than hierarchical clustering. It is based on the assumption that the data fall into a known number (k) of clusters. The method starts by defining initial profiles for the k clusters, sometimes using random values for the clustering characteristics or sometimes using dissimilar cases from the data set. These profiles are called **cluster centers**. Next, cases in the database are assigned to cluster centers based on similarity—each case is assigned to the cluster center to which it is most similar. Now that cases have been added to the clusters, each cluster center is adjusted, based on the cases that belong to its cluster. The new cluster center is recalculated as the average value of each clustering characteristic for the cases in the cluster. Because the cluster centers have been adjusted, some of the cases may now fit better in a different cluster than the one to which they were originally assigned. So the next step is to reassign cases to clusters, again based on similarity measures. After cases are reassigned to clusters, the cluster centers are adjusted again, and the process repeats until no more adjustments are necessary. The final cluster centers represent the "prototypical" profile for each cluster.

The main advantages of the k-means method over the hierarchical method are that it is much quicker to compute, and it gives much more interpretable results for large data sets.

The main drawback of this method is that you have to specify the number of clusters that you want. Sometimes it can be hard to decide how many clusters to ask for if you don't have strong expectations. In such cases, you can often get an idea of the number of clusters in your data by using hierarchical clustering on a small sample of cases. The information derived from the hierarchical analysis can help you identify the ideal number of clusters for the k-means method.

In the clustering example above, you found that there seem to be four substantive clusters in the subsample that you examined. Now, you can perform a *k*-means cluster analysis to see if this clustering fits the entire sample. The first step is to make sure the clustering fields are all measured in a consistent way. In this example, we don't have to worry about this, because all the clustering fields are measured as zero or one. However, this won't always be the case. When your clustering characteristics are measured on different scales, such as *age* and *income*, you need to do something to balance the different scales. Otherwise, the field with the larger scale will overwhelm the field with the smaller scale. For example, *income* would completely wash out any effect of *age*, because income is measured in such large numbers. (Many data mining software packages, including Clementine, will do this rescaling for you automatically, so you don't have to worry about it.)

Figure 12-8
Final cluster centers for k-means cluster solution

Mean

Cluster Number	num_Country_UK	num_Country_USA	num_Gender_F	num_Gender_M	num_Age_21-30	num_Age_31-40	num_Age_51-70	num_Age_71+	num_Buy_for_Family	num_Buy_for_Friends	num_Buy_for_Myself	num_Buy_for_Other	num_Style_Adventure	num_Style_Children	num_Style_Comedy	num_Style_Drama	num_Style_Horror	num_Style_Musical	num_Style_Sci-Fi	num_Style_Western
1	.16	.28	.25	.18	.22	.13	.09	.01	.12	.07	.25	.00	.18	.03	.83	.03	.01	.00	.01	.02
2	.14	.17	.14	.17	.03	.09	.20	.00	.09	.14	.09	.00	.02	.02	.00	.02	.00	.34	.02	.72
3	.33	.05	.20	.18	.00	.04	.34	.00	.04	.05	.28	.00	.00	.00	.00	.67	.35	.00	.00	.00
4	.40	.20	.34	.26	.02	.39	.19	.00	.39	.18	.03	.00	.01	.58	.00	.00	.02	.00	.42	.00

Figure 12-8 shows the final cluster centers for the four-cluster *k*-means cluster model. Here, cluster 1 customers tend to like comedies, roughly corresponding to cluster 3 from the hierarchical cluster model. Cluster 2 customers like musicals and westerns, having something in common with cluster 2 from the hierarchical model. The science fiction fans that we saw in the same cluster in the other model appear to be grouped with cluster 4 here, along with the family buyers. Cluster 3 here corresponds closely to cluster 1 in the hierarchical model.

There is an encouraging amount of agreement between the hierarchical model and the *k*-means model, so the clusters we have discovered are probably real. If there were significant differences between the two models, you would probably want to consider revising the models by using different subsamples for the hierarchical model, different numbers of clusters for the *k*-means models, or both.

With *k*-means models, final cluster centers can be used to score new records. You can classify new records by calculating a distance between each new record and each cluster center. Each new record is predicted to belong to the cluster to which it is closest. This can be useful for carrying over an existing cluster solution to new customers as they make purchases, to help you better predict their needs and desires.

Neural Networks for Clustering

In a nutshell

Purpose: to use a mathematical model of general relationships among a set of characteristics to group similar cases together

Typical application: grouping customers based on their clickstream patterns to identify ways of refining your Web site structure

Strengths: can help determine how many clusters to define; can capture complex relationships; usually produce good predictions

Weaknesses: can be slow to estimate; very difficult to interpret

"Neural Networks for Segmentation" on p. 134 provided a brief overview of neural networks. By choosing a different structure for the neural network, you can also perform clustering tasks. Because the clustering problem doesn't have right and wrong answers that are known ahead of time, you can't estimate the weights of the neural network using errors of prediction—there's no "gold standard" to tell the network when an output is correct or in error. Instead, the network weights are adjusted based on internal constraints. Networks that do not rely on external "teaching" feedback are sometimes called **unsupervised networks** or **self-organizing maps**.

One version of a self-organizing network, known as a **Kohonen network** (after Teuvo Kohonen, the researcher who developed the method), resembles *k*-means cluster analysis. It has the same system of starting with a set of random cluster centers and then updating the centers as they are exposed to the cases in the training data set until it finds a stable set of clusters. The main difference is that the nodes in a Kohonen network are linked together into **neighborhoods** so that clusters that are more similar to each other will be nearer each other in the final network model (after training). For example, a common approach is for the nodes to be arranged in a two-dimensional array. When you present a training case to the network, it decides which node (representing a cluster center) is most similar to that case—you can think of that as the **winning node**. It then adjusts the weights of that node so that it will more closely resemble the training case, but it also adjusts the weights of other nodes in the winning node's neighborhood. The adjustment made to the weight for each node depends on how far the node is from the winning node—the further from the winning node, the smaller the adjustment.

Figure 12-9
Structure of a Kohonen network

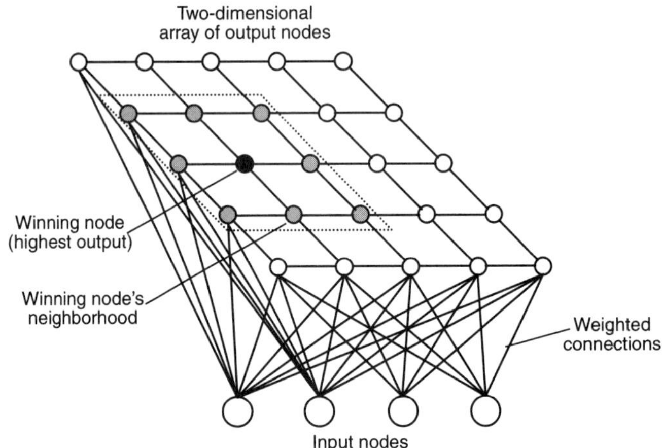

This neighborhood feature allows Kohonen networks not only to identify clusters but also, in a sense, to reduce the dimensionality of the problem. With a two-dimensional array of nodes, the Kohonen network forms a two-dimensional map that attempts to capture most of the variability in the original clustering fields. Examining this mapping can help simplify complex clusters and reveal relationships among the clusters.

Another attractive feature of Kohonen networks is that you don't necessarily have to know the right number of clusters to ask for at the beginning. In general, a Kohonen network will find a good number of clusters, assuming that the cases really do come from homogeneous groups. If there are more output nodes than there are clusters, the network will overlap the nodes so that more than one node may represent a single cluster. If you examine the profiles for the output nodes, you may find that they themselves form clusters, as the "extra" nodes are merged with other nodes, yielding a number of distinct profiles for clusters. This idea is illustrated in Figure 12-10. The array of output nodes is shown with lengths between nodes that have been adjusted based on their similarities—similar nodes are closer together, and dissimilar nodes are further apart. Each of the circled areas represents a single cluster that has "attracted" multiple output nodes. You would conclude from this graph that a three-cluster solution is appropriate. (Of course, with real-world data, the results would probably be a bit messier, but you can still find interesting and usable results with this type of graphic.)

Figure 12-10
Pattern of nodes for a trained Kohonen network

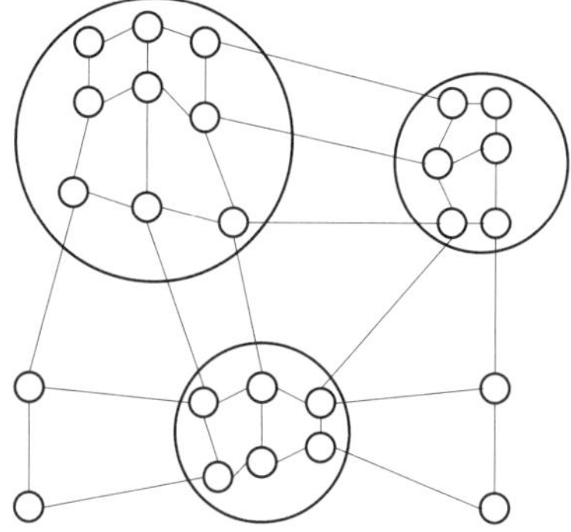

Further Reading

The brief descriptions in this chapter are meant to whet your appetite for these powerful techniques. To learn more about how to use them with real data, you need to learn more about how they work and how to interpret correctly the results that they produce. The following references will give you the background that you need to use these methods effectively and confidently.

Discriminant Analysis

Huberty, C. J. 1994. *Applied discriminant analysis*. New York: John Wiley & Sons, Inc.

Tabachnick, B. and L. Fidell. 1996. "Discriminant Function Analysis." Chap. 11 in *Using multivariate statistics*. New York: HarperCollins College Publishers.

Logistic Regression

Hosmer, D. and S. Lemeshow. 1989. *Applied logistic regression*. New York: John Wiley & Sons, Inc.

Kleinbaum, D. G. 1994. *Logistic regression: A self-learning text*. New York: Springer-Verlag.

Tree-Based Methods

Breiman, L., J. H. Friedman, R. A. Olshen, and C. J. Stone. 1984. *Classification and regression trees*. Belmont, CA: Wadsworth.

SPSS, Inc. 2002. *AnswerTree 3.1 user's guide*. Chicago: SPSS Inc.

Neural Networks for Segmentation

Dayhoff, J. 1990. *Neural network architectures*. New York: Van Nostrand Reinhold.

Ripley, B. D. 1995. *Pattern recognition and neural networks*. New York: Cambridge University Press.

Association Rules

Berson, A. and S. J. Smith. 1997. *Data warehousing, data mining, and OLAP*. New York: McGraw-Hill.

Quinlan, J. R. 1993. *C4.5: Programs for machine learning*. San Mateo, CA: Morgan Kaufmann.

Hierarchical and K-Means Cluster Analysis

Dillon, W. R. and M. Goldstein. 1984. *Multivariate analysis: Methods and applications*. New York: John Wiley & Sons, Inc.

Romesburg, H. C. 1990. *Cluster analysis for researchers*. Melbourne, FL: Krieger.

Neural Networks for Clustering

Dayhoff, J. 1990. *Neural network architectures*. New York: Van Nostrand Reinhold.

Kohonen, T. 1984. *Self-organization and associative memory*. New York: Springer-Verlag.

Ritter, H., T. Martinetz, and K. Schulten. 1992. *Neural computation and self-organzing maps*. Reading, MA: Addison-Wesley.

Chapter

13

Models for Numeric Outcomes

In many situations, you need to be able to make predictions or estimates of important business indicators. For example, you might need to estimate the amount of revenue generated by taxpayers based on various characteristics, or you might need to predict times when your Web server will receive a lot of traffic in order to prevent crashes.

As you saw in the previous chapter, data mining makes use of models to summarize data and make predictions. Just as there are models designed for identifying groups, there are other models designed for predicting numerical outcomes. For example, you can use such models to estimate revenue from particular customer segments, to predict time to attrition for customer accounts, or to predict sales of products for the next three quarters. This chapter will introduce you to some of these models.

Again, as was the case with the models for identifying groups, the modeling methods described here are complex, and the few pages that we devote to each topic do not provide enough detail for you to actually use the methods to make important decisions. This chapter is intended to be an overview of available methods and to familiarize you with the possibilities. If you decide to use one or more of these methods in your data mining, you are encouraged to consult the references at the end of the chapter. They should help you to increase your knowledge so that you can get the greatest benefit from these methods and avoid the potential pitfalls associated with them.

Forecasting Methods

Some of the most interesting data you may have available concerns how things vary over time. For example, you may have a record of customer transactions for several months or years, or you may have data on Web purchases. In these instances, it can be very valuable to be able to make projections or forecasts of future values based on past values. If you are monitoring your e-commerce servers, it would be valuable to be able to predict when there will be surges or lulls in activity so that you can manage your servers better.

ARIMA Models

In a nutshell

Purpose: to identify patterns and make predictions in time series data

Typical application: predicting the ratio of new accounts to closed accounts per month over time

Strengths: allows proper modeling of time series data

Weaknesses: can be difficult to interpret; requires statistical expertise to execute properly

A number of methods are available for dealing with **time series data**. One of the most general methods is called **ARIMA modeling**.[1] An ARIMA model is a combination of three simple models—an autoregressive model (AR), an integration model (I), and a moving average model (MA):

- The **autoregressive model** tries to find relationships between values based on how far apart they are in time. For example, you might find that your inventory for any particular week depends heavily on the inventory for the previous week. Or, if you have a two-week production cycle, you may find that inventory doesn't depend on last week's inventory, but it does depend on the inventory the week before that. The autoregressive portion of the model summarizes such relationships.
- The **integration model** isolates the *absolute level* of the time series value (for example, number of widgets) from the *differences* in that level from one time point to the next (for example, the change in supply of widgets for the month). For example, your supply might be 2,000 widgets in March and 1,800 in April. In this case, 1,800 represents the absolute inventory in April, whereas the difference from the previous time point is –200. (It is negative because the supply went *down* between March and April.) The autoregressive and moving average portions of the

1. ARIMA models are also known as **Box-Jenkins models**, after the statisticians who first described them.

model summarize the pattern of differences, but if there is an overall trend (for example, your inventory tends to swell over the long run), this will throw off the results of the model. The integration part of the model corrects for such "drift" in the overall level of the time series.

- The **moving average** model is a way of smoothing out the bumps—tuning out the noise so that you can see the real pattern. Certain aspects of your day-to-day and month-to-month supply are caused by random, quirky factors such as large orders, spoiled manufacturing lots, and so on. The moving average portion of the model smooths out these quirks, making it easier to examine the underlying factors that influence your process.

ARIMA models can also accommodate seasonal components, where the series tends to move in a cyclical way over time. Such a component doesn't literally have to follow the seasons of the year—it can cycle within days, weeks, or months, as well as years. You can also include other predictors to try to make more accurate predictions or to assess factors that influence your series values. For example, you might include a variable indicating special events to help predict inventory levels.

With these three methods used together, you can often get a fairly good model for predicting near-term future values based on past values. For example, Figure 13-1 shows a time series of subscriber data from a telephone company. The series represents the ratio of new subscribers to dropped subscribers for each month—think of this as a growth rate.

Figure 13-1
Phone company subscriber ratio series (new/dropped subscribers)

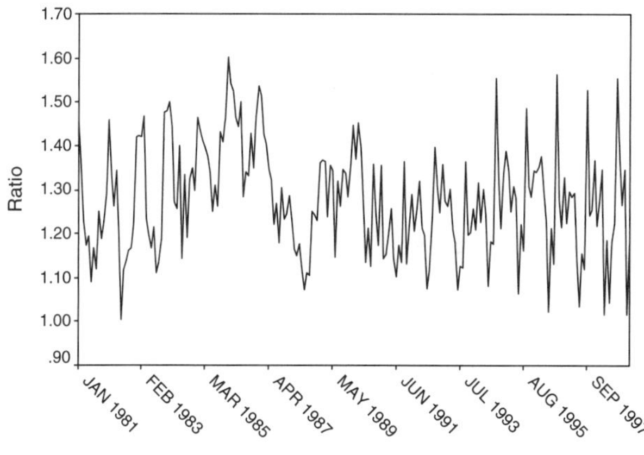

Examining the chart, we discover several things:

- The average growth rate is larger than 1. This implies that the customer base tends to grow from year to year.
- There is **seasonality** in the model. In other words, the ratio depends on what time of year it is. There is a general pattern of a large dip mid-year followed by a peak.
- The model appears not to be **stationary**. This means that the average value is different in different parts of the time span. Specifically, it looks as if overall values are a bit higher for the mid-1980s than they are at other time periods.

The ARIMA model (with a seasonal component) allows you to generate predictions for the next few years. Figure 13-2 shows the actual series and the predictions generated by the ARIMA model. Notice that the ARIMA model does a fairly good job of tracking changes in subscriber ratio for the past (before 1999), and it generates predictions for 1999 through 2001. Looking at the graph, you see that the predictions seem reasonable—they seem to fit into the pattern that your eye picks out quite well. You can then use these projections to allocate service personnel resources or to offer incentives to get customers to subscribe during nonpeak periods.

Figure 13-2
Observed and predicted ratios (new/dropped subscribers)

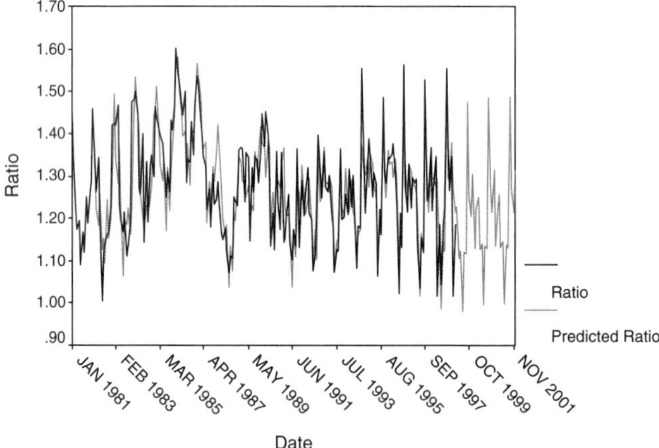

Correlation-Based Models

In a nutshell

Purpose: to measure the strength and direction of the relationship between two characteristics (fields)

Typical application: discovering which services or products tend to be used by the same customers

Strengths: quick to calculate, easy to interpret

Weaknesses: only considers two fields at a time; more complex models are needed for relationships among several fields

Among the simplest models are **correlations**, which examine the extent to which values of one field depend on, or are predicted by, values of another field. Correlations can vary in strength, depending on the fields in question.

An example of a perfect correlation would be engine efficiency measured as miles per gallon and kilometers per gallon for cars. There is a one-to-one correspondence of values from one field to the other—21 miles per gallon always corresponds to 33.6 kilometers per gallon. Of course, the two things are measuring the same underlying characteristic, so you would expect them to vary in the same way.

An example of a moderate correlation is engine displacement and horsepower. Large engines are usually relatively powerful. Conversely, smaller engines tend to be less powerful. The correlation here is not perfect—there are large engines that are not very powerful and small engines that are surprisingly powerful—but there is still a general trend for the two quantities to go up and down together as you look at a sample of cars.

An example of fields with a very weak correlation would be model year and time to accelerate. There is a very slight correlation—newer cars tend to have higher acceleration times. However, many old cars have high acceleration times and many new cars have low acceleration times, so you wouldn't want to base important decisions on this relationship.

Correlations also often have a **direction**—positive or negative. **Positive correlation** means that the fields tend to vary in the same direction; that is, when the value of one field is large, the value of the other also tends to be large. **Negative correlation** means that the fields vary in opposite directions; that is, when the value of one field is large, the value of the other tends to be small. The examples above have a positive correlation. An example of a negative correlation is the fuel efficiency of a car and its horsepower. If a car has a very efficient engine, it usually has low power; if it has a powerful engine, it is usually not very efficient.

Figure 13-3 shows these correlations graphically. In the upper left panel is the plot of miles per gallon and kilometers per gallon. All points fall along a straight line, since these two quantities are just the same thing measured in different units. In the upper right panel is the plot of horsepower and engine displacement. There is a general trend for more powerful engines to be larger, but there is some variability in the extent to which this is true. In other words, the points fall *near* a straight line but not exactly *on* it. In the lower left panel, notice that the relationship between model year and time to accelerate is very weak, as indicated by the general lack of pattern in the points of the graph. Finally, in the lower right panel is the plot of horsepower and miles per gallon. The points cluster around a line, but the line goes down as it goes from left to right, indicating a negative relationship. In other words, *higher* horsepower is usually associated with *lower* efficiency, and vice versa.

Figure 13-3
Example of different correlations

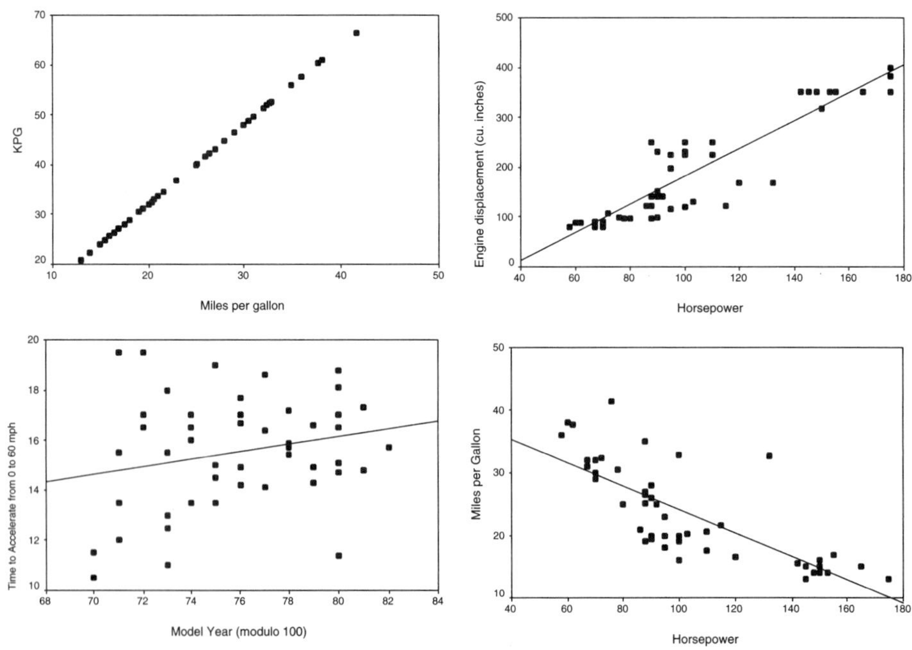

Mathematically, a **correlation coefficient** (or simply **correlation**) is a number that summarizes the size and direction of the linear association between two numeric fields. Values of correlation coefficients range from +1 for perfect positive relationships to –1 for perfect negative relationships, with 0 indicating no relationship.

When looking at correlations across many variables, it is important to remember that your conclusions are based on a sample and that there is always the possibility for error. Most of the time, the estimated correlation you calculate based on your sample will be pretty close to the actual value in the real world, but once in a while, the correlation from your sample will be quite different from the correlation in the larger population. In other words, the correlations you see in your data may appear to be larger or smaller than they are in the real world because of quirks of the specific data you are working with. This is especially important if you are looking at many correlations at the same time. Any time you look at a lot of statistics simultaneously, you are bound to see some that are inflated (or deflated) because of these sampling quirks. Figure 13-4 shows a table of correlations for some randomly generated field values in which there is no true relationship between any of the fields. Each number in the table represents the correlation between the corresponding row and column variables. The entries along the diagonal (from the upper left to the lower right) are blank because those cells represent the correlation of a variable with itself—but a variable always correlates perfectly with itself (with a correlation of 1.0), so these numbers don't give any useful information. Similarly, the entries above the diagonal are omitted because they are redundant with those below the diagonal—the correlation between *V01* and *V02* is the same as the correlation between *V02* and *V01*. Hence, we can remove the diagonal and upper-diagonal correlation values to simplify the table without losing any valuable information.

Figure 13-4

Correlations for 10 unrelated fields

Pearson Correlation

	V01	V02	V03	V04	V05	V06	V07	V08	V09	V10
V01										
V02	-.023									
V03	-.016	.019								
V04	-.014	-.043	-.004							
V05	-.042	-.041	.001	.042						
V06	-.048	.005	.012	.017	-.025					
V07	-.047	.007	.017	.024	-.031	.025				
V08	-.021	-.031	.000	-.051	.059	.004	-.004			
V09	.036	-.026	-.054	-.018	.072*	-.086*	-.049	.040		
V10	-.004	.024	-.016	-.068*	-.011	.011	.001	.047	.009	

*. Correlation is significant at the 0.05 level (2-tailed).

**. Correlation is significant at the 0.01 level (2-tailed).

Notice that three of these correlations (those with asterisks next to them) have been flagged as statistically different from 0, *even though there is no actual relationship between the fields*. This is because the statistical tests can identify only correlations that are *unlikely* to be caused by sampling variation; they cannot say that any particular correlation is *absolutely* not caused by sampling variation. So, evaluating each correlation involves a risk of making an error, saying that a correlation is significant when it actually isn't. The risk is small for each individual comparison, but as you look at more and more correlations, the risks add up. If you look at enough correlations, you can be almost certain that you will make at least one mistake of this type.

For this reason, it is best not to rely solely on statistical hypothesis tests when looking at correlation tables like this. Instead, have an idea in your mind of what constitutes a *useful* level of association, and then look for values that exceed that threshold. This judgment should be based on your domain knowledge of the problem at hand as well as statistical considerations. In the fictitious example above, even the flagged correlations are still very close to 0, indicating that for most purposes, they would be of little value. Keep in mind that borderline correlations (with values very close to your threshold) should be treated cautiously because they may actually be smaller than they appear.

Regression Models

Correlation models are useful for certain situations, but they are somewhat simplistic. They are capable of handling only a few variables at a time, which might cause some patterns to be missed. For more complex situations, a regression model may be more useful. A **regression model** is simply an equation that describes the relationship between a set of predictors and a target field. Suppose you have some demographic information on potential customers and you want to predict how much revenue each customer would generate. A typical regression model would give you a set of coefficients that enable you to make predictions for customers based on the values of the predictors. Each predictor is multiplied by its corresponding regression coefficient, and then those values are summed to give the resulting prediction. Once you have this model, you (or your software) can calculate a prediction for a new potential customer by entering the demographic information into the model.

Several types of models fit into the category of regression models. Some of the more widely used variations include linear regression and Cox regression models. These model types will be discussed below.

Linear Regression Models

In a nutshell

Purpose: to measure the relationship between a set of predictor characteristics (fields) and a numerical target value; also, to provide a model allowing prediction of target values for new cases

Typical application: predicting total profitability for customers

Strengths: quick to calculate; easy to interpret

Weaknesses: limited ability to capture complex relationships

Linear regression models are the most straightforward and easiest to understand of the models in this family. First, consider **simple linear regression**, with only one predictor and one target. Suppose you want to predict total profitability for customers based on various account information. If you have profitability information on existing customers and you have data on the account balances for those same customers, you can plot the two fields against each other, as shown in Figure 13-5.

Figure 13-5
Values for farm income and rainfall, with regression line

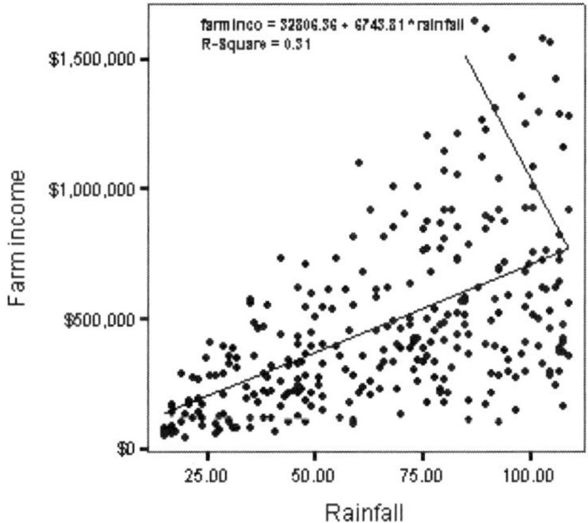

Notice that the points follow a general pattern—lower values for rainfall tend to go along with lower farm income. (You could say that these fields have a positive association.) This pattern can be summarized by a line passing through the cloud of data, as shown in the figure. This line is the **linear regression line** for predicting farm income (*farminco* in the equation) based on rainfall. The computer uses a mathematical method for finding the exact linear regression line that gives the best predictions of target values for given predictor values.[2] The regression model is defined by a formula, also shown in the figure. This regression formula can be used to generate predictions for new cases. To generate a prediction, simply enter the rainfall amount for the new record into the formula, and the formula gives you the prediction for farm income. For example, if you have an applicant in an area with 60 cm of rainfall, that applicant's predicted farm income would be $\$32,806.36 + \$6,743.81 \times 60 = \$437,434.96$. The ***R*-square** reported with the equation is an index of how well the line summarizes the relationship in the data. *R*-square (sometimes written as R^2) varies from 0 to 1—the closer to 1, the stronger the relationship and the better the equation can predict values of the target field. An R^2 close to 0 indicates that the predictors don't give you much information about the target value, and you should consider using either different predictors or a different type of model.

This concept of a regression line can be generalized to situations with more than one predictor. To continue the example, suppose you have additional data about farm size for each applicant. You can use both rainfall and farm size to make predictions about farm income. You now have three variables—two predictors and one target—so now you must visualize the relationship in three dimensions. The two predictors define the two-dimensional "floor," and the value of the target represents the "elevation" above the floor. In this case, the regression equation defines a flat surface (a **plane**) in this three-dimensional space, as shown in Figure 13-6.

2. This method is known as the **method of least squares**. See Appendix A for more information.

Figure 13-6
Regression plane for farm income predicted by rainfall and farm size

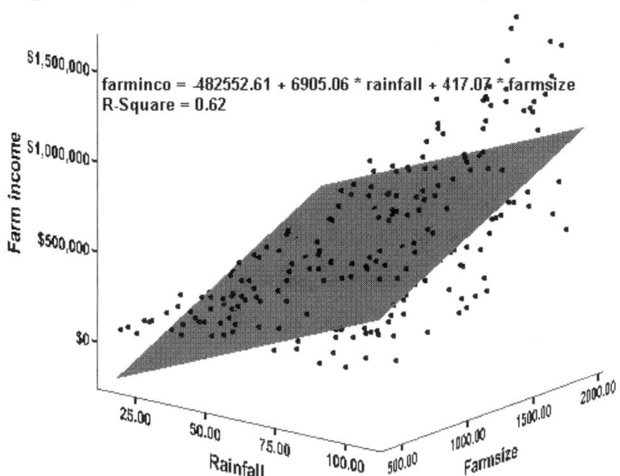

Notice that the regression equation looks similar in form to the previous one except that there is one more part to it, where you add the information you get from farm size to your prediction. Once again, using this regression model, you can calculate predicted farm income for new applicants by plugging the values of rainfall and farm size for those applicants into the formula. For example, if a new applicant had 60 cm of rainfall and their farm was 1,000 acres, the predicted farm income would be $-\$482{,}552.61 + (\$6{,}905.06 \times 60) + (\$417.07 \times 1{,}000) = \$348{,}820.99$.

The concept of linear regression can be generalized further to accommodate basically any number of predictor variables. Regression models with several predictors are sometimes called **multiple regression** models. Of course, it's much harder to visualize a solution in seven-dimensional space, for example, but the principles are the same. The computer finds the best formula for calculating predicted values of the target field based on the values of the predictor fields.

One more important point about linear regression is that the term *linear* in this context refers to a technical mathematical property of the model to be estimated. It does *not* imply that the solution must be a straight line (or a flat plane with multiple predictors). For example, you can include squared terms in the model, which results in a curved line or surface (as shown in Figure 13-7), even though the model is still technically a linear regression model. The formula for the line in the figure is $B = 1.155 - 1.039A + 1.172A^2$.

Figure 13-7
Regression line for a model with a squared term

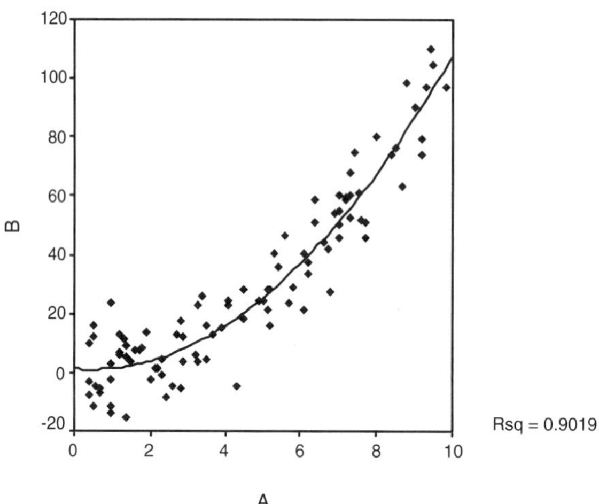

Cox Regression Models

In a nutshell

Purpose: to assess the relationships between a set of characteristics (fields) and the time until a certain event occurs

Typical application: understanding how customer attrition is related to account and demographic characteristics

Strengths: allows proper modeling of time-to-event data

Weaknesses: can be difficult to interpret; requires statistical expertise to execute properly

For some problems, you need to predict the time to a certain event. For example, you might want to test pieces of equipment to find out how long they can run (on average) before they break down. Another example would be predicting time-to-attrition for customer accounts. For problems like this, you might be tempted to measure the time-to-event for a set of items and then just take the average of those values. Unfortunately, this approach works only if every item actually has a measured time-to-event. In the equipment-testing example, every piece of equipment must fail in order for this technique to be valid. Unfortunately, you might have to wait a very long time—longer than you can afford to wait—for every machine to break down. The problem is more clear with the attrition example—many of the customers in your database will still be your customers (that is, they will not have **churned**, or switched to another company) when you need to run the analysis. Those customers have not yet experienced the "event." There may also be other problems that interrupt certain parts of the process that have nothing to do with what you are interested in. In the attrition example, you may lose some customers because they move out of your service area. This type of attrition is beyond your control, so these cases are unlikely to help you find ways to reduce churn. Such cases are called **censored cases** because they haven't (yet) shown the event of interest. You do have *some* useful information for these cases—you know they lasted at least a certain length of time with no event. However, they might go (or have gone) considerably longer if not for these other difficulties; for example, the customer that moved may have remained loyal for many more years if he or she were still in your service area.

A special kind of model, called a **Cox regression model** (also known as a **proportional hazards model**), allows you to use this kind of censored information as well as the uncensored data (cases where the event did occur) to make predictions about how long it will take for something to happen.[3] Instead of trying to predict the length of the time interval directly, Cox regression predicts the **hazard rate** over time. The hazard rate refers to the proportion of cases per unit of time that show the event. For example, at any particular time *t*, the hazard is the proportion of cases that have not shown the event before time *t* but do show the event *at* time *t*. This is then divided by the time interval over which these events occur to give a hazard rate. For example, if you have 2,000 customers who stay for at least one year and there are 96 customers who close their accounts right after their first year, the hazard at one year is $96/2{,}000 = 0.048$, and the hazard rate is 0.048 / 1 month, or 0.048.

By modeling the hazard rate rather than the time-to-event, the model can include information from censored cases up until the time they are censored (that is, the time when you no longer have information on them). For example, suppose that of the 2,000 customers mentioned above, 96 close their accounts but another 150 are censored at one year. This could be because they have been customers for only a year and their accounts are still active, or it could be caused by the customer's death or some other

3. This method and other related methods are often referred to as **survival analysis** because of their common use in medical research to model survival times for patients with certain medical conditions.

unforeseen circumstance not related to customer-retention planning. This leaves us with 2,000 – 96 – 150 = 1,754 customers who make it beyond one year. The next estimate of the hazard rate might be at 13 months, where 102 customers close their accounts. The hazard rate estimate would be $(102/1{,}754)/1 = 0.058$. Notice that the cases that were censored at one year were included in the hazard rate estimate at one year but not in the 13-month estimate. They aren't counted as account closures, though, either—they simply cease to be included in the calculations at all.

Cox regression enables you to include other fields as predictors of the hazard ratio (and thus, indirectly, as predictors of time-to-event). For example, you might include demographic fields, such as age and income, to determine whether there is a demographic pattern to the length of time that customers stay with your institution.

Stepwise Regression Methods

Traditionally, regression methods required you to know something about the pattern you were trying to model. Specifically, you had to specify exactly which fields to use as predictors. However, in data mining, you often don't have such detailed information available. You are trying to chart new territory, to find patterns no one knew about before. "What constitutes a good set of predictors?" is one of the key questions that you hope to answer by mining the data.

For such situations, **stepwise regression** methods can be very helpful. Stepwise methods work by making the computer try different combinations of variables to see which combination gives the best predictions. There are various ways this can be done. The computer can start with no predictors and then add them one by one. It starts with the best single predictor first and keeps adding them until all of the useful predictors have been added. Another method is to go backward, starting with all predictors in the model and then removing those that don't seem to add anything to the predictive accuracy. Some methods combine these approaches so that the model is built in stages; at each stage, the best predictor that isn't already in the model is added, and then the least helpful predictor that *is* in the model is tested to see if it can be removed without degrading the model. Regardless of the details, stepwise methods try to automatically identify the set of predictors that give the best predictions.

There is a danger with stepwise methods, however. Sometimes they work a little *too* well—they fit the random fluctuations in the data as well as the real pattern of interest. This is called **overfitting**. The predictions are very good for the data used to create the model (the **training data**), but the model doesn't generalize well. In other words, the model won't make good predictions on new data, since those new data won't have the same kinds of random fluctuations that appeared in the training data. For this reason, it is very important to test thoroughly how well your model generalizes before you base crucial decisions on it. For stepwise models, you can validate the model by splitting, or **partitioning**, your data into two subsets—a training set and a test set. First, you let the computer build the model based on the training set and then you apply the model to the data in the test set to see whether the model can generate accurate predictions for new data as well. (Even though the test set data isn't really new, it wasn't used to build the model, and therefore it is new to the model.)

For example, refer back to the regression example shown in Figure 13-6. Instead of building the model based on all of the cases, you can split the data into two groups (for example, 70% training set and 30% test set). If you build the model using the training set and validate it using the test set, you will see that the predictions for the test set (in one particular instance, $R^2 = 0.57$) aren't quite as accurate as they are for the training set (for the same instance, $R^2 = 0.64$). This difference is caused by overfitting—the model is mistaking some of the random fluctuations in the training set for an actual pattern. The test set results give a more accurate indication of how well the model will generalize than the training set results.

Remember, before you base any decisions on a model, particularly a model built using stepwise methods, be sure to validate the model using test data. This will give you more confidence that the patterns represented in the model will really generalize to new data.

Neural Networks for Prediction

In a nutshell

Purpose: to build a mathematical model of general relationships between a set of characteristics (fields) and one or more target fields

Typical application: predicting customer longevity based on account and demographic characteristics

Strengths: can capture complex nonlinear relationships; usually produce good predictions

Weaknesses: can be quite slow to estimate and are often difficult to interpret

Using neural networks for prediction is very similar to using neural networks for segmentation (see Chapter 12). The main difference is that a segmentation network has to reproduce a categorical output, but a prediction network has to provide predictions on a continuous scale. Otherwise, the principles are basically the same. Once again, there are many different types of neural networks that can be used for generating predictions, and the choice of which one to use depends on the problem at hand.

As an example, let's consider a straightforward multilayer perceptron (MLP) model to predict customer longevity based on various account characteristics—what types of accounts the customer has, account balances, ratio of deposits to loans, and so on. We trained an MLP using one hidden layer with 23 nodes trained to predict longevity for each customer. Comparing the predictions to actual data showed that the average error was a bit over three years (with longevity scores in the data ranging from less than one year to over 30 years)

Neural networks can also be used for forecasting with time series data. The key is to use the value of the time series at a particular time t as the target and the value at time $t-1$ as a predictor (and perhaps other preceding time points as well). This concept is shown in Figure 13-8.

Figure 13-8
Example of a neural network for forecasting transaction volumes

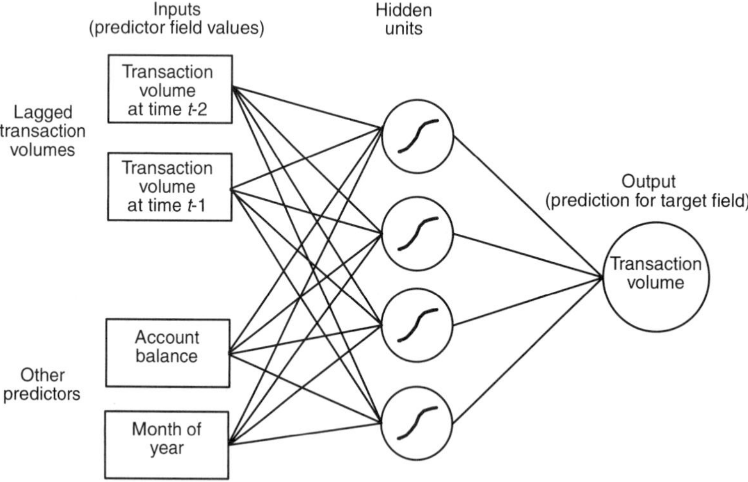

There are other, more complex neural network models that can perform forecasting as well. Such models are beyond the scope of this chapter, but you can find detailed descriptions of them in the references cited at the end of this chapter.

The same advantages and disadvantages discussed in Chapter 12 apply to prediction networks. If you want a model that gives accurate predictions but you don't really care how it works, then a neural network might be just what you need. However, if you want a model that will help you *understand* the process as well as generate predictions, you should probably consider one of the other modeling techniques described here.

Summary

The methods outlined in this chapter are valuable in the data mining process. Reports tell you only *what* happened, but models can tell you *why* it happened. They allow you to generate predictions for either new cases or future events, and in many cases they can also provide you with important insights into the relationships in your data. The ability to make accurate predictions can dramatically increase the effectiveness of your business process and can help you make better decisions.

Further Reading

The brief outlines in this chapter were meant to create an appetite for using these powerful data mining techniques. If you want to learn more about how to use these techniques with real data, you will need to learn more about how they work and how to correctly interpret the results they produce. The following references will give you the background you need to use these methods effectively and confidently.

Correlation Models

Neter, J., M. H. Kutner, C. J. Nachtsheim, and W. Wasserman. 1996. Chapter 15 in *Applied linear regression models.* Chicago: Richard D. Irwin, Inc.

Regression Models

Linear Regression

Draper, N., and H. Smith. 1998. *Applied regression analysis.* New York: John Wiley & Sons, Inc.

Neter, J., M. H. Kutner, C. J. Nachtsheim, and W. Wasserman. 1996. *Applied linear regression models.* Chicago: Richard D. Irwin, Inc.

Cox Regression (Survival Analysis) Models

Kalbfleisch, J. D. 1980. *The statistical analysis of failure time data.* New York: John Wiley & Sons, Inc.

Kleinbaum, D. G. 1996. *Survival analysis: A self-learning text.* New York: Springer-Verlag.

Forecasting/ARIMA

Box, G. E. P., and G. M. Jenkins. 1994. *Time series analysis: Forecasting and control.* Englewood Cliffs, N.J.: Prentice Hall.

Enders, W. 1995. *Applied econometric time series.* New York: John Wiley & Sons, Inc.

Kendall, M., and J. Keith Ord. 1990. *Time series.* New York: Oxford University Press.

Neural Networks for Prediction

Bishop, C. M. 1995. *Neural networks for pattern recognition.* Oxford: Clarendon Press.

Ripley, B. D. 1996. *Pattern recognition and neural networks.* New York: Cambridge University Press.

Appendix

A Brief Review of Statistical Reasoning

What Is Statistical Reasoning?

On a global level, statistical reasoning refers to extracting *general* information from *specific* data. In most research problems, including those faced in data mining, you have a set of data about specific things (such as customers, transactions, and accounts). What you want to do is identify relationships among things (or among properties of things) that are general in nature. In other words, you want to find relationships that apply not only to the things you have measured in your data but to the wider variety of things from which they were chosen—the relationships you find should apply to other potential customers, other potential transactions, etc. You want to be able to make accurate *predictions* about things you haven't seen yet so that you can make better decisions.

Fundamentals of Statistical Reasoning

Several concepts are fundamental to understanding statistical reasoning. The most important are sampling, variation, and probability.

Sampling

Sampling addresses the fact that you don't usually have information on all of the items in which you are interested. You may have records on all of your *current* customers but want to know something about all *possible* customers. You may have records of past transactions but want to know something about all transactions, both past and future. Since you don't have complete data on everything you want to know, you have to make do with the data you have. Because the cases you have data for (called the **sample**) are *similar* to the larger group of cases in which you are interested (called the **population**), you can use statistical methods to draw conclusions about the larger set based on the smaller set.

Variation

Most things that you measure vary from record to record. Accounts have different balances, customers have different buying patterns, transactions have different amounts, and so on. This is called **variation** and is at the heart of data analysis. A field with no variation would be of little value because it would have the same value for all records and thus could not be associated with anything else.

Several possible sources of variation for a particular field include the effects of other things you've measured (that is, other fields), the effects of things you *haven't* measured, and the effects of error, such as measurement error, data entry error, computer failure, or sampling variability. The goal in statistical analysis (and in data mining) is to identify and isolate the variation that you can explain from the variance that is caused by other sources. In this way, you can interpret the measured effects in a meaningful way.

For example, suppose that you are a credit card issuer. You might have a field that indicates revenue generated for each account. These values will vary from account to account—some accounts will generate a lot of revenue, others will generate relatively little. You can explain some of this variation easily—accounts with higher balances will generate more revenue, and factors such as interest rates and annual fees will contribute in predictable ways to account revenues. However, some variability will be difficult or impossible to explain. For example, some customers may use their cards often but pay the balance in full each month. Such customers would show a high balance at any given time but would generate lower revenues because they are not paying finance charges.

There are several ways to measure variation, but the most common are the variance and the standard deviation. (For definitions of these measures, see the glossary.)

Probability

If the things you were interested in behaved in simple, deterministic ways (like billiard balls), you could measure their behavior very precisely and then develop mechanistic models that would explain virtually all of the observed variation. Unfortunately, things are seldom so well behaved. Because there is almost always either error variation or variation caused by unmeasured factors (or both), it is nearly impossible to find such concise explanations for your data. For example, you usually can't say, "All customers who drive red cars will buy *X* and all customers who drive blue cars will buy *Y*." You have to make a statement such as, "Customers who drive red cars are more likely to buy *X* than customers who drive blue cars."

When you talk about things being more likely or less likely to occur, you are using probability to summarize a relationship. **Probability** is a number that represents the likelihood of a particular event. It is measured on a scale from 0 to 1, where 0 probability indicates something that is never true, and 1 indicates something that is always true. A probability of 0.5 indicates something that is equally likely to be true or false (a fifty-fifty chance).[1]

Probability provides a way to talk about the uncertainty in your results. Specifically, it gives you a way to *quantify* the amount of uncertainty associated with a particular conclusion. Since you usually can't make absolute statements based on a sample of data, this probability information is critical to making informed decisions about which conclusions are reasonable and which are not.

Modes of Statistical Reasoning

Two basic modes of statistical reasoning are **statistical testing** and **model building**. These modes were developed for two different kinds of problems; however, the best applications of statistics combine both modes to solve the problem.

Statistical Testing

In many cases, the problem consists of confirming or rejecting a particular conclusion based on the data. For example, you may want to determine whether women are more likely to buy *X* than men are. Or you may want to test the more specific notion that

1. The mathematical definition of probability is quite complex, but the definition given here is adequate to develop a basic idea of the issues involved in statistical reasoning.

women are approximately twice as likely to buy *X* as men are. Or you may want something more general, such as determining whether the likelihood of buying *X* is the same for men and women (regardless of which group has the higher average).

Each of these assertions is called a **hypothesis**. More generally, a hypothesis is a statement about a relationship between fields (or records) that would be expected to show an effect in the data. A hypothesis must be something that can be tested based on the data.

Sampling Variability and Sampling Distributions

Whenever you take a sample from a larger population, you run the risk of getting a sample that doesn't reflect the nature of the population. The magnitude of this risk depends on the size of the sample—the larger the sample, the more likely it is to reflect the nature of the population.[2] For example, if you want to estimate the average income of your potential customers, you calculate the average income for the customers in your database and use that as an estimate of the income of potential customers.

When you have a set of data, you have collected a single sample, and you base your calculations on that sample. But imagine what would happen if you could take samples over and over again—a different sample each time—and repeat your calculations for each sample. There would be some variability in the calculated values, but they would cluster around the true value (the population value). For example, suppose that the true average income for all potential customers is $40,000 per year. If you take a sample of 1,000 customers, you might calculate an average income of $39,698. Now, if you take another different sample of 1,000 customers, you might calculate a slightly different average, perhaps $40,119. If you were to repeat this over and over, you would have a whole set of averages, all of which are estimates of the true value of $40,000. If you repeated this process an infinite number of times and if you plotted the values you observed versus the likelihood of the value occurring, you would generate a plot that is similar to Figure A-1. This is known as a **sampling distribution** because it describes the distribution of calculated values across multiple samples.

2. The risk of getting an unrepresentative sample also depends on *how* the sample is selected. For the moment, assume that the sample was selected randomly from all of the possible items in the population. See "Assumptions" on p. 178 for additional information on problems with sampling.

Figure A-1
Sampling distribution for Income example

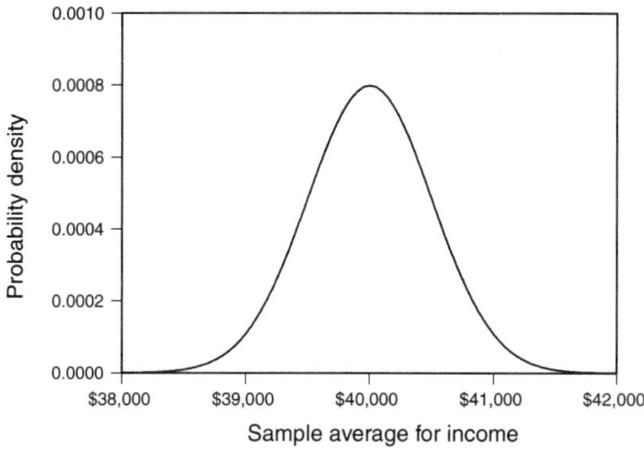

Generally, you have only the one sample that you actually measured. Unfortunately, you can't be sure where your particular sample falls in the sampling distribution. Because of this, you have to use some caution when making direct comparisons between values calculated from samples. For example, you should be careful comparing the average income of people who drive red cars to the average income of people who drive blue cars based on samples of both groups. Figure A-2 shows hypothetical sampling distributions for drivers of red cars and drivers of blue cars, assuming that you have 100 drivers in each sample. Notice that according to the true population values, both groups have equal average income. However, if you happen to get the two means indicated in the graphs from your two samples, the calculated estimates would imply that drivers of red cars have higher income than drivers of blue cars. Noticing this difference, you might be tempted to try to explain why the values are different. In reality, though, the apparent difference is caused by nothing more than the quirks of your samples. In cases like this, statisticians say that the difference is "nonsignificant" or "attributable to chance." In fact, the difference could easily have turned out the other way, with drivers of blue cars appearing to have higher income than drivers of red cars.

Figure A-2
Comparing drivers of red cars to drivers of blue cars

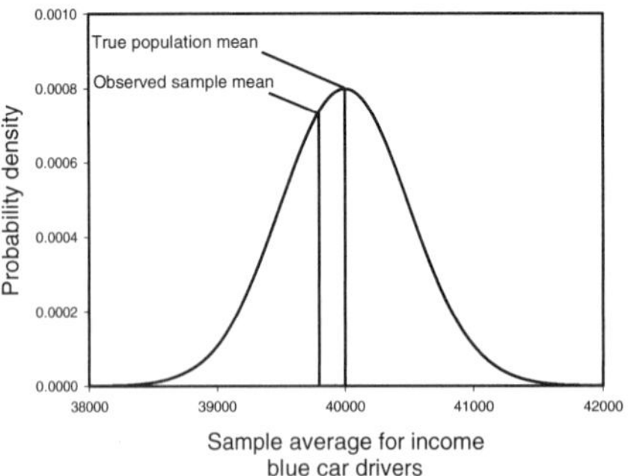

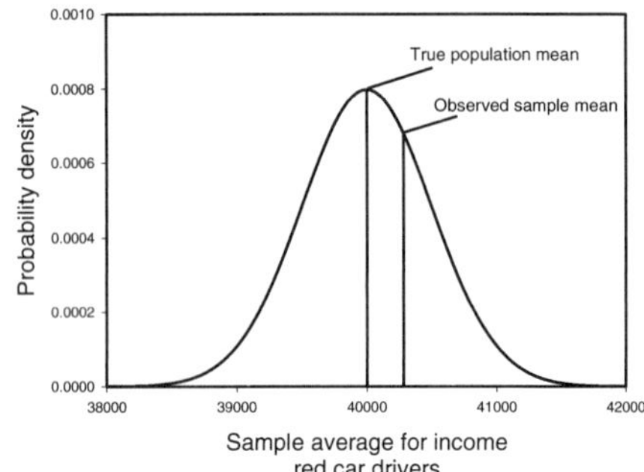

Because of this sampling variability, you should use a probability-based approach to making comparisons. As shown in Figure A-2, you usually find small differences between the average value for a sample and the average value for the true population. You need some way to determine whether a difference is **significant**; that is, whether it is large enough to warrant the conclusion that the difference really exists. The question no longer is, "Is the average value different from *X*?" Rather, the question is, "How likely is it to see the observed average value if the population average is actually *X*?" If that likelihood (measured as a probability) is small enough, then you can assume that the difference is real and you can act accordingly.

The p Value and Statistical Significance

Given the data, how do you calculate this probability? Fortunately, mathematicians discovered a very useful property of the sampling distribution of the average (mean)—if the sample size is large enough, the sampling distribution of the mean is very similar to a specific, well-understood distribution called the **normal distribution**.[3]

Here's how it works. If you know the mean and the standard deviation of a distribution and you know the size of the sample you're taking from the distribution, you can figure out approximately what the sampling distribution looks like. From there, using known properties of the normal distribution, you can use a table or a

3. The claim that the sampling distribution of the mean is approximately normal for large samples is known in statistics as the **central limit theorem**. For more details, see Hays (1988) or Hogg and Craig (1978).

mathematical formula to calculate the probability associated with getting a value equal to or more extreme than any particular value.

To clarify this, let's say that you know something about car drivers in general—their average (mean) income is about \$40,000 per year. Now suppose that you draw a sample of 100 drivers with red cars and then calculate a sample mean of \$40,625 and a standard deviation of \$5,000. The sampling distribution for the mean, assuming a true population value of \$40,000 and a standard deviation of \$5,000, is now similar to Figure A-3.

Notice that the observed value of \$40,625 is marked in the sampling distribution. To calculate the probability of getting that sample value (or one that is more extreme) if the true value is \$40,000, the computer calculates the area under the curve from \$40,625 to infinity. In this example, that calculated probability is approximately 0.11. This probability is often referred to as a ***p* value**.

Figure A-3
Calculating the probability of a sample value, assuming a true mean of \$40,000

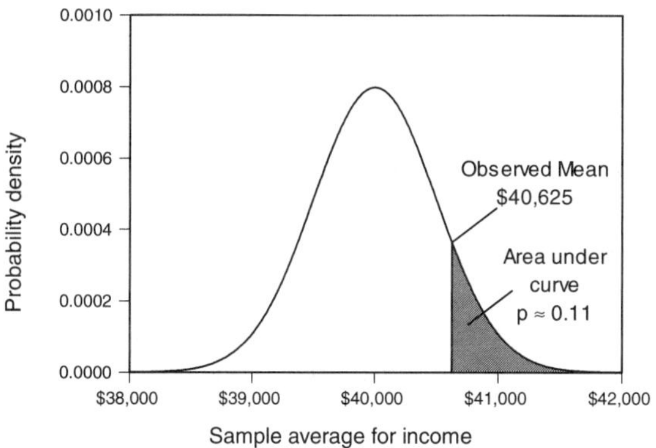

When you use a statistical test, you need a criterion for deciding when a difference is real and when it might be caused by sampling error (that is, due to chance). The smaller the probability, the less likely the difference is due to chance and the more likely it is to be caused by some kind of systematic effect. To be objective, you need a criterion that is more concrete than "small enough," so you choose a specific probability value as the criterion and then use it as a cutoff for making the decision about whether an observed difference is real. This criterion is sometimes called **alpha**, or the **significance level**. A calculated probability that is *smaller* than the significance level indicates that the sample you observed is unlikely to come from a population with the hypothesized mean. In this case, you can say that the difference between hypothesized mean and actual mean is **statistically significant**. Some customary values for alpha are 0.05 or 0.01. The specific value chosen may vary from situation to situation, depending on the relative costs of making different mistakes. (See "Types of Errors" on p. 179 for more information.)

Suppose you choose 0.05 as your significance level in testing whether the difference between the income of drivers of red cars and the hypothesized value of $40,000 is real. In this example, where the sample mean is $40,625, the probability of seeing a sample like this is about 0.11 if the true population mean for all drivers of red cars is $40,000. Since this value is larger than our significance level of 0.05, you cannot say conclusively that the difference is real. If the population has a mean of $40,000, there is about an 11% chance of choosing a sample of 100 cases with a mean of $40,625 (assuming a standard deviation of $5,000). Thus, even though the risk of the difference being due to sampling error is rather small, it is not small enough for us to be confident that it is *not* due to sampling error.

Modeling

Usually, you want to know something more explicit than simply whether a difference is statistically significant. You often want to make specific predictions about events, based on the knowledge you have about certain aspects of the events. For example, you might want to predict whether a credit applicant is likely to default on a loan, based on various information you have about his or her income, employment, credit history, and so on. To make predictions such as these, you need a way to relate the information you have to the information you want to predict. You do this by building a model.

Various models are used in statistics, but usually a model is expressed in the form of an equation. You have the values that you want to use to make the prediction (the predictors), and you have the value(s) that you want to predict (the target).[4] The equation specifies the nature of the relationship between the predictors and the target. One of the most commonly used models in statistics is a linear regression model, which assumes that the relationship between the predictors and the target follows a straight line (or a plane in multiple dimensions, when the model has more than one predictor). The equation for this model follows the general pattern

4. Statisticians call the fields you use in making your prediction **independent variables** because they are assumed not to be affected by other variables in the model. The field being predicted is called the **dependent variable** because it is assumed that values of this field are dependent on the values of the predictor fields.

$$\hat{y} = B_0 + B_1 \cdot X_1 + B_2 \cdot X_2 + \ldots + e$$

where $\hat{y}$ is the predicted target value for a case, $X_1 \ldots X_n$ are the predictors, e is the random error term (since you usually don't get perfect predictions), and $B_1 \ldots B_n$ are the **parameters** of the model. The parameters are computer-generated estimates based on the data, and they define the relationships between individual predictors and the target. Using the equation with the estimated parameters, you can generate predictions for new cases. Simply enter the values for the predictors, and the computer calculates a predicted target value based on the equation.

Other examples of models include a discriminant analysis model for categorical data, a C5.0 tree, or a neural network. Not all of these models take the form of an equation, but they all involve estimation of parameters that are used to predict values for the target field.

Estimating Model Parameters

Model parameters are estimated mathematically, based on the data. This is done by selecting values that give the best predictions—in other words, values that minimize the discrepancy between predicted values and actual values. This discrepancy between predicted and actual values can be measured in different ways, depending on aspects of the model and the data. For basic linear regression models, the discrepancy is measured as the square of the difference between the predicted and actual values (the squared error). The parameters of the model (known as the **regression coefficients**) are calculated so that they minimize the average squared error across all cases. Because the model minimizes the squared errors, it is sometimes called the **method of least squares**.

Other more complex models require different measures of discrepancy and use different methods to minimize them. Logistic regression models for categorical data use a method called **maximum likelihood**, which tries to find the model that is most likely to have generated the observed data. In other words, the measure of discrepancy is the *inverse* of the probability that a given model generated the observed data. (Minimizing the inverse of the probability is the same as maximizing the probability.) However, there is no direct solution to find the parameters that lead to maximum likelihood, so models like this must be estimated iteratively. A series of models is generated, each one better than the last, until it is not possible to improve the model any more. The last model is then presented as the final model.

Other methods of model building use other measures of discrepancy and other estimation methods, but the end result is the same—a set of parameters that allow you to generate predictions for the target field based on values for the predictor fields.

Evaluating Models

Once you have estimated a model, you have to determine whether it does an adequate job of making predictions. A lot of factors affect a model's ability to predict, including the selection of predictor fields, the appropriateness of the model type, the estimation method, problems with the data, and so on.

The most straightforward way to evaluate a model is to assess how close the predicted values are to the observed values. If the differences between predicted and observed values are small, then you may decide that the model is adequate. However, if the differences are large, you probably need to consider using different predictors, trying a different model type, or checking your data for errors or inconsistencies.

The discrepancies can be examined either case by case or in aggregate. By examining case-by-case discrepancies, you sometimes get a sense of the specific mistakes the model is making. For example, discrepancies that are often larger for men than for women may indicate that different factors are at work among men, and you may need to develop separate models for men and women. You can also gain important insight with an aggregated index of discrepancy, which summarizes discrepancies across all cases. Such a summary goodness-of-fit statistic can tell you if your model is off the mark or if it is actually good for most cases.

One advantage of global goodness-of-fit statistics is that they tend to be measured on a consistent scale, making it easier to compare models to see which is making better predictions. Such measures are often computed to have an intuitive meaning. One of the most common goodness-of-fit measures is the proportion of variance accounted for by the model. For regression models, this is equal to the square of the multiple correlation for the model (R^2). This allows you to compute the R^2 values for separate models and identify the model with the higher R^2 as the better predictive model.

Another important aspect of evaluating models is testing whether they can be generalized. In some cases, a model may fit a particular sample of data quite well but may not give good results when applied to new data. This is called **overfitting**. It happens because the model fits some of the random fluctuations (the error variance) in the original data in addition to the real pattern of interest. Those random fluctuations are specific to the original data, which means that they won't be found in new data and that the predictions of the model will suffer for it. Since the whole purpose of generating a model is to make predictions for new cases, this would seriously undermine the usefulness of a model. Two approaches to testing for this problem are partitioning and cross-validation.

Partitioning consists of splitting your data into two parts—a training sample and a test sample. The training sample is used to estimate the model, and the model is then applied to the test sample. If the prediction is adequate for the test sample, then you can assume that the model will generalize fairly well to new data.

Cross-validation is done by splitting your data into more than two samples, all of about the same size. For each sample, a model is estimated based on all of the cases *except* the ones in the selected sample, and the model is then tested on the selected sample. This is repeated for each of the samples, and the average of the goodness-of-fit statistics for the samples tells you how well a model based on all of the data is likely to perform on new data.

Combining Statistical Testing with Model Building

For certain situations, you need more from a model than just a way to predict future values. You might want to know which predictors are most important for generating accurate predictions, or you might want to know whether one particular model allows you to make better predictions than another model. In cases like this, you can apply statistical testing techniques to your model to get the answers you are looking for.

If you want to know which predictors in the model are important and which are not, you can test the parameters and identify those that are most likely to be different from 0. In many cases, the theoretical sampling distributions for model parameters are known, which means that you can compute *p* values for each of the parameters and then use the *p* values to draw conclusions about the parameters.

You can also use statistical testing to compare models to determine whether one model is significantly better than another. This can be useful in situations where a complex model is a little better than a simpler one. It's often true that complex models give better prediction than simple ones, but a statistical test can help you decide whether the increase in prediction is worth the difficulties associated with more complex models.

Some Pitfalls of Statistical Reasoning

Statistical reasoning is a complex process, and if you are not diligent, you can easily go astray. Several conditions must be satisfied for statistical methods to work the way they are designed to work. Statistical reasoning has an important place in the process of generating knowledge from data, but it cannot work in a vacuum—it requires careful planning, consideration of the strengths and weaknesses of the various statistical methods, domain knowledge, and common sense to get good, actionable results.

Assumptions

All statistical methods require you to make assumptions about the data and about the real-world processes that are described by the data. Without these assumptions, it would be impossible to summarize the data. Assumptions vary from method to method, but some assumptions are common to most statistical methods. One of the most important assumptions is that the sample you have is representative of the larger population about which you want to make predictions. In other words, the sample must be similar to the population in all important aspects. If this assumption doesn't hold, standard statistical methods may give misleading results. For example, suppose you have been selling men's shoes, and you decide to begin selling women's shoes as well. You might be tempted to build a marketing campaign based on the information you've gained from your database of male customers. However, that information may not apply at all to the female customers you want to target. In this case, your sample (men) probably differs from the target population (women) in significant ways. In order to successfully apply statistics or data mining to this type of problem, you would need to get some data on potential female customers.

Each statistical method is based on a unique set of assumptions. Because there isn't space here to detail the assumptions for every statistical method, we suggest that when you use a statistical method, you should check your software's documentation or a statistics manual to find out what assumptions are required and how to check your data to see that the assumptions are reasonable for your particular situation.

Types of Errors

When you make a decision based on statistical tests, there are four possible outcomes, as summarized in Table A-1.

Table A-1
Outcomes for statistical decision making

		Your decision	
		No difference	Difference
True state of the world	No difference	Correct	False alarm
	Difference	Miss	Correct

Notice that there are two ways in which your decision can be wrong—you can claim the difference is real when it is not (a **false alarm**), or you can claim a difference is *not* real when it *is* (a **miss**).[5] Because it is usually more interesting when there is a difference than when there isn't, people are careful about calling a difference real only if they are very confident that it is. But it is equally important to remember that there is also a risk of error when you decide a difference is due to chance.

In some cases, there are different consequences to the two types of errors, and those considerations should influence how you make decisions. For example, suppose that it costs $1 to contact a potential customer but that customer can generate $5 in profits if she responds to the offer. Now, suppose that there are two groups of customers—one group who appears unlikely to buy according to your statistical model but would buy nevertheless, and another group who appears likely to buy but will not. It costs more if you eliminate the first group from your campaign (the $5 – $1 = $4 that you would have earned from each one if you had sent to them) than it costs if you include the second group (the $1 each that it costs to contact them). Therefore, in this situation, you would want to use a fairly liberal criterion for deciding which potential customers to send to.

Statistical Significance and Practical Significance

Remember that statistical significance applies only to whether a difference is likely to be real. It doesn't say anything about whether that difference is important or useful. Keep in mind that statistical testing depends heavily on the size of the sample being used. The bigger the sample, the better the test is at identifying small differences as

5. Statisticians call these **Type I** and **Type II** errors, respectively.

real. For example, with 100 cases, you might be able to detect a $1 difference, but with 100,000 cases, you can detect a difference of one-tenth of a cent. In data mining, of course, you usually have large data sets, so you can detect very small differences. The problem with this is that it can lead to a lot of "so what?" results. You can find that two groups differ by one-tenth of a cent and that the difference is statistically significant, but in some situations, it may not be enough of a difference to justify taking action.

The *importance* of a difference is not a statistical question. You have to put the statistical results in the context of the substantive problem to make decisions about which differences are important and which ones are useful for answering your questions or helping you to improve your business practices.

Cause and Effect

It is often tempting to make attributions about cause and effect based on statistical results. However, you must be very careful in making such attributions. Sometimes the path of cause and effect isn't as clear as it seems at first glance. In fact, just because you find a significant association between two things doesn't necessarily mean that there's any causative relationship between them at all. As an absurd example, consider the relationship between the number of shoe salespeople in a city and the number of fires in the city over a period of years. The positive relationship between the two things does not imply that shoe salespeople are arsonists, nor does it imply that fires drive people to sell shoes. It is simply the result of the city's growth over the years. As the city grows, more shoe stores open and hire salespeople, and the growing number of buildings increases the number of fires you are likely to see in a given period of time.

For a more realistic example, suppose you analyze some data and discover that there seems to be a positive relationship between income and frequency of medical checkups. There are three possible explanations for this finding:

- More affluent people can afford optional checkup visits, whereas poor people can afford to go to the doctor only when they are really sick (income causes checkup frequency).
- People who actively maintain their health—for example, by getting regular checkups—are able to get and keep better jobs than those who neglect their health (checkup frequency causes income).
- This relationship is caused by a third element, such as population density—affluent people tend to live in the city where health care is more accessible.

You would have to make further investigations, using additional information, to determine which possibility is the most likely explanation for the relationship.

Statistics and Data Mining

Statistical methods clearly have a central role in data mining. They provide powerful techniques for choosing, estimating, and testing models. However, the use of statistical methods in data mining is somewhat different from traditional statistical practice. Consider some of the following differences between traditional applications of statistical methods and their use in data mining.

Control over data. In traditional statistical applications, the researcher usually has control over some or all of the data—how it is collected, what fields are measured, and how it is processed—and each investigation tends to be encapsulated; that is, the data from one investigation are kept separate from data for other investigations. In contrast, the data miner rarely has control over the data. Data are taken as they are from whatever data stores are available. Data miners often must piece together data from various sources, and they have little or no say in how it is coded, organized, or combined with other data. Data miners typically spend a great deal of time taking these original data sources and getting them into shape for data mining.

Amount of data. Traditional statistics were designed to deal with small data sets, with efficiency as a primary consideration. Indeed, many of the most commonly used statistical methods were developed before the widespread use of computers and were designed to be accessible to researchers with only a desk calculator (if even that). In addition, data collection is expensive, and it is common for traditional researchers to try to find ways to answer their questions using as little data as possible. On the other hand, the data miner usually has huge amounts of data. In fact, the amount of data can sometimes be problematic; for example, it may take several days to analyze a data set with millions of records, even with a fast computer.

The role of theory. Traditional researchers specify theories about relationships first and then seek to verify those relationships using statistical methods. They know exactly what they are looking for when they start. While data mining can also be done in this way, it is much more common for data miners to go to the data first, looking for patterns that can generate new theories. Data miners often have only a general idea of what they are looking for; they use the data to help them fill in the details.

You don't have to be a statistician to do data mining. However, knowing something about the fundamentals of statistical reasoning enables you to get the most out of your data mining efforts while minimizing the risks of misinterpreting or misusing your data mining results.

Appendix

Guide to SPSS Products Used in Data Mining

The following is a brief summary of data mining software packages available from SPSS. For more details, see the SPSS Web site at *http://www.spss.com.*

Clementine/Clementine Server

Purpose. To provide a complete data mining workbench with functionality for all phases of the data mining process.

Target audience. Knowledge workers and model builders.

Methods available. A variety of data access features, including reading data directly from databases, comprehensive data management, reporting and graphs, and data mining methods including neural networks, C5.0, C&RT, association rules, logistic regression, linear regression, clustering, sequence rules, and PCA/factor analysis. When reading from a database, Clementine can use SQL pushback to take advantage of the highly optimized DBMS routines for data preparation. Clementine also provides a powerful scripting facility. Clementine Solution Publisher allows you to deploy your Clementine models with ease, and Clementine Server provides highly scalable data mining capabilities.

Comments. Clementine provides a complete data mining solution, from data access and manipulation to modeling and deployment. The stream format of Clementine sessions allows you to see at a glance what you've done so far and how it all fits together, making it easier to focus on your business objectives instead of programming.

SPSS/SPSS Server

Purpose. To provide advanced statistical analysis capabilities in addition to reporting and graphical analysis.

Target audience. Knowledge workers, model builders, developers.

Methods available. Data management, Database Capture Wizard for accessing databases and data warehouses, interactive report generation, a wide variety of statistical methods including linear regression, analysis of variance, curve estimation, discriminant analysis, factor analysis, cluster analysis, and nonparametric statistics. Additional functionality is available in various options that can be added to SPSS. SPSS Server provides scalable data analysis capabilities.

Comments. A complete data analysis solution well suited to statisticians, which includes data access, sophisticated statistical analysis, and presentation-quality output. Results can be distributed and viewed by others using the SPSS SmartViewer or the SmartViewer Web Server.

Options for SPSS

If you need statistical functionality beyond that found in the SPSS Base system, the following options can be added to SPSS:

Tables. Allows you to create a variety of presentation-quality tabular reports, including complex tables and displays of multiple-response data.

Regression Models. Provides techniques for analyzing data that do not fit traditional linear statistical models. It includes procedures for logistic regression, nominal regression, weighted least-squares regression, and general nonlinear regression.

Advanced Models. Focuses on techniques used in sophisticated experimental and biomedical research, including general linear models (GLM), variance components analysis, loglinear analysis, and survival analysis (for time-to-event data).

Trends. Performs comprehensive forecasting and time-series analyses with multiple curve-fitting models, smoothing models, and methods for estimating autoregressive functions.

Categories. Useful for optimal scaling of categorical data, including correspondence analysis.

Conjoint. Performs conjoint analysis.

Exact Tests. When the assumptions for analyzing crosstabulated data or using nonparametric statistics are not valid, exact tests can be used to derive exact p values for statistical results.

Missing Value Analysis. Describes patterns of missing data, estimates means and other statistics, and imputes values for missing observations.

Maps. Plot and analyze spatial data to find geographical patterns.

SmartViewer

Purpose. To allow others to view and interact with results from SPSS.

Target audience. Information consumers.

Methods available. Interaction with pivot tables, viewing of charts and tables.

Comments. This client program allows others who need information to view and manipulate results created in SPSS. SmartViewer users are able to interact with pivot tables as if they were running SPSS. This eliminates the need to repackage and summarize results for distribution to decision makers.

SmartViewer Web Server

Purpose. To allow others to view and interact with results from SPSS.

Target audience. Information consumers.

Methods available. Interaction with pivot tables, viewing of charts and tables.

Comments. This server program allows others who need information to view and manipulate results created in SPSS, using common Web-browsing software such as Microsoft Internet Explorer or Netscape Communicator. SmartViewer Web Server users are able to interact with pivot tables within their Web browser. This eliminates the need to repackage and summarize results for distribution to decision makers and has the added benefit of presenting information through the familiar Web browser interface.

AnswerTree/AnswerTree Server

Purpose. To provide segmentation and prediction using tree-based models.

Target audience. Model builders.

Methods available. CHAID, Exhaustive CHAID, C&RT, QUEST.

Comments. Provides a highly interactive environment for generating classification and regression trees. AnswerTree works by splitting your sample into homogeneous subgroups. You can use your domain knowledge to customize your tree models for your business problem. Rules for assigning subgroups and computing predicted target values can be generated and exported in SPSS, SQL, or decision rule formats for fast, easy scoring of new cases. AnswerTree Server provides highly scalable model building.

Neural Connection

Purpose. To estimate and generate predictive models based on neural networks and related methods.

Target audience. Model builders.

Methods available. Multilayer perceptrons, radial basis functions, Kohonen networks, Bayesian networks, closest class mean classifier, multiple regression, principle components analysis.

Comments. Neural networks are particularly useful for problems where simple linear models don't work well. Neural Connection's unique interface makes it easy to create neural network models and generate the output necessary to interpret the results.

DecisionTime/WhatIf?

Purpose. To create forecasts for time series data.

Target audience. Model builders.

Methods available. Exponential smoothing and ARIMA time series models.

Comments. Making predictions for data that vary over time requires specialized methods like those found in DecisionTime. The modeling wizard helps you select the best model for your data. Forecasts created in DecisionTime can be used to test scenarios using WhatIf? There is also a server version of DecisionTime for tackling large time series problems.

LexiQuest Mine

Purpose. To mine textual data, such as Web pages, e-mail, or other unstructured documents.

Target audience. Model builders.

Methods available. Natural Language Processing technology.

Comments. LexiQuest's NLP technology works on a deep level to identify concepts in documents and find patterns among those concepts. It allows you to find crucial information in the complexities of textual data.

Glossary

aggregate data. Data that have been aggregated; summarized data.

aggregation. The process of combining data across groups. Aggregation is used to create summaries.

Apriori. An algorithm for inducing association rules from data. The algorithm is based on finding frequent items and building up rules based on these frequent items.

association. The extent to which values of one field depend on or are predicted by values of another field.

association rules. Rules, usually of the form

if a [and b and c...] then x

that summarize relationships in the data. These rules are inferred from the data using algorithms such as Apriori and GRI.

balancing. Leveling the distribution of an attribute (normally symbolic) in a data set by discarding records with common values or duplicating records with rare values. *See also* stratified sampling.

Boolean field. A field that can take only two values, *true* or *false* (often encoded as 1 and 0, respectively). *See also* dichotomous field and flag.

boosting. A technique used to increase the accuracy of a model. The technique uses multiple models built sequentially. The first model is built normally. The data are then weighted to emphasize the records for which the first model generated errors, and the second model is built. The data are then weighted again based on the second model's errors, and another model is built, and so on, until the specified number of models has been built. The boosted model consists of the entire set of models, with final predictions determined by combining the individual model predictions.

boxplot. A plot that shows a summary of the shape of the values for a field (variable). The line in the middle of the box splits the data into two equal parts; the ends of the box split each half again. The end of the "whiskers" indicate the largest value within 1.5 box lengths of the mean (above and below). Outliers are indicated by points beyond the ends of the whiskers.

business understanding. The first phase of the CRISP-DM process model. Involves determining business objectives, assessing the situation, determining data mining goals, and producing a project plan.

C5.0. An algorithm for creating a decision tree based on minimization of entropy measures.

case. A single object or element of interest in the data set. Cases might represent customers, transactions, manufactured parts, or other basic units of analysis. With denormalized data, cases are represented as records in the data set.

categorical field. A field (variable) where values are restricted to a finite list of possible values. Examples are gender (male, female), U.S. state (Arizona, California, etc.), and product name. Categorical fields can be either unordered (nominal) or ordered (ordinal).

cell. In a display table, the intersection of one row and one column. In an OLAP cube, the subset of cases defined by a single value for each dimension in the cube.

CHAID. An algorithm for creating a decision tree for categorical data based on statistical tests.

chi-square. A test statistic used to evaluate the association between categorical variables. It is based on differences between predicted frequencies and observed frequencies in a crosstabulation.

classification. A process of identifying the group to which an object belongs by examining characteristics of the object. In classification, the groups are defined by some external criterion (contrast with clustering).

classification and regression trees (C&RT). An algorithm for creating a decision tree based on minimization of impurity measures. Also known as CART.

classification tree. A type of decision tree where the goal of the tree is classification.

clustering. The process of grouping records together based on similarity. In clustering, there usually is no external criterion for groups (contrast with classification).

column. A measured quality about records in a database. Also known as a variable, feature, or attribute.

confusion matrix. A crosstabulation of predicted values versus observed values for a given classification model. Shows the different types of errors made by the model.

continuous field. A field (variable) that can take a wide range of numeric values. Such fields are treated as real numbers in statistical calculations.

correlation. A statistical measure of the linear association between two continuous fields. Values range from –1 to +1. A correlation of 0 means no relationship between the two fields.

Cox regression. A special type of regression model used with time-to-event data, such as time to breakdown or time to customer attrition. Also called a proportional hazards model. This model is part of a family of methods collectively called survival analysis because of their common use in medical research.

CRISP-DM. Stands for CRoss Industry Standard Process for Data Mining. A standardized approach to applying data mining to solve real-world problems.

crosstabulation. A table showing counts based on categories of two or more categorical fields. Each cell of the table indicates how many cases have a specific combination of values for the fields. *See also* OLAP cube and multidimensional table.

cross-validation. A technique for estimating the accuracy of a model on new data when a test sample is not available. It involves splitting the training data into *n* subsets, or "folds," and then holding out each subset as a test set for a model built on the rest of the data. The accuracy estimates are averaged across all *n* models, and the average is taken as the estimate of how accurate a model built on all the training data will be for new data.

data cleaning. The process of checking data for errors and correcting those errors whenever possible.

data mart. A database extracted from a larger, broader data store for a specific purpose (such as marketing decision support).

data mining. A process for extracting information from large data sets in order to solve business problems.

data preparation. The third phase in the CRISP-DM process model. Involves selecting, cleaning, constructing, integrating, and formatting data for modeling.

data quality. The extent to which data have been accurately coded and stored in the database. Factors that adversely affect data quality include missing data, data entry errors, program bugs, etc.

data set. A set of data that has been prepared for analysis, usually by denormalizing the data and importing it as a flat file into an analysis program.

data understanding. The second phase of the CRISP-DM process model. Involves collecting initial data, describing the data, exploring the data, and verifying data quality.

data visualization. A process of examining data patterns graphically. Includes use of traditional plots as well as advanced interactive graphics. In many cases, visualization allows you to easily spot patterns that would be difficult to find using other methods.

data warehouse. A large database created specifically for decision support throughout the enterprise. It usually consists of data extracted from other company databases. These data have been cleaned and organized for easy access. Often includes a metadata store as well.

database management system. A software system for managing, entering, storing, and manipulating data. Common examples are systems from Oracle, Sybase, and Informix.

datum. Singular for data. Usually refers to an individual piece of information—a single field from a single record.

DBMS. *See* database management system.

decision tree. A class of statistical models that classify records based on various field values. The entire sample of cases is split according to a field value, and then each subgroup is split again. The process repeats until further splits cease to improve classification accuracy or until other stopping criteria are met. *See also* CHAID, C&RT (classification and regression trees), QUEST, and C5.0.

demographics. Descriptive data about people. Examples include age, race, gender, income, etc.

denormalized data. Data that have been extracted from a relational database (that is, normalized data) and converted to a single table in which each row represents one record and each column represents one field. A file containing denormalized data is called a flat file. This is the type of data typically used in data mining.

dependent variable. A variable (field) whose value is assumed to depend on the values of other variables (fields). Also known as a target field or variable.

deployment. Actual application of data mining results to your business process to make improvements. Also, the last phase of the CRISP-DM process model. Involves planning the deployment, planning for monitoring and maintenance of the deployed results, producing a final report, and reviewing the project.

derived field. A field that is calculated or inferred from other fields. For example, if you have share price and earnings per share for stocks in your database, you could divide the former by the latter to get the P/E ratio, a derived field.

description. A process for summarizing the overall characteristics of existing data without regard to whether the observed patterns generalize to other data or situations. Contrast with inference.

dichotomous field. A field (variable) that has only two possible values. An example of a dichotomous field is one indicating response to a promotion; possible values are response or nonresponse.

dimension. In an OLAP cube, any of the fields used to define categories to break down the summaries. Compare with measure and variable.

distribution. A characteristic of a field (variable) defined by the pattern of values observed in the data for that field. The distribution of a field can be examined graphically with boxplots and histograms or by using statistical summaries such as the mean, standard deviation, skewness, and kurtosis. The distribution of a field has important implications for selecting data mining techniques for use with that data.

domain knowledge. Knowledge and expertise that you possess related to the substantive business problem under consideration, as distinguished from knowledge of statistical or data mining techniques.

drill down. To examine successively deeper levels of detail in a multidimensional table. You start at the top level with aggregate data and then select subsets of the data for closer examination.

error. For a model, error is a measure of the model's tendency to make predictions that are dissimilar to the true values. For a classifier, error is a measure of the classifier's tendency to make incorrect classifications.

evaluation. The fifth phase in the CRISP-DM process model. Involves evaluating results, reviewing the modeling process, and determining the next steps.

factor analysis. A data reduction technique, closely related to principal components analysis, that works by deriving a small number of fields that capture most of the information contained in a much larger set of fields.

feature. An attribute of a case or record. In database terms, synonymous with field. *See also* variable.

field. A datum associated with a record in a database. A measured characteristic of the object represented by the record. *See also* feature and variable.

flag. A Boolean field.

flat file. A data set represented by a single table with a row for each record and a column for each field. Composed of denormalized data.

genetic algorithm. A method for optimizing a model. The method involves generating a large set of competing models, selecting those that perform the best, and combining those to form new models. The best of the new models are again selected and recombined, and the process proceeds iteratively until a suitably good model is generated.

gigabyte (GB). A unit measuring data size, consisting of approximately one billion bytes (1024 megabytes). Compare with megabyte and terabyte.

GUI. Graphical user interface. A system for interacting with the computer using menus, windows, a mouse-controlled cursor, etc.

hazard rate. Describes the probability that an event will happen at a particular point in time, based on the use of survival analysis with time-to-event data. An example of a question that the hazard rate would help to answer is, "How likely is it that a customer who has been with us for two years will switch to a different company this month?"

histogram. A graphical display of the distribution of values for a numeric field. It is created by dividing the range of possible values into subranges called bins, and a bar is plotted for each bin, which indicates the number of cases having a value within the range of the bin.

homogeneous. Being of consistent composition. A characteristic of a group whose members are all similar to one another in some relevant way. A common goal of data mining is to identify homogeneous groups in order to make decisions about how to treat members of the group.

hypothesis test. A formal statistical procedure that estimates the probability of obtaining the observed data if a particular hypothesis (the null hypothesis) is assumed to be true. If the probability is small enough, we claim that the null hypothesis is unlikely to be true, and we reject it in favor of an alternative hypothesis. (See Appendix A for more details on statistical tests.)

impurity. An index of how much variability exists in a subgroup or segment of data. A low impurity index indicates a homogeneous group, where most members of the group have similar values for the criterion or target field.

inference. The process of deriving information from a sample of data in order to apply that information to a larger population of cases. Inference involves assumptions about the data sample and the fields it contains. Contrast with description.

input field. A predictor field in a model. Also called an independent variable.

interaction. In a model, an interaction is a type of effect involving two or more fields (variables) in which the effect of one field in predicting the target depends on the level of the other field(s). For example, if you are predicting response to a marketing campaign, you may find that high price leads to decreased response for low-income people but increased response for high-income people.

intranet. A special internal network of resources, based on the same protocols used by the Internet. An intranet allows sharing of documents and files (including data mining results) via commonly available Web browsers and other Internet software.

iterative. Involving repeated applications of a step or a series of steps. Counting is a simple iterative procedure, which works by taking the step "add one to the previous value" and applying it repeatedly. An iteration is a single pass through the steps of an iterative process.

k-means. An approach to clustering that defines *k* clusters and iteratively assigns records to clusters based on distances from each cluster's mean until a stable solution is found.

Kohonen network. A type of neural network used for clustering. Also known as a self-organizing map (SOM).

kurtosis. A statistic that indicates an aspect of a field's distribution. Kurtosis is a measure of how much the tails of the distribution differ from the tails of a corresponding normal distribution. A large kurtosis (positive or negative) indicates that the distribution cannot be successfully approximated by a normal distribution.

lift. Improvement in expected return caused by the use of a classifier or model over that expected with no classification or prediction. The higher the lift, the better the classifier or model.

linear model. A model that assumes that the relationship between fields follows a straight line (or a flat surface, for models with more than one predictor).

logistic regression. A special type of regression model used when the target field is categorical.

market basket analysis. An application of association-based models that attempts to describe pairs or clusters of items that tend to be purchased by the same customer at the same time.

mean. The average value for a field (variable). The mean is a measure of the center of the distribution for a field. The mean is technically valid only for continuous fields, but it can be applied to ordinal categorical fields if you are willing to assume that the ordinal values of the field act as if they were numbers in a continuous scale. Compare with median and mode.

measure. In an OLAP cube, any of the values being summarized. Compare with dimension.

median. The value for a field below which 50% of the observed values fall; the value that splits the data into an "upper half" and a "lower half." The median is a measure of the center of the distribution for a field. The median is valid for continuous or ordinal categorical fields. Compare with mean and mode.

megabyte (MB). A unit measuring data size, consisting of approximately one million bytes. Compare with gigabyte and terabyte.

metadata. Literally, data about data. Metadata is information about the data in your data store. It typically contains descriptions of fields and records, and relationships between fields, as well as information about how the data store was assembled and how it is maintained.

mode. The most frequently observed value for a field. The mode is a measure of the center of the distribution for a field. The mode is technically valid for any type of field (nominal, ordinal, or continuous). However, its usefulness can be limited for certain kinds of continuous fields, especially in cases where it is rare for two records to have the same value for the field. Compare with mean and median.

model. A mathematical equation that describes the relationship among a set of fields. Models are usually based on statistical methods and involve assumptions about the distributions of the fields used in the model, as well as the mathematical form of the relationship.

modeling. The fourth phase in the CRISP-DM process model. Involves selecting a modeling technique, generating a test design, building models, and assessing the models.

multidimensional table. A table that represents data broken down by several different fields. Pivot tables are a special kind of multidimensional table that allows you to interact with the table to dynamically change the way the dimensions are arranged in the table. In some contexts, they are referred to as OLAP cubes.

multilayer perceptron (MLP). A common type of neural network, used for classification or prediction. Also called a backpropagation network.

nearest neighbor classifier. An analytical method that categorizes unknown cases by identifying a similar case (or cases) in a set where the category is known, and using the category (or categories) of those similar cases to derive a predicted category for the new case.

neural network. A mathematical model for predicting or classifying cases, using a complex mathematical scheme that simulates an abstract version of brain cells. Rather than calculating the specifics of the model directly, as is done with regression models, a neural network is trained by presenting it with a large number of observed cases, one at a time, and allowing it to update itself repeatedly until it learns the task.

nominal field. A categorical field in which the categories are unordered. That is, there is no direct sense that one category is higher or lower than any other. Examples are gender (male, female) and country of origin.

normal distribution. A special distribution that has been well studied and is often used to simplify statistical analysis. This is the so-called bell-shaped curve.

normalized data. Data that have been broken into logical pieces that are stored separately to minimize redundancy. For example, information about specific products may be separated from order information; by doing this, the details of each product appear only once, in a products table, instead of being repeated for each transaction involving that product. Normalized data are usually stored in a relational database, with relations defining how records in different tables refer to one another. Contrast with denormalized data.

OLAP. *See* online analytical processing.

OLAP cube. A multidimensional table used in the context of online analytical processing.

OLTP. *See* online transaction processing.

online analytical processing (OLAP). A method of examining data, usually involving multidimensional tables (called OLAP cubes). The method is based on summarizing data to multiple levels of abstraction and providing techniques to allow the user to manipulate the view interactively to search for interesting relationships.

online transaction processing (OLTP). An automated system for processing transactions that stores a record of each transaction as it is processed. Such systems are often used as a data source for a data warehouse.

open database connectivity (ODBC). A data exchange interface, allowing programs of various types to exchange data with each other. For example, if your database system and data mining software are both ODBC compliant, the task of transferring data from one to the other is made much simpler.

ordinal field. A categorical field with ordered categories. That is, the values of the categorical field have a sense of higher and lower, although the differences between adjacent categories may not all be the same. For example, consider a field describing years of education. It is clear that 12 years of education are greater than 11; however, it is equally clear that the difference between 10 and 11 years of education is not the same as the difference between 11 and 12 years. Contrast with nominal field and continuous field.

outlier. A record with extreme values for one or more fields. Various technical definitions are used for determining which specific cases are outliers. The most common criterion is that any case with a value greater than three standard deviations from the mean (in either direction) is considered an outlier.

output field. The field whose values you want to predict. Also called the target or the dependent variable.

overfitting. A potential problem with model estimation in which the model is influenced by some quirks of the data sample. Ideally, the model encodes only the true patterns of interest. However, sometimes data sets contain systematic errors that can end up encoded in the model as well. Cross-validation is a method for detecting overfitting in a model.

Pareto chart. A bar chart in which categories are sorted by descending value. Pareto charts are useful for identifying the most important factors for a particular outcome.

pivot table. An interactive multidimensional table. Pivot tables allow the user to change the level of summarization or the format of the table "on the fly," making examination of your data fast and easy.

population. The group that is the target of inference, the set of cases you are ultimately interested in. A data sample is selected from a population, and inferences based on the sample are applied to the population. For example, the cases in your customer database represent a sample of customers from the population of all potential customers.

prediction. An estimate of the value of some target field for an unknown case, based on a model and the values of other fields for that case.

predictor. A field in the data set that is used in a model or classifier to predict the value of some other field (the target).

principal components analysis (PCA). A data reduction technique that works by deriving a small number of fields that effectively summarize the information contained in a larger set of fields.

probability. A measure of the likelihood of an event occurring. Probability values range from 0 to 1; 0 implies that the event never occurs, and 1 implies that the event always occurs. A probability of 0.5 indicates that the event has an even chance of occurring or not occurring.

proportional hazards model. A special type of regression model used with time-to-event data, such as time to breakdown or time to customer attrition. Also called Cox regression. This model is part of a family of methods collectively called survival analysis because of their use in medical research.

query. A formal specification of data to be extracted from a database, data warehouse, or data mart. Queries are often expressed in structured query language (SQL). For example, to analyze records for only your male customers, you would make a query on the database for all records in which customer's gender has the value *male*, and then analyze the resulting subset of the data.

QUEST. An algorithm for creating a decision tree based on statistical tests.

record. A row in a database; for denormalized data, synonymous with case.

regression. A mathematical technique for estimating a linear model for a continuous target field.

regression tree. A tree-based algorithm that splits the sample of cases repeatedly to derive homogeneous subsets, based on values of a continuous target field.

relational database. A data store designed for normalized data. A relational database usually consists of a set of tables and a set of relations that define how records from one table are related to records from other tables. For example, a product ID may be used to link records in a transactions table with records in a product detail table.

report OLAP. The use of OLAP cubes to summarize and break down information. *See also* multidimensional table.

row. A record (or case) in a database.

rules. Specifications that indicate relationships between values of fields, or how cases are to be classified. Used especially with decision trees.

rule induction. The automatic construction of association rules from data, using an algorithm such as Apriori.

sample. A subset of cases selected from a larger set of possible cases (called the population). The data you analyze are based on a sample; the conclusions you draw are usually applied to the larger population.

scatterplot. A data graph that plots two (or sometimes three) numeric fields against each other for a set of records. Each dot in the scatterplot represents one case. Relationships between fields can often be readily seen in an appropriate scatterplot.

scoring. The process of producing a classification or prediction for a new, untested case. An example is credit scoring, where a credit application is rated for risk based on various aspects of the applicant and the loan in question.

segment. A group or subgroup having some set of properties in common. Usually used in a marketing context to describe homogeneous subsets of the population of potential customers.

segmentation. A process of identifying groups of records with similar values for a target field. The process takes the whole set of records and divides them into subgroups or segments based on characteristics of the records.

set field. A categorical field whose values are members of a set.

significance (statistical). A statement regarding the probability that an observed difference is attributable to random fluctuations (that is, attributable to chance). (See Appendix A.)

skewness. A statistic that describes how "off-center" a distribution is, compared to the symmetrical normal distribution. A field with positive skewness has a small number of cases with very high values; a field with negative skewness has a small number of cases with very low values.

standard deviation. A measure of the variability in the values of a field. It is calculated by taking the difference between each value and the overall mean, squaring it, summing across all of the values, dividing by the number of records (or sometimes by the number of records minus one), and then taking the square root. Sometimes symbolized as s (for samples) or σ (for populations). The standard deviation is equal to the square root of the variance.

standardized variable. A variable or field that has been rescaled so that its mean is 0 and its standard deviation is 1. Positive values represent cases that are above the mean, and negative values represent cases that are below the mean. The fundamental characteristics of the data are not changed, but standardization allows comparisons among variables with different scales (for example, age and income). Values of standardized variables are sometimes called z scores.

statistics. Generally, a set of methods used to derive general information from specific data. The term is also used to describe the computed values derived from these methods.

stratified sampling. A procedure that selects a specific number of records from each of several groups (strata) in a data set in order to control the relative proportion of records from each group in the resulting sample. *See also* balancing.

structured query language (SQL). A specialized language for selecting data from a database. This is the standard way of expressing data queries for most database management systems.

survival analysis. A family of methods for analyzing time-to-event data. *See also* proportional hazards model.

symbolic field. A field whose values represent categories. Set fields and flags are both types of symbolic fields. Also known as a categorical field.

target. The field you want to predict, whose value is assumed to be related to the values of other fields (the predictors). Also known as the dependent variable or output field.

terabyte (TB). A unit measuring data size, consisting of approximately one trillion bytes (1024 gigabytes). Compare with megabyte and gigabyte.

time series analysis. In general, techniques applied to data where measurements are taken on the same unit at several points in time. Also, the application of these techniques.

transformation. A formula applied to values of a field in order to alter the distribution of values. Some statistical methods require that fields have a particular distribution. When a field's distribution differs from what is required, a transformation (such as taking logarithms of values) can often fix the discrepancy.

variable. In general, any measured characteristic that can vary across records. Variables are represented as fields in a database; for most purposes, variable and field are synonymous. In report OLAP, a variable is any of the values being summarized—a measure.

variance. A measure of the variability in the values of a field. It is calculated by taking the difference between each value and the overall mean, squaring it, summing across all of the values, and dividing by the number of records (or sometimes by the number of records minus one). Sometimes symbolized as s^2 (for samples) or σ^2 (for populations). The variance is equal to the square of the standard deviation.

visualization. *See* data visualization.

z score. *See* standardized variable.

Bibliography

References Cited in Text

Applied Technology Group. 1997. *Data warehousing technology glossary.* Natick, MA: Applied Technology Group. (Also available at *http://www.techguide.com/.*)

Berry, M. J. A. and G. Linoff. 1997. *Data mining techniques for marketing, sales, and customer support.* New York: John Wiley & Sons, Inc.

Berson, A. and S. J. Smith. 1997. *Data warehousing, data mining, and OLAP.* New York: McGraw-Hill.

Claritas, Inc. 2000. *PRIZM cluster narratives.* Ithaca, NY: Claritas, Inc.

Dalal, S. R., E. B. Fowlkes, and B. Hoadley. 1989. Risk analysis of the space shuttle: Pre-Challenger prediction of failure. *Journal of the American Statistical Association,* 84: 945–957.

Glymour, C., D. Madigan, D. Pregibon, and P. Smyth. 1997. Statistical themes and lessons for data mining. *Data Mining and Knowledge Discovery,* 1: 11–28.

Hays, W. 1988. *Statistics (4th ed.).* Orlando, FL: Harcourt Brace Jovanovich.

Hogg, R. and A. Craig. 1978. *Introduction to mathematical statistics (4th ed.).* New York: Macmillan.

Kohavi, R., C. Brodley, B. Frasca, L. Mason, and Z. Zheng. 2000. KDD-Cup 2000 organizers' report: Peeling the onion. SIGKDD Explorations, 2:2, 86-98. *http://www.ecn.purdue.edu/KDDCUP.*

Kohonen, T. 1984. *Self-organization and associative memory.* New York: Springer-Verlag.

Selvin, H. and A. Stuart. 1966. Data dredging procedures in survey analysis. *The American Statistician,* 20:3, 20–23.

Tappin, L. 1994. Analyzing data relating to the Challenger disaster. *Mathematics Teacher,* 87: 423–426.

Two Crows Corporation. 1998. *Introduction to data mining and knowledge discovery.* Potomac, MD: Two Crows Corporation.

Wilson, L. 1997. Canadian bank mines for gold. *Computerworld,* 31:42, 73–74.

Books on Data Mining

Berry, M. J. A. and Linoff, G. 1997. *Data mining techniques for marketing, sales, and customer support.* New York: John Wiley & Sons, Inc.

Berry, M. J. A. and Linoff, G. 1999. *Mastering data mining.* New York: John Wiley & Sons.

Berry, M. J. A. and Linoff, G. 2002. *Mining the Web: Transforming customer data.* New York: John Wiley & Sons.

Berson, A. and S. J. Smith. 1997. *Data warehousing, data mining, and OLAP.* New York: McGraw-Hill.

Berson, A., K. Thearling, and S. J. Smith. 1999. *Building data mining applications for CRM.* New York: McGraw-Hill.

Fayyad, U. M., G. Piatetsky-Shapiro, P. Smyth, and R. Uthurusamy. 1996. *Advances in knowledge discovery and data mining*. Cambridge, MA: MIT Press.

Groth, Robert. 1997. *Data mining: A hands-on approach for business professionals.* Englewood Cliffs, NJ: Prentice Hall.

Hand, D., H. Mannila, and P. Smyth. 2000. *Principles of data mining.* Cambridge, MA: MIT Press.

Hastie, T., R. Tibshirani, and J. H. Friedman. 2001. *The elements of statistical learning: Data mining, inference, and prediction.* New York: Springer Verlag.

Mena, J. 1999. *Data mining your Website.* New York: John Wiley & Sons.

Pyle, D. 1999. *Data preparation for data mining.* San Francisco: Morgan Kaufmann.

Quinlan, J. R. 1993. *C4.5: Programs for machine learning.* San Francisco: Morgan Kaufmann.

Weiss, S. and N. Indurkhya. 1998. *Predictive data mining: A practical guide.* San Francisco: Morgan Kaufmann.

Westphal, C. and T. Blaxton (1998). *Data mining solutions.* New York: John Wiley & Sons.

Books on OLAP

Berson, A. and S. J. Smith. 1997. *Data warehousing, data mining, and OLAP.* New York: McGraw-Hill.

Thomsen, Erik. 1997. *OLAP solutions: Building multidimensional information systems.* New York: John Wiley & Sons, Inc.

Books on Data Visualization

Cleveland, W. 1985. *The elements of graphing data.* Monterey, CA: Wadsworth.

_____. 1993. *Visualizing data.* Summit, NJ: Hobart Press.

du Toit, S. H. C., A. G. W. Steyn, and R. H. Stumpf. 1986. *Graphical exploratory data analysis.* New York: Springer-Verlag.

Tufte, E. 1983. *The visual display of quantitative information.* Cheshire, CT: Graphics Press.

Books on Statistical Modeling

Agresti, A. 1996. *An introduction to categorical data analysis.* New York: John Wiley & Sons, Inc.

Box, G. E. P. and G. M. Jenkins. 1994. *Time series analysis: Forecasting and control.* Englewood Cliffs, NJ: Prentice Hall.

Draper, N. and H. Smith. 1998. *Applied regression analysis.* New York: John Wiley & Sons, Inc.

Enders, W. 1995. *Applied econometric time series.* New York: John Wiley & Sons, Inc.

Fienberg, S. E. 1980. *The analysis of cross-classified categorical data.* Cambridge, MA: MIT Press.

Kalbfleisch, J. D. 1980. *The statistical analysis of failure time data.* New York: John Wiley & Sons, Inc.

Kleinbaum, D. G. 1996. *Survival analysis: A self-learning text.* New York: Springer-Verlag.

Moore, D. S. and G. P. McCabe. 1998. *Introduction to the practice of statistics.* New York: W. H. Freeman.

Neter, J., M. H. Kutner, C. J. Nachtsheim, and W. Wasserman. 1996. *Applied linear regression models.* Chicago: Richard D. Irwin, Inc.

Tabachnick, B. and L. Fidell. 1996. *Using multivariate statistics.* New York: HarperCollins College Publishers.

Books on Neural Networks

Bigus, J. P. 1996. *Data mining with neural networks: Solving business problems from application development to decision support.* New York: McGraw-Hill.

Bishop, C. M. 1995. *Neural networks for pattern recognition.* Oxford: Clarendon Press.

Dayhoff, J. 1990. *Neural network architectures.* New York: Van Nostrand Reinhold.

Kohonen, T. 1997. *Self-organizing maps.* New York: Springer-Verlag.

Ripley, B. D. 1995. *Pattern recognition and neural networks.* New York: Cambridge University Press.

Ritter, H., T. Martinetz, and K. Schulten. 1992. *Neural computation and self-organizing maps.* Reading, MA: Addison Wesley.

Resources on the World Wide Web

About Data Mining at Two Crows
http://www.twocrows.com/about-dm.htm
ACM Special Interest Group on Knowledge Discovery in Data and Data Mining (SIGKDD)
http://www.acm.org/sigkdd/
Complete Data Mining Solution from SPSS Inc.
http://www.spss.com/datamine/
Data Miners
http://www.data-miners.com/
Data Mining Home Page on St@tServ
http://www.statserv.com/datamining.html
Data Warehousing Knowledge Center
http://www.datawarehousing.org/
FedStats—The U.S. Government Clearinghouse for Publicly Accessible Data
http://www.fedstats.gov/
KDNuggets Directory: Data Mining and Knowledge Discovery Resources
http://www.kdnuggets.com/
PlugIn Datamation Section on Data Mining
http://itmanagement.earthweb.com/datbus
Statistics on the Web
http://www.execpc.com/~helberg/statframes.html
The Data Mine
http://www.the-data-mine.com/
The Data Mining Group
http://www.dmg.org/

Index

accuracy, 11
Advanced Models (SPSS option), 184
aggregate data, 189, 193
aggregation, 56, 189
Agresti, A., 205
alpha
  in statistical testing, 173
alternative hypothesis, 194
AnswerTree, 186
AnswerTree Server, 186
appending data, 57
application developers, 9
Applied Technology Group, 203
Apriori, 189
ARIMA, 150–152
artificial intelligence, 5
assessing models, 70
assessing the situation, 24
association rules, 136–138, 189
  confidence, 137
association-based models, 153–156, 196
associations, 189
assumptions, 25
assumptions of statistical methods, 178
attributes
  derived, 54
autoregressive model, 150
averages, 14
  in multidimensional tables, 98

backpropagation networks, 197
balancing, 47, 189
bar charts, 105–107
benefits (of data mining), 28
Berry, M. J. A., 203
Berson, A., 203, 204
Bigus, J. P., 205
Bishop, C. M., 166, 205
Blaxton, T., 204
Boolean data, 35
Boolean fields, 189
boosting, 189
Box, G. E. P., 166, 205
Box-Jenkins models. *See* ARIMA
boxplots, 189, 193
Breiman, L., 148
Brodley, C., 203
building models, 67–70
business objectives, 23
business success criteria, 23
business understanding, 18, 21–32, 190

C5.0, 190
cases, 190
categorical fields, 190, 197, 198
Categories (SPSS option), 184
cause and effect, 180
cells, 97, 190
censored cases, 161
central limit theorem, 172
CHAID, 132, 190, 192
charts. *See* graphics
chi-square statistic, 190
churning, 161
Claritas, Inc., 203

classification, 126–136, 190
classification and regression trees (C&RT), 132, 190, 192
classification tree, 190
classifiers, 193
cleaning data, 49–53
Clementine, 183
Clementine Server, 183
Cleveland, W., 204
cluster centers, 143
clustering, 126, 138–147, 190
  hierarchical, 139–142
  k-means, 143–145
  neural networks, 145–147
  references, 148
coding schemes, 35, 39, 52
coefficients
  regression, 175
column, 190
confidence
  association rules, 137
confirmation, 6
confusion matrix, 129, 190
Conjoint (SPSS option), 185
constraints, 25
constructing data, 53–57
contingencies, 26
continuous fields, 191, 196
correlation coefficient, 155
correlations, 153, 191
costs (of data mining), 28
counts
  in multidimensional tables, 97
coverage
  in association rules, 137
Cox regression, 191
Cox regression models, 160–162
Craig, A., 203
CRISP-DM, 191
  business understanding, 18, 21–32
  data preparation, 19, 43–59
  data understanding, 18, 33–41
  deployment, 19, 83–91
  evaluation, 19, 77–82
  general process model, 18
  modeling, 61–75
  overview, 17–20
crosstabulation, 191
cross-validation, 177, 191, 198

Dalal, S. R., 203
data, 10–15
  appending, 57
  Boolean, 35
  characteristics, 10
  cleaning, 49–53, 191
  coding schemes, 35, 39, 52
  collecting, 33
  constructing, 53–57
  defining test data, 66
  denormalized, 13, 192, 194
  describing, 34
  errors, 39, 51
  exploring, 36
  formatting, 58
  integrating, 57–58
  merging, 57
  missing values, 50
  normalized, 12, 192, 197, 200
  numeric, 34
  organization, 11–13
  partitioning, 67
  quality, 39, 191
  selecting, 43
  shape, 13
  symbolic, 35
  terminology, 12
data marts, 191
Data Mine, The (Web site), 206
data mining, 191
  defined, 1–2
  history, 4–6
  hype, 4
  methods, 93
  types of users, 8–9
data mining goals, 29

data mining process, 17–20
data mining success criteria, 29
data preparation, 19, 43–59, 191
data quality, 11
data reduction, 55
data set, 190, 191
data understanding, 18, 33–41, 192
data warehouses, 5, 192
Data Warehousing Knowledge Center, 206
database management system (DBMS), 192
databases
  birth of, 4
Datamation, 206
datum, 192
Dayhoff, J., 148, 205
decision trees, 132–134, 192, 199, 200
  C&RT, 190
  CHAID, 190
  QUEST, 199
  references, 148
DecisionTime, 186
defining test data, 66
demographics, 192
denormalized data, 13, 190, 192, 194
dependent variables, 174, 192, 201
deployment, 19, 83–91, 192
  monitoring and maintenance, 85
  planning, 83
derived attributes, 54
derived fields, 193
describing the data, 34
description, 193
determining business objectives, 21
dichotomous fields, 193
Dillon, W. R., 148
dimensions, 193
  in OLAP cubes, 95
direction of association, 153
discovery, 6
discriminant analysis, 127–130
  references, 147
discriminant functions, 128
distance score, 139
distribution, 13, 193, 194, 195, 196, 202
  sampling, 170
domain knowledge, 193
Draper, N., 165, 205
drilling down, 193
du Toit, S. H. C., 204

Enders, W., 166, 205
error bars, 120
errors, 193
  in statistical tests, 179
evaluating model results, 77
evaluation, 19, 77–82, 193
Exact Tests (SPSS option), 185
example data mining projects, 20
exploring the data, 36

factor analysis, 55, 193
false alarms, 179
Fayyad, U. M., 204
features, 193
FedStats, 206
Fidell, L., 147, 205
fields, 194
  derived, 54, 193
Fienberg, S. E., 205
final report, 87
findings, 77
flag (field type), 194
flat files, 191, 192, 194
forecasting, 149–165
  ARIMA, 150–152
  neural networks, 163–165
formatting data, 58
Fowlkes, E. B., 203
Frasca, B., 203
Friedman, J. H., 148, 204

generated records, 56
genetic algorithms, 194
gigabytes (GB), 194
Glymour, C., 203
goals
  data mining, 29
Goldstein, M., 148
goodness of fit, 176
graphical user interface (GUI), 194
graphics, 192
  bar charts, 105–107
  chart enhancements, 120–122
  line charts, 111–112
  Pareto charts, 108–109
  pie charts, 112–113
  point charts, 115–120
  reference lines, 122
  selecting a chart, 122–124
  symbols, shapes, and colors, 121
Groth, R., 204

Hand, D., 204
Hastie, T., 204
Hays, W., 203
hazard rate, 161, 194
hierarchical clustering, 139–142
histograms, 13, 193, 194
Hoadley, B., 203
Hogg, R., 203
homogeneous, 194
Hosmer, D., 147
Huberty, C. J., 147
hypothesis tests, 7, 169–174, 194

impurity, 190, 195
imputation, 50
independent variables, 174
Indurkhya, N., 204
inference, 195, 199
information consumers, 9
inner joins (merging data), 57
input field, 195
integrating data, 57–58
integration model, 150
interaction, 195
intranet, 195
inventory of resources, 24
itemset, 138
iteration, 195
iterative, 195

Jenkins, G. M., 166, 205

Kalbfleisch, J. D., 166, 205
KDNuggets Directory, 206
Kendall, M., 166
key fields, 12
Kleinbaum, D. G., 147, 166, 205
k-means clustering, 143–145, 195
knowledge discovery, 6
knowledge workers, 9
Kohavi, R., iv
Kohonen networks, 145–147, 195
Kohonen, T., 203, 205
kurtosis, 193, 195
Kutner, M. H., 165, 205

LANs, 5
layers
  in multidimensional tables, 101
least squares
  method of, 175
Lemeshow, S., 147
LexiQuest Mine, 187
lift, 195
line charts, 111–112
linear discriminant analysis. *See* discriminant analysis

linear models, 195, 199
linear regression, 157–160
Linoff, G., 203
logistic regression, 130–131, 196
  references, 147
logit, 130
loglinear models, 160–162

Madigan, D., 203
Mannila, H., 204
Maps (SPSS option), 185
market basket analysis, 196
Martinetz, T., 148, 205
Mason, L., 203
maximum likelihood, 175
maximum value, 100
McCabe, G. P., 205
mean, 14, 98, 193, 196
  in multidimensional tables, 98
measurement errors, 39
measures, 193, 196
  in OLAP cubes, 95
median, 196
megabyte (MB), 196
Mena, J., 204
merging data, 57
metadata, 36, 39, 53, 196
method of least squares, 158
minimum value, 100
misclassification table, 129
misses, 179
missing data, 39
Missing Value Analysis (SPSS option), 185
missing values, 50
mode, 196
model builders, 9
model building, 7
modeling, 61–75, 149–166, 196
  ARIMA, 150–152
  association-based, 153–156
  assumptions, 63
  Cox regression, 160–162
  CRISP-DM, 19
  forecasting, 149–165
  in statistics, 174
  linear regression, 157–160
  loglinear models, 160–162
  measuring goodness of a model, 64
  references, 165–166
models, 193, 196
  accuracy, 64
  assessing, 70
  association-based, 196
  building, 67–70
  evaluating results, 77, 176–177
  model description, 70
  parameter settings, 68, 73
  regression, 199
  supervised, 64
  unsupervised, 65
monitoring and maintenance of deployed results, 85
Moore, D. S., 205
moving average, 151
multidimensional tables, 95–103, 191, 193, 197, 198, 200
  cells, 97
  contents, 102
  dimensions, 95
  layers, 101
  measures, 95
  structure, 101
  variables, 95
multilayer perceptron (MLP), 197
multinomial logistic regression. *See* logistic regression
multiple regression, 159
  See also regression models

Nachtsheim, C. J., 165, 205
nearest neighbor classifier, 197
negative associations, 153
neighborhoods
  in Kohonen networks, 145

Neter, J., 165, 205
Neural Connection, 186
neural networks, 134–136, 195, 197
  for clustering, 145–147
  for prediction, 163–165
  for segmentation, 134–136
  references, 148
next steps
  determining, 81
nominal fields, 197
normal distribution, 172, 195, 197, 200
normalized data, 12, 192, 197, 200
null hypothesis, 194
numeric data, 34

OLAP cubes, 95–103, 191, 193, 196, 197, 198, 200
Olshen, R. A., 148
online analytical processing (OLAP), 5, 198
online transaction processing (OLTP), 4, 198
open database connectivity (ODBC), 198
Ord, J. K., 166
ordinal fields, 196, 198
outer joins (merging data), 57
outliers, 198
output field, 198
overfitting, 66, 162, 176, 198

p value, 172
parameter settings (models), 68, 73
parameters
  in statistical modeling, 175
Pareto charts, 108–109, 198
partitioning, 67, 130, 163, 177
PCs, 5
percentages
  in multidimensional tables, 97
Piatetsky-Shapiro, G., 204
pie charts, 112–113
pivot tables, 197, 198
plots. *See* graphics
point charts, 115–120
polynomial regression, 159
populations, 168, 195, 199, 200
positive associations, 153
prediction, 199
predictor fields, 199
Pregibon, D., 203
principal components analysis (PCA), 199
PRIZM codes, 56
probability, 169, 194, 199
project plan, 30
proportional hazards models, 191, 199
proportional hazards models. *See* Cox regression models
Pyle, D., 204

quality of data, 39
queries, 199
QUEST, 192, 199
Quinlan, J. R., 204

R^2, 158
random sampling, 47
range, 100
records, 199
  generated, 56
regression, 199
regression coefficients, 175
regression models, 156–163
  Cox regression, 160–162
  linear regression, 157–160
  loglinear, 160–162
  stepwise, 162–163
Regression Models (SPSS option), 184
regression trees, 199
relational databases, 12, 192, 197, 200
  See also normalized data
report OLAP, 200
requirements, 25
resources
  inventory of, 24

reviewing the data mining process, 80
reviewing the project, 90
RFM score, 56
Ripley, B. D., 148, 166, 205
risks (in data mining), 26
Ritter, H., 148, 205
Romesburg, H. C., 148
rows, 200
rule induction, 200
rules, 200

sample, 168, 200
sampling, 10, 45–48, 167–168, 195, 198, 199, 200
  advantages, 46
  disadvantages, 46
  random, 47
  sampling distribution of a statistic, 170
  stratified, 47
scatterplot, 116, 200
scatterplot matrix, 118
Schulten, K., 148, 205
scoring, 129, 145, 200
seasonality, 152
segmentation, 126, 126–136, 200
  decision trees, 132–134
  discriminant analysis, 127–130
  logistic regression, 130–131
  neural networks, 134–136
selecting a modeling technique, 61
selecting data, 43
self-organizing map (SOM), 145, 195
Selvin, H., 203
sensitivity analysis, 136
service paradigm, 5
set field, 200
significance
  practical, 179
  statistical, 172, 179, 200
significance level
  of a statistical test, 173
simple random sampling, 47
situation
  assessing, 24
skewness, 193, 200
Smith, H., 165, 205
Smith, S. J., 203, 204
smoothers, 119
Smyth, P., 203, 204
SPSS, 184
  optional modules, 184–185
  Web site, 206
SPSS SmartViewer, 185
SPSS SmartViewer Web Server, 185
St@tServ, 206
standard deviation, 100, 168, 193, 201
standardized variables, 201
statistics, 201
  assumptions, 178
  hypothesis testing, 169–174
  in data mining, 3
  modeling, 174
  statistical reasoning, 167–181
  statistical significance, 172
  types of errors, 179
Statistics on the Web (Web site), 206
stepwise regression, 162–163
Steyn, A. G. W., 204
Stone, C. J., 148
stratified sampling, 47, 201
structure
  multidimensional tables, 101
structured query language (SQL), 199, 201
Stuart, A., 203
Stumpf, R. H., 204
success criteria
  business, 23
  data mining, 29
sums
  in multidimensional tables, 98
supervised models, 64
support
  in association rules, 137

survival analysis, 191, 194, 201
  See also Cox regression models
symbolic data, 35
symbolic field, 201

Tabachnick, B., 147, 205
Tables (SPSS option), 184
Tappin, L., 203
target fields, 192, 201
terabytes (TB), 201
terminology, 27
test data
  defining, 66
test design
  generating, 64
test set, 130
Thearling, K., 204
Thomsen, E., 204
Tibshirani, R., 204
time series, 111, 150
time series analysis, 202
tools and techniques
  assessing, 31
training set, 130
transformations, 202
trees. *See* decision trees
Trends (SPSS option), 184
Tufte, E., 204
Two Crows Corporation, 203
Type I and Type II errors, 179

unsupervised models, 65
unsupervised networks, 145
Uthurusamy, R., 204

validation, 3
variability, 13, 168
  measures of, 100
variables, 193, 202
  dependent, 174, 192
  in OLAP cubes, 95
  independent, 174
  standardized, 201
variance, 100, 168, 202
variation, 168
verifying data quality, 39
visualization, 192

Wasserman, W., 165, 205
Weiss, S., 204
Westphal, C., 204
WhatIf, 186
Wilson, L., 203

z scores, 201, 202
Zheng, Z., 203